Dudley W. Curry
Ph.D., C.P.A., Southern Methodist University

STUDENT GUIDE

COST ACCOUNTING
A MANAGERIAL EMPHASIS

FIFTH EDITION

Charles T. Horngren
Ph.D., C.P.A., Stanford University

PRENTICE-HALL, INC., *Englewood Cliffs, New Jersey 07632*

Printed in the United States of America

10 9 8 7 6 5

ISBN 0-13-179630-5

Prentice-Hall International, Inc., *London*
Prentice-Hall of Australia Pty. Limited, *Sydney*
Prentice-Hall of Canada, Ltd., *Toronto*
Prentice-Hall of India Private Limited, *New Delhi*
Prentice-Hall of Japan, Inc., *Tokyo*
Prentice-Hall of Southeast Asia Pte. Ltd., *Singapore*
Whitehall Books Limited, *Wellington, New Zealand*

Contents

To the Student

This student guide is designed for use with the textbook, *Cost Accounting: A Managerial Emphasis,* fifth edition, by Charles T. Horngren. For each textbook chapter there is a corresponding guide chapter containing a brief survey, a detailed review summary, and a comprehensive set of self-test and practice exercises.

The solutions to all these exercises are at the back of the student guide. They provide immediate feedback to reinforce your understanding.

Please note that this guide is intended for use with the textbook, not as a substitute for the textbook. Therefore, do not rely on the guide to the exclusion of the book in your study of accounting or in your preparation for quizzes and exams.*

Comments and suggestions from users are welcome.

Dudley W. Curry
Southern Methodist University

*Also helpful is another Prentice-Hall supplement that is aligned with the textbook chapters: *Professional Examination Questions and Answers: A Self-Study Approach* by John K. Harris.

Angela Phillips

53/57 = 93%

1 The Accountant's Role in the Organization

THIS FIRST CHAPTER is designed to give us a useful perspective concerning modern systems of cost accounting. We distinguish between internal reporting to managers for planning and controlling operations (**management accounting**) and external reporting to stockholders, creditors, and others (**financial accounting**). Cost accounting generally includes management accounting plus the function of costing products for measuring inventories and determining income for both internal and external users.

The chapter describes the basic elements of management control systems and introduces one of the major themes of the entire book: the **cost-benefit approach** to obtaining information for management decisions. In addition, a helpful explanation is provided of the management accountant's role in large business organizations.

REVIEW SUMMARY

A. In almost every organization, the accounting system is the *major quantitative information system.*
  1. Successful accounting systems provide information for three broad purposes:
     a. Reporting to managers for planning and controlling routine operations.
     b. Reporting to managers for making special decisions and formulating major plans and policies.
     c. Reporting to stockholders, creditors, government agencies, and other outside parties. This is essentially a custodial or stewardship function.
  2. Note how the primary targets of these purposes are different:
     a. The first two purposes deal with the *internal* use of information by managers: *management accounting.*
     b. The third purpose is concerned mainly with the *external* use of information by investors: *financial accounting.*
     c. *Modern cost accounting systems* generally include the first two purposes plus part of the third purpose: the costing of products for measuring inventories and determining income.

B. Our book deals with the systems for the management planning and control of operations.

1. Such a system is often simply called a *control system.*
2. *Planning* includes:
   a. Setting of goals and objectives.
   b. Predictions of results.
   c. Decisions on how to achieve goals.
3. *Control* includes:
   a. Actions to carry out planning decisions.
   b. Evaluating performance through *feedback.*
4. There are two main instruments for aiding managers in operating a control system:
   a. *Budgets,* which are formal quantifications of plans.
   b. *Performance reports,* which are measurements of actual results in comparison with budgets.
   c. Deviations of actual results from the budgeted data are called *variances.*
   d. Analysis of these variances can reveal the most serious deviations and can help managers to practice *management by exception.*

C. The basic elements of a management control system are related as shown in the textbook diagram (Exhibit 1-1).
1. The *superior,* who oversees the work of subordinates.
2. The *subordinate,* who supervises one or more processes.
3. The *operating process,* which is a group of related activities or decisions.
4. The *environment,* which consists of various existing conditions that are *uncontrollable,* such as weather and competitor reactions.
5. *Performance,* which is a continuing evaluation of the results of operating processes.
6. And *feedback,* the key to control, which is often represented by a comparison of actual results with the budget. Feedback can be useful in making changes to improve:
   a. Selection of goals and objectives.
   b. Means and procedures for performing routine activities.
   c. Ways of arriving at decisions.
   d. Formulations of predictions.
   e. Operating processes (management operations).
   f. Measuring and rewarding performance.
7. Management control is essentially a *human activity* that aims at helping people in their work.

D. It is important to use the *cost-benefit approach* to obtain information for management decisions.
1. Like other economic goods, accounting information is a commodity with a price.
2. Therefore, the cost of obtaining information should be compared with the expected benefits to be obtained.
3. The optimal accounting system or technique is one that produces the most net benefit after the costs of obtaining the information are deducted.
   a. The choice depends on the circumstances in each situation.
   b. *Thus, the appropriate system or technique is not simply the one that appears to be "most accurate" or "necessary," regardless of its costs.*

E. The chief accounting executive, or chief management accountant, is often called the *controller.*
1. The principal functions of the controller are:
   a. Planning for control
   b. Reporting and interpreting
   c. Evaluating and consulting
2. In contrast, the principal functions of the *corporate treasurer* are:

    a. Provision of capital
    b. Investor relations
    c. Short-term financing, banking, etc.
  3. Note that the controller deals more directly with the *operating problems* of a company than does the treasurer, who is concerned more with *financial matters.*
  4. The controller has duties somewhat analogous to those of a *ship's navigator.*

F. A general distinction should be observed between *line authority* and the *staff function.*
  1. Line managers, such as sales and production executives, are directly responsible for the principal operations of a business.
  2. As shown in textbook Exhibit 1-2, the controller's authority is basically of the *staff* type—that is, giving advice and service to other departments:
    a. Service departments, such as the storekeeper and purchasing agent, which aid the work of producing departments
    b. Producing and operating departments, such as the production superintendent and the assembly foreman.
  3. As shown in Exhibit 1-3, the controller has *direct* or *line* authority over only the members of his own department, such as those employees who conduct internal audits, keep cost records, or prepare payrolls.

G. Two principal roles must be performed simultaneously by the chief accountant of an organization:
  1. The *watchdog role* for top managers:
    a. This is the *scorekeeping task* of accumulating and reporting data, a regular day-to-day routine involving large volumes of work and many completion deadlines.
    b. Examples are indicated in Exhibit 1-3: general accounting procedures and maintenance of cost records.
  2. The *helper role* for all managers:
    a. This role includes the *attention-directing and problem-solving tasks* of experienced accountants who work directly with management decision makers on nonroutine problems.
    b. Examples indicated in Exhibit 1-3 are, respectively, performance analysis and special reports.
  3. The controller's responsibility for playing both these roles often requires large organizations to divide accountants' duties into the specialties shown by Exhibit 1-3.

SELF-TEST AND PRACTICE EXERCISES*

I For each of the following multiple-choice and true-false statements, select the single most appropriate answer, and enter its identification letter in the space provided:

d 1. A modern cost accounting system should be designed for the main purpose of (a) planning by stockholders, (b) developing historical costs for inventory valuations, (c) providing data for income tax returns, (d) aiding internal decisions makers.

b 2. The field of cost accounting today excludes the functions of inventory measurement and income determination: (a) true, (b) false.

~~d~~ b 3. Cost accounting is constrained by (a) generally accepted accounting principles, (b) the cost-benefit criterion, (c) both of the above, (d) neither of the above.

a 4. The planning function includes (a) choosing goals and objectives, (b) evaluating management performance, (c) both of the above, (d) neither of the above.

d 5. The control function includes (a) predictions of results, (b) preparing budgets, (c) both of the above, (d) neither of the above.

*Answers and solutions to all self-test and practice exercises are given in the back of the *Student Guide.*

18/20

____ 6. Deviations of actual results from budget figures are called (a) differences, (b) exceptions, (c) variances, (d) unplanned amounts.

____ 7. Managerial control and engineering control are synonymous: (a) true, (b) false.

____ 8. In a management control system, the basic element that is uncontrollable is called (a) the subordinate, (b) performance, (c) feedback, (d) the environment.

____ 9. In a management control system, feedback can be valuable in improving (a) predictions, (b) goals, (c) decisions methods, (d) all of the above.

____ 10. Management control is an activity that usually cannot be carried out exclusively by the use of sophisticated data processing systems: (a) true, (b) false.

____ 11. Because an accounting system must be maintained to meet the requirements of income taxation and external reporting, the cost of obtaining accounting information may be safely ignored in making management decisions: (a) true, (b) false.

____ 12. The choice of an appropriate accounting system or technique should be based mainly on (a) what is necessary under the particular circumstances, (b) what is the best reflection of economic reality, (c) what is the most accurate measurement, (d) all of the above, (e) none of the above.

____ 13. Control is defined in our course as the process of setting maximum limits on financial expenditures: (a) true, (b) false.

____ 14. The controller's authority is basically of the (a) staff type, (b) line type.

____ 15. The controller has direct authority over (a) various line departments, (b) members of the accounting department, (c) both of the above, (d) neither of the above.

____ 16. The controller is most aptly likened to the ship's (a) captain, (b) engineer, (c) cook, (d) navigator, (e) executive officer.

____ 17. The principal functions of the controller include (a) providing capital, (b) arranging short-term financing, (c) both of the above, (d) neither of the above.

____ 18. The controller's office furnishes advice and service to (a) producing departments, (b) service departments, (c) both of the above, (d) neither of the above.

____ 19. The "watchdog" function of managerial accountants usually includes the task(s) of (a) scorekeeping, (b) attention directing, (c) problem solving, (d) all of the above.

____ 20. The "helper" role of managerial accountants is usually performed via the tasks of (a) attention directing, (b) problem solving assistance, (c) both of the above, (d) neither of the above.

II Complete each of the following statements:

1. Modern systems of cost accounting may be called ____________________

2. CMA stands for ____________________

3. The management practice of concentrating on areas that deserve attention and ignoring areas that are running smoothly is called ____________________ ____________________

4. The two major accounting tools included in planning and control systems for managers are:

(a) ____________________

(b) ____________________

5. The key to the management control process is ____________________

6. The information that is produced by a planning and control system for the possible improve-

11/11

ment of the system is called feedback

7. The optimal accounting measure or system for management decision purposes should be determined through the cost/benefit approach.

8. The chief accounting executive, or chief management accountant is often called controller

9. The two principal roles that must be performed simultaneously by the chief accountant of an organization are the watchdog role for top managers and the helper role for all managers.

III For each of the following activities within a company, identify the main function that is being performed:

PS: problem solving
AD: attention directing
SK: scorekeeping

AD 1. Preparing a comparative schedule for a department store of advertising expenses incurred, by sales departments and by months.

SK 2. Entering deposits in the cash receipts journal of a record shop.

PS 3. Estimating future cash inflows and cash outflows relating to the contemplated investment of an oil company in an international joint venture.

SK 4. Computing and recording the end-of-year adjustments of a wholesale appliance company for its expired fire insurance premiums.

SK 5. Tabulating the disposition of traffic tickets issued by the police of the City of Plano.

AD 6. Analyzing deviations from the budget of wages paid to clerks in the clearing department of a large city bank.

6/6

IV For each of the following employees of a large hospital, use the code below to indicate the major type of duty that usually would be performed:

SK: scorekeeping
AD: attention directing
PS: problem solving

SK 1. billing clerk

PS 2. cost analyst AD

AD 3. head of special reports and studies PS

SK 4. vouchers payable bookkeeper

AD 5. head of internal auditing

V For each of the following pairs of personnel of a farm machinery manufacturer, use the code shown below to indicate the usual type of authority of the first-named person over the second-named person:

L: line authority
S: staff authority
N: no authority

N 1. manufacturing vice-president L
plant maintenance foreman

S 2. controller
production superintendent

L 3. assistant controller
internal auditor

L 4. controller
billing clerks

N 5. production superintendent
payroll clerks

N 6. financial vice-president S
shipping foreman

L 7. manufacturing vice-president
drill press foreman

S 8. assistant controller
storekeeper

N 9. chief inspector
controller

N 10. president
chairman of the board

8/10

VI Classify each of the following departments of a large manufacturing company either as a service department (S) or as a producing department (P):

S 1. plant personnel

S 2. toolroom

P 3. parts assembly

S 4. machinery maintenance

S 5. plant air conditioning

P 6. material cutting

S 7. chief inspector

S 8. power plant

P 9. product grinding

P 10. curing process

10/10

2 An Introduction to Cost Terms and Purposes

IN CHAPTER TWO we continue our preliminary exploration of management accounting systems by studying some basic cost concepts used throughout the book. No single kind of cost is exclusively useful in all situations, because there are many different costs for many different purposes.

The chapter explains the fundamental relationships among decision alternatives, cost objectives, and the design of a management accounting system. Also included is a description of the contrasting behavior of fixed and variable costs and an important survey of the basic cost terminology for manufacturing operations. Be sure you understand the important distinction between **product-costs** (inventoriable costs) and **period costs** (noninventoriable costs).

REVIEW SUMMARY

A. *Costs* are generally defined as resources sacrificed or foregone to achieve specific objectives.

1. A *cost objective* is any activity for which a separate measurement of costs is desired.
2. The particular decision alternatives that managers expect to consider have a direct influence on the determination of cost objectives against which costs will be accumulated by the accounting system.
3. Modern cost accounting systems are built around probable cost objectives that can be anticipated (such as products and departments) to serve routine uses:
   - **a.** For inventory valuation and income determination.
   - **b.** For management planning and control decisions.

B. Among the most useful concepts in the entire field of management accounting are those concerning the behavior of different kinds of costs when there are changes in the level or volume of activity of a chosen cost objective, such as units of products sold, tons shipped, or hours worked.

1. *Variable costs* are those costs that *change in total* in direct proportion to changes in the volume of activity.
   - **a.** Variable costs are the *same per unit* of activity at different levels of activity.
   - **b.** Examples of variable costs are direct materials used, direct labor, and sales commissions.

c. Notice how variable costs can be graphed against cost objectives in textbook Exhibits 2-1 and 2-2.

2. *Fixed costs* are those costs that are the *same in total* over a wide range of activity volume within a given time period.
   a. Therefore, fixed costs are *not the same per unit* of activity at different levels of activity; instead, fixed costs on a per-unit basis will vary inversely with changes in activity volume.
   b. Examples of fixed costs are executive salaries, fire insurance, and straight-line depreciation.
   c. The wide range of activity volume over which total fixed costs would not change is called *the relevant range.*
   d. The relevant range can be defined as the band of activity in which budgeted sales and expense relationships will be valid.
   e. Exhibits 2-3 and 2-4 illustrate some of these ideas graphically.

3. An identification of *cost-behavior patterns* (*cost functions*) helps describe the relationships between total costs and cost objects.
   a. For simplicity, we assume at this stage that all costs can be classified as fixed or variable.
   b. In addition, cost functions are usually assumed to be *linear* (straight-line), rather than curvilinear.
   c. Further, in practice, activity is assumed to be measurable in *only one specified dimension,* such as product units, labor hours, sales dollars, etc.

4. *Unit cost* figures often represent *averages* based on a total cost that includes both fixed and variable elements.
   a. For this reason, unit cost data should be used with great caution for predictive and decision purposes—as pointed out in the textbook example of the $1,000 party fee for a musical group.

C. As a useful background for the later study of planning and control concepts—which are equally applicable to both manufacturing and nonmanufacturing activities—we review some basic cost terminology for manufacturing operations.

1. The cost to manufacture a tangible product has three basic elements.
   a. *Direct-material costs* are the costs of all materials that are physically observable as being identified with the finished good and that may be traced to the finished good in an economically feasible way. Examples are lumber and hardware for a furniture manufacturer.
   b. *Direct-labor costs* are the costs of all labor that is physically traceable to the finished good in an economically feasible manner. Examples are the labor of lathe operators and product assemblers.
   c. *Indirect manufacturing costs* are all costs other than direct materials and direct labor that are associated with the manufacture of the finished good. Examples are factory supplies, supervisory labor, and depreciation of manufacturing facilities.
   d. Indirect manufacturing costs are also called *factory overhead, factory burden, manufacturing overhead, manufacturing expenses,* and so forth.
   e. Some indirect manufacturing costs are variable and some are fixed.
   f. Direct material plus direct labor is called *prime cost;* direct labor plus factory overhead is called *conversion cost.*

2. Note in Exhibit 2-5 how the three basic elements of cost are typically shown in a company's schedule of cost of goods manufactured.

D. A fundamental distinction must be made between two general types of costs, as summarized in Exhibit 2-6.

1. *Product costs are inventoriable costs.*
   a. These costs are measures of inventories until the inventories are sold and become *cost of goods sold,* which is an *expense.*
   b. The main kinds of product costs are direct materials, direct labor, and factory overhead.
2. *Period costs are noninventoriable costs.*
   a. These costs are expenses incurred, without having been previously classified as costs of inventory.
   b. Typical period costs are selling and administrative expenses, which appear in the income statement after the gross margin figure.
3. Instead of the single merchandise inventory of a merchandising company, a manufacturing company could show three inventory items in its balance sheet:
   a. Direct materials
   b. Work in process
   c. Finished goods
4. There are two basic ways of accounting for inventories:
   a. The *perpetual-inventory method* requires a continuous record of inventory transactions.
   b. The *periodic-inventory method* relies on physical inventory counts.
   c. Both methods can produce the same measure of cost of goods sold (Exhibit 2–7).

E. There is some additional cost terminology you should become familiar with:
1. *Manufacturing expenses,* a misnomer, is often used as a substitute for *factory overhead.*
   a. Factory overhead, of course, is *not* an expense, but is part of the product costs.
   b. Such costs are transformed into expense (cost of goods sold) only when the products are sold.
2. *Cost of sales* is often used as a synonym for cost of goods sold.
3. *Indirect-labor costs* usually account for a major part of factory overhead.
   a. These include the wages and salaries of various factory service employees, idle time of direct labor, and even overtime premium of direct labor.
   b. Such overtime premium is not part of direct labor cost, despite the association of the overtime with specific jobs, provided such association is due to the *random scheduling* of the jobs instead of the special characteristics of the jobs themselves.
4. *Payroll fringe costs,* such as payroll taxes and the cost of employee benefits, are generally classified as factory overhead.

SELF-TEST AND PRACTICE EXERCISES

I For each of the following multiple-choice and true-false statements, select the single most appropriate answer and enter its identification letter in the space provided:

____ 1. Costs that vary inversely with changes in the volume of activity include: (a) total variable costs, (b) total variable costs divided by activity volume, (c) total fixed costs, (d) total fixed costs divided by activity volume, (e) none of the above.

____ 2. Total fixed costs are $80,000 when 5,000 product units are produced. When 8,000 units are produced, fixed costs would tend to be: (a) $128,000 in total, (b) $16 per unit, (c) $48,000 in total, (d) $10 per unit.

____ 3. Total variable costs are $120,000 when 15,000 product units are produced. When 20,000 units are produced, variable costs would tend to be: (a) $6 per unit, (b) $120,000 in total, (c) $8 per unit, (d) $80,000 in total.

____ 4. Within the relevant range: (a) total fixed costs would tend to stay the same, (b) unit variable costs would tend to stay the same, (c) both of the above, (d) neither of the above.

5. In practice, cost behavior patterns are usually assumed to relate to: (a) unidimensional measures of activity volume, (b) multidimensional measures of activity volume, (c) both of the above, (d) neither of the above.

6. Prime cost is direct labor cost plus indirect material cost: (a) true, (b) false.

7. Conversion cost is factory overhead cost plus: (a) direct material cost, (b) indirect labor cost, (c) direct labor cost, (d) none of the above.

8. Examples of factory overhead cost could include: (a) lubricants for factory machinery, (b) salary of factory superintendent, (c) both of the above, (d) neither of the above.

9. In practice, cost-behavior patterns are usually assumed to be: (a) linear, (b) curvilinear, (c) both of the above, (d) neither of the above.

10. Unit costs often represent averages that include: (a) fixed costs, (b) variable costs, (c) both of the above.

11. In general, if unit costs are multiplied by the number of product units at a certain level of activity, the result would be a total cost that is also appropriate for a different level of activity: (a) true, (b) false.

12. The three basic elements of manufacturing cost are direct materials, direct labor, and: (a) indirect materials and labor, (b) selling and general expenses, (c) fixed factory overhead, (d) cost of goods sold, (e) none of the above.

13. In general, factory-overhead costs are: (a) direct manufacturing costs, (b) indirect manufacturing costs, (c) both of the above, (d) neither of the above.

14. Examples of direct labor include wages of: (a) raw material handlers, (b) product assemblers, (c) both of the above, (d) neither of the above.

15. Cost of goods sold is: (a) an expense, (b) an asset, (c) a period cost, (d) all of the above.

16. In general, the idle time of direct labor should be included as direct-labor cost: (a) true, (b) false.

17. The overtime premium earnings of direct-labor employees are usually included as part of factory-overhead cost: (a) true, (b) false.

18. When inventories are accounted for by keeping a continuous record of changes in them, the method is called: (a) perpetual-inventory method, (b) periodic-inventory method, (c) both of the above, (d) neither of the above.

19. For a manufacturing company, the cost of goods available for sale during a given period is: (a) the beginning inventory of finished goods, (b) the cost of goods manufactured during that period, (c) the sum of the above, (d) none of the above.

20. Total manufacturing costs incurred plus the decrease in work-in-process inventory is equal to cost of goods manufactured: (a) true, (b) false.

21. A factory assembly worker's wage is $12 per hour for straight time and $18 per hour for time over 40 hours per week. In one week, the worker accumulated 45 hours. The overtime premium is: (a) $72, (b) $90, (c) $570, (d) $30, (e) none of the above.

22. A lathe operator in a furniture factory is randomly assigned to various jobs. The straight-time wage rate is $18 per hour with time and one-half for time over 40 hours per week. How much of these earnings should be charged to factory overhead if 48 hours are worked in one week? (a) $864, (b) none, (c) $72, (d) $144, (e) some other amount.

II Complete each of the following statements:

1. Cost is defined as ______________________________

2. The two main purposes for which modern cost accounting systems accumulate costs are:

(a) Inventory valuation Income determination

(b) Management planning + control

3. Any activity for which a separate measurement of costs is desired is called cost objective

4. The collection of costs in an organized way by an accounting system is called Cost Accumulation

5. Cost-behavior patterns may be called cost functions

6. Prime cost is the total of two types of cost:

(a) Direct Materials

(b) Direct Labor

7. Direct-labor cost plus factory-overhead cost is called conversion cost

8. Minor materials that become part of a manufactured product but that cannot feasibly be traced to specific physical units are called Indirect materials

13/14 = 93%

9. Sales less cost of goods sold is equal to Gross Profit (or Margin) on Sales

10. Product costs are synonymous with inventoriable costs.

11. The three major inventory classifications that might appear among the assets shown on the balance sheet of a manufacturing company are:

(a) Direct Materials

(b) Work-in-Process

(c) Finished Goods

12. Such items as payroll taxes and the costs of employee benefits are usually included as part of factory-overhead cost and are called Indirect labor payroll fringe costs.

13. The cost of goods available for sale less the ending inventory of finished goods is equal to Cost of Goods Sold

14. In a merchandising company, merchandise purchases plus the beginning inventory of merchandise is equal to Cost of Goods Available for Sale

III The operating statements of Queensview Corporation included these items:

Selling expenses	$64,000
Direct labor cost	84,000
General administrative expenses	36,000
Direct materials used	68,000
Fixed factory overhead costs	44,000
Variable factory overhead costs	20,000
Interest expense	8,000
Income tax expense	24,000

Compute the following amounts:

(a) Prime cost . . . . $ 152,000

(b) Conversion cost . . . . $ 148,000

(c) Total product costs . . . . $ 216,000

(d) Total period costs . . . . $ 96,000

IV Classify each of the following costs of Glen Lakes Company in two ways: (a) as variable costs (V), or fixed costs (F); (b) as inventoriable costs (I), or noninventoriable costs (N):

	(a) V or F	(b) I or N
0. Example: Direct labor	V	I
1. Commissions paid to salesmen		
2. Overtime premium of lathe operators		
3. Straight-line depreciation of factory equipment		
4. Straight-line depreciation of trucks used for delivery of sales to customers		
5. Idle time of assembly labor		
6. Salary of company controller		
7. Fire insurance on direct materials		
8. Property taxes on finished goods held for sale		
9. Direct materials		
10. Rent paid for store building		

V Sphinx Company's operating data for a year includes $180,000 of conversion cost and $132,000 of prime cost. If factory overhead was 50% larger than direct material cost, compute each of the following:

(a) Direct material cost

(b) Direct labor cost

(c) Factory overhead cost

VI Rather Corporation reported the following operating data for a year:

Manufacturing costs incurred	$250,000
Increase in inventory of work in process	28,000
Decrease in inventory of finished goods	23,000

Compute:

(a) Cost of goods manufactured

(b) Cost of goods sold

VII You are given the following data for Board Game Manufacturing Company for 19__2.

Sales		$350,000
Depreciation of machinery		4,000
Direct factory labor		70,000
Factory heat, light, and power		3,000
Factory supplies used		2,000
Indirect factory labor		28,000
Miscellaneous manufacturing expenses		1,000
Purchase of direct materials		88,000
Rent, factory building		12,000
Selling and administrative expenses		120,000
Inventories:	Dec. 31, 19__1	Dec. 31, 19__2
Direct materials	$22,000	$ 20,000
Finished goods	39,000	45,000
Work in process	18,000	12,000

1. Prepare in good form a schedule of cost of goods manufactured for 19__2.

2. Prepare in good form the 19__2 income statement, ignoring income taxes.

3 Cost-Volume-Profit Relationships

THIS CHAPTER EXAMINES several basic concepts and decision models that are widely used by managers for planning and control. The principal technique described here is often called **breakeven analysis,** but it is actually more broadly applicable than this name suggests. It deals with the relationships among activity volume, variable expenses, fixed expenses, and net income. Thus, breakeven analysis may more aptly be called **cost-volume-profit analysis.**

The key to understanding this subject is **contribution margin,** which is the excess of sales over variable expenses. This excess can be expressed in various terms: total dollars, dollars per product unit, percentage of sales, or ratio to sales.

The chapter also introduces **sensitivity analysis, variable costing, the contribution approach** to income statements, and **sales mix.**

REVIEW SUMMARY

A. The *breakeven point* is that point of activity (level of sales volume) where total revenues equal total expenses. At this point there is neither profit nor loss.

1. The *equation method* of determining the breakeven point is based on the fundamental relationships among the principal elements of the income statement:

a.

Sales		xxx
Less:		
Variable expenses	xxx	
Fixed expenses	xxx	xxx
Net income		xxx

b. One equation form of this income statement is:

Sales = Variable Expenses + Fixed Expenses + Net Income

c. Example: selling price \$5, variable cost per unit \$2, total fixed costs \$600, breakeven units X:

$$\$5X = \$2X + \$600 + 0$$
$$\$3X = \$600$$
$$X = \frac{\$600}{\$3}$$
$$X = 200 \text{ units}$$

d. The breakeven point in total dollar sales for this example is 200 units times \$5 = \$1,000. Prove this by filling these blanks:

		500,000
Sales (200 × \$ 5)	350,000	\$ 4,000
Less expenses:		
Variable (200 × \$ 2)	\$ 400	
Fixed	600	1,00
	(35,000)	
Net income		\$ - 0 -

2. Instead of using the equation method, one can often find the breakeven point more quickly and more easily by using an equivalent, streamlined approach called the *contribution-margin method.* This merely utilizes one form of the basic equation:

$$\text{Sales} = \frac{\text{Fixed Expenses + Net Income}}{\text{Contribution Margin}}$$

a. The breakeven point in terms of *product units* is computed simply by dividing total fixed expenses by the *contribution margin per product unit:*

$$\frac{\$600}{\$5 - \$2} = \frac{\$600}{\$3} = 200 \text{ units}$$

b. The breakeven point in terms of *total dollar sales* is determined simply by dividing total fixed expenses by the *contribution-margin ratio* or *percentage of sales:*

$$\frac{\$600}{\$3 \div \$5} = \frac{\$600}{.6} = \$1,000$$

3. The *graphic approach* (textbook Exhibit 3–1), which is useful in visualizing the concept of breakeven analysis, can utilize either of two methods for plotting expenses:
   a. Placing fixed expenses below variable expenses, or
   b. Placing fixed expenses above variable expenses (preferred by many because it depicts more clearly the key concept of contribution margin).
4. The sales in terms of product units or total sales dollars that must be made to attain a certain *target net income* can be computed either by the equation method or by the contribution-margin method.
   a. The equation method would be the same as described above except that the target net income is used instead of zero net income.
   b. The contribution-margin method is the same as described above except that the target net income is combined with total fixed expenses before dividing by the contribution margin per unit, ratio, or percentage.

B. Certain important cost-volume-profit assumptions are customarily made when breakeven charts are prepared.

1. The relationships between total sales and total expenses are usually assumed by accountants to be those that would apply only to the *relevant range:* the rather wide band of activity volume within which total fixed costs and unit variable costs would remain the same.

2. In contrast to the somewhat simplified relationships implied by accountants' breakeven charts, the economists' breakeven charts usually reflect the more realistic *curvilinear relationships* between sales and variable expenses over a more complete range of activity volume.
3. Essentially, accountants, assume *linear behavior of total costs and revenues:*
   a. All costs are divisible into the strictly fixed and variable elements defined in Chapter 2.
   b. Unit selling prices, unit variable costs, and total fixed costs are constant at different activity levels.
   c. No changes in efficiency and productivity occur at different volume levels.
   d. Activity volume is the only relevant factor affecting costs.

C. Because costs, volume, and profits are interrelated, a change in any factor could affect the breakeven point and net income.
1. Unpredictable changes in operating conditions could alter both fixed and variable costs and affect the contribution margin, breakeven point, activity volume, and net income.
2. In order to cope with such uncertainty, a manager can apply a *sensitivity analysis* to a cost-volume-profit model.
   a. Different predictions and assumptions are made for various critical factors in a given case.
   b. Computations are then made to measure the effects of these changes.
   c. Thus, sensitivity analysis can help managers focus on the most sensitive aspects of a particular plan of action before making potentially costly commitments.

D. There are two major methods of product costing:
1. *Absorption costing treats fixed manufacturing overhead as an inventoriable cost.*
2. *Variable costing* (also called direct costing and marginal costing) *treats fixed manufacturing overhead as a period cost.*
3. *However, both methods treat all variable manufacturing costs as inventoriable costs.*
4. See the important diagram in textbook Exhibit 3-2.
5. Variable costing is useful for management planning and control, but it is not acceptable for external reporting or for income tax purposes.

E. These two methods of product costing affect the income statement:
1. The *traditional income statement* uses absorption costing:
   a. Expenses are classified by *management function:* manufacturing, selling, administrative.
   b. Manufacturing costs are deducted from sales to obtain a *gross profit* or *gross margin.*
   c. Selling and administrative expenses are then deducted to obtain net income.
2. The *contribution income statement* uses variable costing.
   a. Expenses are classified by *cost behavior:* variable and fixed.
   b. All variable costs are deducted from sales to obtain a *contribution margin.*
   c. All fixed costs are then deducted to obtain net income.
3. In contrast to the traditional structure of the income statement, the measurement and reporting of contribution margins can provide important advantages to management.
   a. Contribution margins and ratios can help management identify the products to emphasize or redesign and those to de-emphasize or drop.
   b. Contribution margins may aid management in making decisions concerning selling-price changes and special sales promotions.
   c. Contribution-margin data can be useful in deciding how to utilize most profitably machines, materials, and other resources.
   d. In general, the contribution approach enables management to understand more

clearly the cost-volume-profit relationships and therefore to determine more realistically the combination of products, selling prices, and sales volume necessary to attain target profits.

F. A *profit-volume graph,* or *P/V chart* (Exhibit 3–3), is often helpful in understanding the impact of volume changes on net income.

1. The horizontal scale or axis of the P/V chart shows units of volume; the vertical scale shows net income in dollars.
2. A net-income line is plotted so that it indicates the breakeven point where it crosses the horizontal scale.

G. The activity volume of an organization can be measured in different ways.

1. If the entire physical volume is measurable in *uniform terms,* such as product units, patient-days, or student credit hours, the breakeven volume can be computed:
   - **a.** In terms of these units, as illustrated above in A.1.c.
   - **b.** In terms of total sales dollars, by multiplying the breakeven units by the uniform selling price per unit, as illustrated in A.1.d.
2. However, if the entire physical volume is not measurable in uniform terms (or if data in units are *not* available), the breakeven volume in *total sales dollars* can nevertheless be computed:
   - **a.** First, determine the total contribution margin at any particular sales level (within the relevant range).
   - **b.** Divide this contribution margin by the total sales at that level. This is the *contribution-margin percentage or ratio.*
   - **c.** Divide the total fixed costs by this percentage or ratio.

SELF-TEST AND PRACTICE EXERCISES

I For each of the following multiple-choice and true-false statements, select the single most appropriate answer and enter its identification letter in the space provided:

___ 1. The breakeven point is defined as the sum of variable expenses and fixed expenses: (a) true, (b) false.

___ 2. The main purpose of breakeven analysis is: (a) to judge operating performance, (b) to explain operations to stockholders, (c) to make operating plans, (d) to delegate responsibility for operating decisions.

___ 3. Castle Corporation has sales of $500,000, variable expenses $350,000, and fixed expenses $135,000. Contribution margin is: (a) $15,000, (b) 70 percent, (c) $365,000, (d) 30 percent.

___ 4. See above. The breakeven sales for Castle Corporation would be: (a) $485,000, (b) $192,857, (c) $450,000, (d) none of the above.

___ 5. Contribution margin is: (a) sales minus fixed expenses, (b) sales divided by variable expenses, (c) variable expenses minus fixed expenses, (d) none of the above.

___ 6. The number of product units that must be sold to earn a specified amount of net income can be calculated by dividing the contribution margin per product unit into: (a) total fixed expenses, (b) the specified amount of net income, (c) the sum of the above, (d) none of the above.

___ 7. Given for Glen Company (in thousands): sales $650, fixed expenses $330, variable expenses $390, number of product units sold 130. Compute the breakeven point: (a) 110 units, (b) $825, (c) 220 units, (d) $720.

___ 8. See above. If Glen Company is to achieve a net income of $70, its sales must be: (a) $1,500, (b) 500 units, (c) $790, (d) 200 units.

___ 9. The accountant's breakeven charts are usually: (a) linear, (b) nonlinear, (c) curvilinear, (d) none of the above.

___ 10. The economist's breakeven charts usually depict: (a) constant unit selling prices at different activity levels, (b) constant unit variable costs at different activity level, (c) both of the above, (d) neither of the above.

___ 11. The breakeven charts used by accountants usually assume: (a) unchanging total fixed expenses, (b) unchanging unit variable costs, (c) both of these, (d) neither of these.

___ 12. Accountants' breakeven charts usually assume that, as the activity level changes: (a) efficiency changes, (b) productivity changes, (c) both efficiency and productivity change, (d) neither efficiency nor productivity change.

___ 13. Given for Lake Corporation: sales $600,000, fixed expenses $399,000, and variable expenses $180,000. Compute the breakeven point: (a) $570,000, (b) $579,000, (c) $133,000, (d) $1,330,000.

___ 14. See above. If Lake Corporation is to achieve a net income of $42,000, its sales must be (a) $612,000, (b) $621,000, (c) $630,000, (d) none of the above.

___ 15. Sensitivity analysis is designed to help determine: (a) the effects of proposed plans on human behavior, (b) the financial consequences of possible prediction errors, (c) the defects of decision models, (d) who is to blame for unsuccessful operations.

___ 16. As sales exceed the breakeven point, a low contribution-margin percentage would result in lower profits than would a high contribution-margin percentage: (a) true, (b) false.

___ 17. The breakeven point for a given case would be decreased by an increase in: (a) total fixed costs, (b) the contribution-margin percentage, (c) either of the above, (d) neither of the above.

___ 18. The vertical axis of the P/V chart shows: (a) units of volume, (b) costs in dollars, (c) contribution margin in dollars, (d) margin of safety in dollars, (e) none of the above.

___ 19. The contribution approach to the income statement makes a primary classification of expenses according to: (a) cost behavior, (b) management function, (c) relative sizes of the expenses, (d) none of the above.

___ 20. In multi-product firms, a shift in sales mix from products with high contribution-margin ratios to products with low contribution-margin ratios would cause the breakeven point to be: (a) lower, (b) higher, (c) unchanged, (d) different, but underterminable.

___ 21. Both absorption costing and variable costing treat as inventoriable costs: (a) all variable manufacturing costs, (b) fixed manufacturing overhead, (c) all variable selling and administrative expenses, (d) none of the above.

___ 22. All fixed costs are treated as period costs when variable costing is used: (a) true, (b) false.

___ 23. All fixed costs are treated as product costs when absorption costing is used: (a) true, (b) false.

___ 24. Absorption costing is acceptable for: (a) income tax purposes, (b) external reporting, (c) both of the above, (d) neither of the above.

___ 25. Given for Clubb Company (in thousands): sales $530, manufacturing costs $220 (half fixed), and selling and administrative expenses $270 (two-thirds variable). Ignore inventories and compute gross margin: (a) $260, (b) $310, (c) $40, (d) none of the above.

___ 26. See above. Compute for Clubb Company the contribution margin: (a) $330, (b) $310, (c) $40, (d) $240.

___ 27. A company produces and sells two products at contribution margins of $4 for A and $10 for B. Fixed costs are $21,000. If the planned mix is five units of A for each unit of B, the breakeven point in terms of *total* units would be: (a) 4,200, (b) 9,000, (c) 1,800, (d) some other number.

___ 28. A company produces a product for sale at $24 per unit. Costs are $48,000 for total fixed costs and $16.00 for variable costs per unit. The number of units to be produced and sold to obtain a $14,400 profit after income taxes of 40 percent would be: (a) 7,500, (b) 3,000, (c) 9,000, (d) 3,750.

___ 29. As the activity level increases within the relevant range, fixed costs will: (a) remain the same per unit, (b) increase in total, (c) decrease per unit, (d) none of the above.

___ 30. As the activity level decreases within the relevant range, variable costs will: (a) increase in total, (b) decrease per unit, (c) increase per unit, (d) none of the above.

II Complete each of the following statements:

1. The key concept that is most useful in understanding breakeven analysis is ______________________________

2. In the usual breakeven graph, the horizontal scale or axis represents ______________________________

3. The linearity assumption for breakeven charts is likely to be most accurate within the ______________________________ of activity volume.

4. Breakeven analysis by accountants usually assumes that the only relevant variable affecting cost is ______________________________

5. The expected values of a decision model will be affected by changes or errors in critical data inputs. A technique that measures this effect is called ______________________________

6. An increase in total fixed costs in a given case would cause the breakeven point to ______________

7. In multi-product companies, the relative combinations of products sold is called the ______________________________

8. Gross margin is ______________ minus ______________

9. Contribution margin is ______________ minus ______________

10. Net income is contribution margin minus ______________________________

III The relevant range of Country Corporation's activity volume lies between 20,000 units and 40,000 units. Fill these blanks:

Activity Volume	Total Variable Costs	Variable Costs Per Unit	Total Fixed Costs	Fixed Costs Per Unit
24,000	$______(a)	$______(b)	$______(c)	$______(d)
30,000	120,000	______(e)	90,000	______(f)
36,000	______(g)	______(h)	______(i)	______(j)

IV Given for Flexible Products, Inc.:

Sales price per product unit	$ 70
Variable expenses per product unit	50
Total fixed expenses	4,800

Find:

1. Contribution margin per product unit . . . . $ ______

2. Breakeven sales in units . . . . ______ units

3. Sales in units that would produce a net income of $1,200. . . . . ______ units

4. Sales in units that would produce a net income of 20% of sales . . . . ______ units

5. Net income, if 600 product units were sold . . . . $ ______

6. The breakeven sales in units, if variable expenses were increased by $5 per unit and if total fixed expenses were decreased by $1,200 . . . . ______ units

7. If the company desires a net income of $1,800 on a sales volume of 300 units, what must the unit selling price be, assuming no changes in the $50 variable expenses per unit or the $4,800 total fixed expenses? . . . . $ ______

V Given for Monument Sales Company:

Sales	$60,000
Total fixed expenses	12,000
Total variable expenses	42,000

Find:

1. Net income when sales are $60,000 (as above) . . . . . $ ______

2. Contribution-margin ratio or percentage . . . . . ______ %

3. Breakeven sales . . . . . $______

4. Sales that would produce a net income of $9,000, assuming no changes in the contribution-margin ratio or in total fixed expenses . . . . . $ ______

5. Sales that would produce a net income of 20% of sales, assuming no changes in the contribution-margin ratio or in total fixed expenses . . . . . $ ______

6. Breakeven sales if total fixed expenses are reduced by $2,000 and if selling prices are reduced by 10% per product unit, assuming no changes in variable expenses per product unit . . . . . $ ______

VI Given for Paper Toys, Inc. (in thousands):

Sales	$750
Manufacturing expenses	400
Selling and administrative expenses	300

Of the manufacturing expenses, 40 percent are fixed, and 30 percent of the selling and administrative expenses are fixed. Compute the following, assuming that all inventories are negligible:

1. Total fixed manufacturing expenses .... $ ______

2. Total variable manufacturing expenses .... $ ______

3. Total fixed selling and administrative expenses .... $ ______

4. Total variable selling and administrative expenses .... $ ______

5. Total fixed expenses .... $ ______

6. Total variable expenses .... $ ______

7. Gross profit .... $ ______

8. Contribution margin .... $ ______

9. Net income .... $ ______

VII Canasta Products, Inc. produces and sells two products as follows:

	J	K
Selling prices per unit	$18	$10
Variable costs per unit	13	7

Total fixed costs are $31,500.

Compute the breakeven point in terms of *total* units for each of these planned sales mixes:

1. Three Js for each K ______ units

2. Three Ks for each J ______ units

3. Five Js for every three Ks ______ units

VIII Given for Iconoclast Potteries:

Product selling price per unit	$ 50
Variable expenses per unit	30
Total fixed expenses	16,000
Target net income after taxes	9,000
Income tax rate	40%

Compute the number of product units that must be sold to achieve the target net income after taxes.

IX Given for Dual-View Lens Corporation for 19__8:

	Fixed	Variable	Total
Manufacturing cost of goods sold	$80,000	$120,000	$200,000
Selling expenses	20,000	80,000	100,000
Administrative expenses	30,000	10,000	40,000
Sales			365,000

1. Prepare an income statement in the traditional form:

2. Prepare an income statement using the contribution approach:

3. Compute the operating income if sales volume increased 10% without any change in unit selling prices:

4 Job, Process, and Operation Systems

THE FRAMEWORK of the three basic systems of product costing for a manufacturing company is presented in this chapter. Described are the principal records and procedures involved in management planning and control and in the accumulation of costs for inventory valuation and income determination. Also illustrated are the typical transactions and their entries in the accounts.

The diagram in Exhibit 4-5 of the textbook is an excellent focal point for the study of a cost system, because it includes the principal accounts used in manufacturing accounting and it clearly shows the flow of costs from the originating accounts, through the inventories, and to the cost of goods sold. Using this diagram for a background aids immensely in understanding this chapter and many of the other chapters that follow.

REVIEW SUMMARY

A. In management accounting systems, costs are usually accumulated to meet both internal management needs and external reporting requirements.

1. A major aim of such systems is the accumulation of costs *by departments or cost centers* to assist planning and control by pinpointing responsibility.
2. Another major objective is the accumulation of costs *by products* for purposes of inventory valuation and income determination.
3. *Job-order costing* is suitable for use by companies that manufacture custom-made products that are readily identified by individual units or batches, each of which receives varying inputs of direct materials, direct labor, and factory overhead.
   - **a.** Such products would include furniture, machinery, highway bridges, drilling platforms for off-shore oil exploration, and space modules for voyages to the moon.
   - **b.** Nonmanufacturing situations for which the job-order system would be suitable include advertising agencies, auto repair, public accounting practice, social welfare cases, and research projects.
4. In contrast to job-order costing, *process costing* is appropriate when there is a mass production of uniform units, which usually flow continuously through a series of standard production steps called processes.

a. Such products would include textiles, chemicals, petroleum products, cement, bricks, newsprint, ice cream, and breakfast foods.
b. Nonmanufacturing situations for which the process system would be appropriate include banks, insurance companies, schools, libraries, and many government services.

5. Some features are common to both job-order and process-costing methods:
   a. Product costs per unit are determined by averaging (process-costing operations typically use larger denominators for this purpose than job-costing operations).
   b. In addition to accumulating costs by products, each costing method also accumulates costs in cost centers or departments for planning and control purposes.
6. A third product costing system is used by many companies.
   a. This system is called *operation costing.*
   b. It contains elements of both job-order costing and process costing.
   c. Materials are specifically allocated to identifiable batches of products.
   d. However, conversion costs are identified with the particular manufacturing operations through which the material batches flow.

B. Several basic forms and documents are used in a typical job-order cost system.
1. The central document is the *job-order* or *job-cost sheet,* textbook Exhibit 4–1.
   a. The job-order or job-cost sheet is used to accumulate product costs by identifiable lots of product.
   b. The file or collection of job orders for uncompleted jobs serves as the subsidiary ledger for Work-in-Process Control, a general-ledger account.
   c. In effect, the file of these cost sheets for uncompleted jobs is a perpetual book inventory of work in process.
2. Two other perpetual book inventories are also usually maintained in subsidiary ledgers:
   a. The *stores cards* (Exhibit 4–6), which represent costs and quantities of materials on hand, are controlled by the Stores Control account in the general ledger.
   b. The *finished-goods stock cards,* which measure costs and quantities of completed goods held for sale, are controlled by the Finished Goods Control, a general-ledger account.
3. The individual *factory department overhead cost sheets* (Exhibit 4–7), which contain the details of various kinds of manufacturing expenses actually incurred, make up a subsidiary ledger, which is controlled by the Factory Department Overhead Control account.
4. *Stores requisitions, labor work tickets,* and *labor clock cards* (Exhibits 4–2, 4–3, and 4–4) serve two basic purposes:
   a. They are used as bookkeeping media for charging direct costs to jobs and indirect costs to overhead departments.
   b. They are used to aid in fixing responsibility for the control and usage of both direct and indirect materials and labor.

C. In practice, the general-ledger entries for transactions of job-order cost systems are typically oriented toward measuring inventory costs rather than serving the needs of management responsibility and cost control.
1. Usually the charges for *prime costs* (direct material and direct labor) are taken directly to the Work-in-Process Control and not through intermediate department accounts for responsibility and cost control (Exhibit 4–8).
2. However, costing for control is not overlooked in job-order cost systems, but is usually accomplished by the preparation of daily or weekly summaries of the source documents for material and labor costs (material requisitions, labor work tickets, and labor clock cards).

D. Most factory-overhead costs are indirect manufacturing costs and thus cannot easily be identified with specific jobs.

1. Therefore, the amount of factory-overhead cost applicable to specific jobs must be estimated by using rates based upon total direct-labor cost, total direct-labor hours, total machine-hours, or some other base for allocating indirect costs to jobs.

2. *Rather accurate* overhead cost rates for a given period could be calculated at the end of such period by using actual overhead costs and actual overhead allocation bases, but the resulting cost information would usually *not be available on a timely basis* for several important purposes:

a. Making interim measurements of product inventory costs and operating net income,

b. Currently relating factory-overhead costs to products for purposes of planning and control, and

c. Using manufacturing cost as one of the important factors in setting selling prices of products finished during the period.

3. Therefore, instead of using the more accurate *actual* or *historical* rates for applying overhead costs to production, most companies use the less accurate but more timely *predetermined* rates that are based upon forecasted or budgeted amounts of factory-overhead costs and the overhead rate base (such as budgeted total direct-labor costs or hours).

4. These predetermined factory-overhead cost rates are typically used on an *annualized basis* rather than a monthly basis for two important reasons:

a. To overcome the volatility in computed unit costs due to changes in the level of volume (the denominator reason), and

b. To avoid the volatility in computed unit costs due to seasonal variations in total factory-overhead costs (the numerator reason).

E. Accounting for total factory-overhead costs involves actual overhead, applied overhead, and the difference between these two amounts.

1. *Actual overhead cost* is the amount of overhead cost incurred on the accrual accounting basis.

a. Actual overhead cost is debited to Factory Department Overhead Control and its subsidiary ledger, the factory department overhead cost sheets.

b. The offsetting credit entries are made to such accounts as Stores Control, Accrued Payroll, Unexpired Insurance, Allowance for Depreciation, and Accounts Payable. See Exhibit 4–5.

2. *Applied overhead cost* is found by multiplying the predetermined overhead rate by the actual (historical) amount of the overhead rate base (such as total direct-labor costs or hours).

a. Applied overhead cost is debited to Work-in-Process Control and its subsidiary ledger, the individual job-cost sheets.

b. The offsetting credit is made to Factory Overhead Applied, a contra or offset account to Factory Department Overhead Control.

3. The difference between applied and actual overhead is called either:

a. *Overapplied overhead* or *overabsorbed overhead,* if the applied amount is greater than the actual amount, or

b. *Underapplied overhead* or *underabsorbed overhead,* if the applied amount is less than the actual amount.

4. *At the end of the year,* there is typically only a small amount of under- or overapplied overhead cost, and it is usually closed out by a debit or credit, respectively, to Cost of Goods Sold, in contrast to the more accurate method of prorating the amount over

three accounts in proportion to the unadjusted overhead portions of their balances:
   a. Cost of Goods Sold
   b. Finished Goods
   c. Work in Process

F. The procedures described above for factory overhead illustrate the difference between two basic costing approaches for manufacturing companies:
   1. *Normal absorption costing* uses *predetermined overhead rates* for applying factory overhead to production.
   2. *Actual absorption costing* uses the *actual factory overhead costs* for products manufactured.
   3. Both of these approaches use the actual costs of direct materials and direct labor for products manufactured.
   4. *The normal system measures more realistic costs of individual products at the time they are manufactured.*

G. The key to both the process costing system and the operation costing system is *equivalent units.*
   1. This is the expression of output in terms of *doses* or *amounts* of resources applied to the output.
   2. For example, if the conversion costs have been fully applied to 300 units completed in a process but only 40 percent applied to the ending inventory of 100 units partially completed, the equivalent units would be 300 + 40% (100) = 300 + 40 = 340 units.
      a. Total costs are divided by the number of equivalent units to arrive at unit costs.
      b. Unit costs are then used to allocate total costs between completed production and the ending inventory of work in process. See the textbook illustration.

SELF-TEST AND PRACTICE EXERCISES

I For each of the following multiple-choice and true-false statements, select the most appropriate answer and enter its identification letter in the space provided:

____ 1. Costs are always accumulated by responsibility center for control purposes when the type of cost system used is: (a) job-order costing, (b) process costing, (c) operation costing, (d) any of these types of cost systems.

____ 2. When varying inputs of direct labor and factory overhead are received by individual product units or batches, the most appropriate type of cost system to use is: (a) job-order costing, (b) process costing, (c) operation costing.

____ 3. A-C Corporation produces six sizes of air conditioning filters. Each size requires different kinds and quantities of direct materials, but requires identical kinds and quantities of direct labor and factory overhead. The most appropriate type of cost system to use is: (a) job-order costing, (b) process costing, (c) operation costing.

____ 4. Companies engaged in the mass production of like product units that require identical quantities and kinds of direct materials and that flow continuously through a series of uniform production steps would usually cost such products by: (a) the job-order costing method, (b) the process costing method, (c) the operating costing method.

____ 5. Accounting systems for manufacturers accumulate costs for the purposes of: (a) planning and control, (b) valuing inventories, (c) measuring net income, (d) all of the above.

____ 6. Examples of products for which a job-order costing system would probably be suitable include: (a) newsprint, (b) auto repairs, (c) both of the above, (d) neither of the above.

___ 7. Examples of operations for which a process costing system would probably be suitable include: (a) oil refining, (b) mining, (c) both of the above, (d) neither of the above.

___ 8. Product costs per unit are determined by an averaging process in: (a) a job-order cost system, (b) a process cost system, (c) an operation costing system, (d) all of the above.

___ 9. When a job-order cost system is used, costs are usually also accumulated in cost centers or departments: (a) true, (b) false.

___ 10. The file of cost sheets for uncompleted jobs serves as a perpetual book inventory of direct materials: (a) true, (b) false.

___ 11. A perpetual book inventory is represented by: (a) the finished-goods stock cards, (b) the stores requisitions, (c) both of the above, (d) neither of the above.

___ 12. Under the job-cost system described in the textbook, purchases of direct material are debited to: (a) Purchases, (b) Work in Process, (c) Factory Overhead, (d) some other account.

___ 13. Under the job-cost system described in the textbook, issues of direct materials are debited to: (a) Factory Overhead, (b) Stores, (c) Work in Process, (d) some other account.

___ 14. Under the job-cost system described in the textbook, issues of indirect materials are debited to: (a) Factory Overhead, (b) Stores, (c) Work in Process, (d) some other account.

___ 15. Documents that are used as a basis for charging costs to jobs and overhead departments include: (a) stores cards, (b) labor work tickets, (c) both of the above, (d) neither of the above.

___ 16. The subsidiary ledger for Factory Department Overhead Control contains entries for applied factory overhead: (a) true, (b) false.

___ 17. Indirect labor used should be debited in a job-cost system to: (a) Accrued Payroll, (b) Work in Process, (c) Finished Goods, (d) some other account.

___ 18. When direct-labor employees are paid in a job-cost system, cash should be credited, and the debit should be to: (a) Accrued Payroll, (b) Work in Process, (c) Finished Goods, (d) some other account.

___ 19. Under the job-order cost system, when factory overhead is applied by a predetermined rate, (a) Factory Overhead is debited, (b) Work in Process is credited, (c) Factory Overhead Applied is credited, (d) none of the above.

___ 20. A historical rate for applying factory-overhead cost to products would be preferred to a predetermined rate if the only criteria used consisted of (a) accuracy, (b) timeliness, (c) both of the above, (d) neither of the above.

___ 21. In a job-order cost system, costing for control purposes is usually accomplished by the frequent preparation of summaries of the source documents for labor and material costs: (a) true, (b) false.

___ 22. When predetermined rates are used for applying factory overhead to production, they should usually be calculated to cover: (a) a month, (b) a quarter, (c) a year, (d) any of the above periods.

___ 23. When a job-order cost system is used, the accounting entry for jobs completed would include: (a) a debit to Cost of Goods Sold, (b) a credit to Finished Goods, (c) a debit to Work in Process, (d) a debit to Finished Goods.

___ 24. The accounting entry under a job-order cost system, when finished goods are sold, would include: (a) a credit to Finished Goods on a selling price basis, (b) a credit to Cost of Goods Sold on a cost basis, (c) a debit to Sales on a selling price basis, (d) none of the above.

___ 25. Smokestack Products computed for a certain year: $608,000 total factory overhead budgeted, $621,000 total factory overhead incurred, and $614,000 total factory overhead applied. The factory overhead for the year was: (a) underapplied by $7,000, (b) overapplied by $6,000, (c) underapplied by $13,000, (d) overapplied by $13,000.

___ 26. Overapplied factory overhead is the excess of applied factory overhead over the amount of: (a) budgeted factory overhead, (b) predicted factory overhead, (c) forecasted factory overhead, (d) all of the above, (e) none of the above.

___ 27. The usual end-of-year treatment of underapplied factory overhead is to: (a) debit Cost of Goods Sold, (b) credit Cost of Goods Sold, (c) debit Cost of Goods Sold and appropriate inventory accounts, (d) credit Cost of Goods Sold and appropriate inventory accounts, (e) none of the above.

___ 28. The amount of under- or overapplied factory overhead would, in general, tend to be larger at the end of the year than at any interim date: (a) true, (b) false.

___ 29. A *normal* absorption costing system provides for charging Work in Process with actual direct material costs and with applied factory overhead costs: (a) true, (b) false.

___ 30. An *actual* absorption costing system provides for charging Work in Process with actual direct labor costs and applied factory overhead costs: (a) true, (b) false.

___ 31. Fluid Manufacturing Company's Laminating Process completed 550 units in May and showed an ending inventory of 150 units, which were 60 percent completed as to conversion costs and 100 percent completed as to material costs. Material costs were $2,450, and conversion costs were $3,200. What is the unit conversion cost? (a) $5.00, (b) $4.57, (c) $3.83, (d) some other amount.

___ 32. See the preceding item. What is the unit material cost? (a) $3.83, (b) $4.00, (c) $3.50, (d) some other amount.

___ 33. See the two preceding items. What is the cost of the ending inventory in process? (a) $765, (b) $975, (c) $1,275, (d) some other amount.

II Complete each of the following statements:

1. Companies that manufacture products that are readily identified by individual units or batches, each of which receives varying inputs of direct materials, direct labor, and factory overhead, would usually find the ____________ costing system more suitable than the ____________ ____________ costing system.

2. For planning and control purposes, costs can be accumulated in ____________

3. The subsidiary ledger for Work-in-Process Control consists of ____________

4. A document used to aid in fixing responsibility for the control and usage of materials is ____________ ____________

5. Applied factory overhead should be debited to ____________ Control and to ____________

6. The predetermined factory-overhead rate can be determined by dividing ____________ cost by ____________

7. Applied factory-overhead cost is calculated by multiplying ____________ by ____________

8. At the end of the year, if the overapplied factory-overhead cost is to be handled in a theoretically accurate manner, it should be prorated by ____________ entries to three accounts: ____________, ____________, and ____________

III Given for Prognosis Instruments, Inc.:

Budgeted factory-overhead cost	$550,000
Budgeted direct-labor hours	440,000 hrs.
Actual factory-overhead cost	$562,000
Actual direct-labor hours	460,000 hrs.

Find:

1. Predetermined overhead rate . . . . $ ______
2. Applied factory-overhead cost . . . . $ ______
3. Amount of underapplied factory-overhead cost or overapplied factory-overhead cost . . . . $ ______

IV The Prolific Production Company presents the following selected general-ledger accounts showing balances at April 1 of the current calendar year:

Cash	
10,000	

Accrued Payroll	
	-0-

Work-in-Process Control	
41,000	

Unexpired Insurance	
1,000	

Stores Control	
32,000	

Finished Goods Control	
148,000	

Allowance for Depreciation	
	70,000

Factory Dept. Overhead Control	
62,000	

Cost of Goods Sold	
200,000	

Accounts Payable	
	27,000

Factory Overhead Applied	
	63,000

Sales	
	310,000

Correct balances at April 30 of the current year include:

Accrued Payroll	$ 3,000(Cr.)
Stores	$ 30,000(Dr.)
Work in Process	$ 47,000(Dr.)
Finished Goods	$152,000(Dr.)

The April transactions of the company are summarized as follows:

(a)	Cash sales	$105,000
(b)	Materials purchased on account	42,000
(c)	Direct materials used	39,000
(d)	Direct factory labor incurred	16,000
(e)	Indirect materials used	______
(f)	Indirect factory labor incurred	______
(g)	Factory insurance expired	300
(h)	Factory depreciation	1,700
(i)	Factory utility services purchased on account	3,000
(j)	Factory overhead applied: 125% of direct-labor cost	______
(k)	Accounts payable paid	49,000
(l)	Factory payroll paid	22,000
(m)	Cost of goods manufactured	______
(n)	Cost of goods sold	______

Required:

1. Calculate the dollar amounts to fill the five blanks in the above list of transactions (e, f, j, m, n).

2. Post the amounts for all April transactions to the general-ledger accounts on the preceding page, using each transaction letter to cross-reference your posted debits and credits. Journal entries are not necessary.

V Adherence Glue Works presented the following data for the June operations of its Mixing Process:

Materials added	$13,200
Conversion costs	$17,952
Beginning inventory in process	none
Ending inventory in process	1,200 units
Units started	6,000 units
Units completed and transferred out	4,800 units
Units lost from spoilage	none

The ending inventory is 40 percent completed as to conversion costs and 100 percent completed as to materials.

Compute:

1. Equivalent units for conversion costs . . . . . $ ______

2. Equivalent units for materials . . . . . $ ______

3. Unit conversion cost . . . . . $ ______

4. Unit material cost . . . . . $ ______

5. Cost of work completed and transferred out . . . . . $ ______

6. Cost of ending work-in-process inventory . . . . . $ ______

7. Proof of total costs allocated: $13,200 + $17,952 = $31,152.

5 Master Budget and Responsibility Accounting

IN THIS CHAPTER we study the **budgeting system** of planning and control. A budget is a plan of action that quantifies an organization's goals in terms of specific financial and operating objectives. The **master budget** is a comprehensive set of detailed operating forecasts for all segments of an organization. In addition to systematizing the planning function, budgets also provide criteria for measuring performance and improving internal communication and coordination.

This chapter describes the general framework of the master budget and explains the important connections between budgets and the behavioral aspects of a control system, including such concepts as **responsibility accounting, controllability of costs,** and **management by objectives (MBO).**

REVIEW SUMMARY

A. A *budget* is a quantitative expression of an organization's plan of action and an aid to the coordination and implementation of the plan.

1. The budget is helpful to management in making two broad types of decisions:
   - **a.** *Financing decisions* deal with the obtaining of funds for acquiring resources.
   - **b.** *Operating decisions* are concerned with the acquisition and utilization of scarce resources.
2. The budget is valuable to very small units as well as to large organizations.
3. Budgets have several significant advantages when properly used:
   - **a.** They compel management to face the task of planning.
   - **b.** Budgets aid in translating plans into explicit terms that can be useful as a basis for evaluating actual performance in the future.
   - **c.** Budgets also serve to communicate management plans, to coordinate these plans, and to carry them out.

B. Budgets can be classified in at least two ways:

1. They may be classified as to the length of time covered.
   - **a.** The usual period for planning and control budgets is one year, which can be divided into months or quarters and which can also be kept continuously extended for one year in advance.

b. Long-term budgets of ten or more years can be used for basic changes in products and manufacturing facilities.

2. The budgeted financial statements, sometimes called *pro forma statements,* may be classified also as to general type of budget. See the textbook Exhibit 5–1:
   a. *Operating budgets,* such as the sales, production, and expense budgets, are elements of the budgeted income statement.
   b. *Financial budgets* include the capital budget, the budgets for cash receipts and disbursements, the budgeted balance sheet, and the budgeted changes in financial position.

C. A helpful perspective of the *master budget* is provided by the textbook illustration of its preparation in a step-by-step approach.
1. The final master budget is the product of several preliminary drafts, each of which may lead to decisions that require an additional draft.
2. Several basic steps are typically followed in preparing the final budget exhibits:
   a. Make the forecast of sales by products in both units and dollars.
   b. Prepare the budget for the number of units to produce that, with beginning inventories, will meet the needs of sales and also bring ending inventories up to the target levels.
   c. Construct schedules for material, labor, and overhead costs to support the production activity determined in the preceding step.
   d. Make the cost-of-goods-sold budget.
   e. Prepare the various expense budgets.
   f. Construct the budgeted income statement.
   g. Make cash budgets that show, in addition to expected cash receipts and disbursements, financing plans involving loans and temporary investments (textbook Appendix 5A).
   h. Prepare a balance sheet that is projected to the end of the budget period (Appendix 5A).

D. The forecast of sales volume is usually the keystone of the entire budget structure, but it is often difficult to predict reliable sales figures.
1. Many factors should be considered, such as:
   a. Past sales volume,
   b. General economic and industry conditions,
   c. Market research studies,
   d. Pricing policies, and
   e. Advertising, competition, and other factors.
2. Usually, in forecasting sales, it would be wise not to rely entirely upon a single procedure, but to use some suitable combinations of three particular procedures:
   a. Individual salesmen and sales managers of the organization combine their predictions after considering such factors as previous sales volumes, economic indicators, and competitive conditions.
   b. Predict sales by using a statistical approach such as trend measurements, cycle projections, and correlation analysis.
   c. The top executives and administrators of the organization hold a meeting, express their opinions, and arrive at a group judgment as to predicted sales.

E. Master budgets are helpful foundations for the construction of computer-based simulation models that are often called *financial planning models.*
1. Such models are mathematical statements of relationships among a company's activities and selected related factors, both internal and external.
2. The models are used not only for preparing and revising budgets, but also for comparing the effects of various decision alternatives (*sensitivity analysis*).

3. The degree of sophistication of such models ranges from the standard general-purpose simulators, available on a rental basis, to the more comprehensive models that must be designed to meet the complex requirements of specific organizations.
4. As in all information decisions, the selection of computer-based simulation models should be determined by a *cost-benefit approach.*

F. When decision making with a given organization is subdivided into certain areas of management responsibility (cost centers, profit centers, and investment centers), some form of *responsibility-accounting system* should usually accompany this subdivision.

1. Because the design of a system and the design of an organizational structure are actually interdependent, they should not be designed separately.
2. Responsibility-accounting systems (also called profitability-accounting systems or activity-accounting systems) recognize various decision centers throughout an organization and trace costs (and revenues, assets, and liabilities, where appropriate) to the individual manager who is primarily responsible for making decisions about the costs in question.
3. Responsibility reports (performance reports) should be prepared periodically to provide the manager of each decision center with figures on those items subject to his control, as illustrated in textbook Exhibit 5-3.
4. Such reports may show only the budgeted amounts and the variances of actual amounts from budgeted amounts.
   a. This focus on the variances illustrates *management by exception.*
   b. Managers thus need not waste their time and effort on those parts of the reports that reflect the smoothly running phases of operations.

G. It is important but difficult to distinguish between controllable and uncontrollable costs.

1. *Controllable costs are costs directly influenced by a given manager within a given time span.*
2. In practice it is often not easy to fix responsibilty or controllability for a given cost.
3. In general, the length of the time period involved must be considered in determining the management level at which a cost is controllable.
4. However, remember that variances arising from a responsibility-accounting system should not be used to "fix the blame," but rather to help suggest possible causes of variances or to identify persons who should be asked to explain the variances.
5. Helpful in measuring and evaluating performance is a system of *management by objectives* (MBO).
   a. Budget goals and plans for attaining them are set jointly by manager and superior for specific conditions and periods.
   b. Subsequent evaluation of performance is then made in light of these specifics.
   c. Obvious benefits can flow from a joint effort that enhances the credibility and validity of goals and plans as perceived by participants in the MBO process.

SELF-TEST AND PRACTICE EXERCISES

I For each of the following multiple-choice and true-false statements, select the most appropriate answer and enter its identification letter in the space provided:

___ 1. The usual starting point in the preparation of a master budget is: (a) production forecasts, (b) cash flow forecasts, (c) expense forecasts, (d) none of the above.

___ 2. A budgeted balance sheet would be classified as: (a) an operating budget, (b) a financial budget, (c) either of the above, (d) neither of the above.

___ 3. Operating budgets would include: (a) the production budget, (b) the selling expense budget, (c) both of the above, (d) neither of the above.

___ 4. In making a production budget for a given period, one should give consideration to: (a) predicted beginning inventories of the period, (b) desired ending inventories of the period, (c) both of the above, (d) neither of the above.

___ 5. Wool Products Company has a desired inventory of 14,500 units of a certain product at the end of its budget period, a beginning inventory of 20,000 units, and projected sales of 64,500 units. Budgeted production should be: (a) 70,000 units, (b) 64,500 units, (c) 59,000 units, (d) none of the above.

___ 6. As a basis for judging operating results, it is usually better to use expected performance than to use past performance: (a) true, (b) false.

___ 7. In the construction of a master budget, the last step is usually the preparation of the forecasted: (a) income statement, (b) cash receipts, (c) sales, (d) production, (e) balance sheet.

___ 8. It is usually feasible to forecast sales without considering: (a) general economic conditions, (b) competition, (c) both of the above, (d) neither of the above.

___ 9. Arriving at a sales forecast by forming a group judgment composed of the opinions of top company officers is usually: (a) a fast method, (b) an excellent method, (c) both of the above, (d) neither of the above.

___ 10. Norm Manufacturing Company has a $126,000 balance of accounts receivable at the beginning of its budget period. It expects to make $219,000 of sales on account and to collect $143,500 of cash on account during the budget period. Compute the forecasted ending balance of accounts receivable: (a) $236,500, (b) $201,500, (c) $219,000, (d) none of the above.

___ 11. See the preceding item. Assume that no other cash inflows are expected, that total cash payments during the budget period are expected to be $179,000, and that the minimum increase desired in the cash balance is $10,000. What is the amount necessary to borrow? (a) $45,500, (b) $44,500, (c) $24,500, (d) some other amount.

___ 12. A usually effective way of forecasting sales is to rely entirely on the predictions of the individual salesmen and sales managers of the organization: (a) true, (b) false.

___ 13. Ordinarily, a master budget would include: (a) predicted income tax expenses, (b) predicted income tax liability, (c) both of the above, (d) neither of the above.

___ 14. Potential cash deficiencies would usually be determined by: (a) the sales budget, (b) the pro forma balance sheet, (c) the expense budgets, (d) the projected income statement, (e) none of the above.

___ 15. Units of materials to purchase would be equal to budgeted materials usage: (a) plus the desired ending inventory of materials and minus the beginning inventory of materials, (b) plus the beginning inventory of materials and minus the desired ending inventory of materials, (c) both of the above, (d) neither of the above.

___ 16. New Fabrications, Inc. desires to reduce its inventory of a certain raw material by 40 percent. The inventory at the beginning of the budget period is 120,000 units, and the company plans to manufacture 84,000 product units. Each of these requires 2.5 units of the raw material. How many units of the raw material should be purchased during the budget period? (a) 138,000 units, (b) 36,000 units, (c) 90,000 units, (d) some other quantity.

___ 17. A financial planning model can be used: (a) in the preparation and revision of budgets, (b) for sensitivity analysis, (c) both of the above, (d) neither of the above.

___ 18. For evaluating performance and planning it is best to compare current results with: (a) historical records of the organization, (b) average performance of similar organizations, (c) budget data.

___ 19. Controllable costs are equivalent to variable costs: (a) true, (b) false.

___ 20. The variances developed in a responsibility-accounting system should be used primarily to help identify: (a) persons who can be blamed for the variances, (b) persons who made or approved the budget forecasts, (c) both of these, (d) neither of these.

II Complete each of the following statements:

1. Budgets may be called projections, forecasted statements, predicted statements, or ______ ______ statements.

2. Budgets should help to communicate management ______, to coordinate these ______, and to implement them.

3. A budget that always shows a 12-month forecast by adding a month or quarter in the future as the month or quarter just ended is dropped is called a ______ budget.

4. In preparing a master budget, it is usually best to start with a forecast of ______ ______

5. Budgeted units of product to manufacture may be determined by adding ______ ______ to budgeted sales and subtracting ______ ______ from this total.

6. Cash budgets can be helpful to managers in avoiding unnecessary cash ______ ______ and ______ cash balances.

7. Computer-based simulation models constructed on the foundation of master budgets are often called ______

8. The selection of computer-based simulation models should be determined by a ______ approach.

9. In ______ accounting systems (also called profitability-accounting systems or activity-accounting systems), costs are traced to various decision centers of the organization.

10. In performance reports to managers of decision centers, the focus on ______ of actual amounts from budgeted figures illustrates a form of "management by ______."

11. Costs that are directly influenced by a manager during a given time span are called ______ costs.

III Given for the Eight Seas Company:

Beginning inventory (cost)	$120,000
Expected sales	$510,000
Desired ending inventory (cost)	$145,000

Find the cost of budgeted purchases, assuming that inventory cost is marked up by 70 percent of cost to obtain the sales prices at which goods are sold to customers . . . . $ ______

IV Given for Mort Sanger Stores:

Cash discounts allowed to customers who pay in month of sale: 2%

Collection experience: 50% pay in month of sale, 30% in next month, and 20% in following month.

Budgeted sales: January $300,000, February $250,000, March $400,000

Compute: 1. Budgeted cash collections for March . . . . $ ______

2. Balance of accounts receivable at March 31 . . . . $ ______

V Given for Gabbert Tapestries:

	Case 1	Case 2
Beginning cash balance	$ 4,200	$ 2,700
Expected cash receipts	98,000	73,600
Expected cash disbursements	87,000	80,800
Minimum ending cash balance desired	8,000	8,500
Find the estimated amount necessary to borrow or available for repayment of loans and interest	______	______

VI Given for Summ-Totall Material Company:

	Finished Product X	Finished Product Y
Number of units to be produced	2,000 units	3,000 units
Number of pounds of Material A needed for each finished product unit	10 lb	15 lb
Number of square feet of Material B needed for each finished product unit	20 ft	6 ft

	Material A	Material B
Beginning inventories of materials	6,000 lb	15,000 ft
Desired ending inventories of materials	10,000 lb	8,000 ft
Purchase price of materials per pound, per square foot	$4.00	$6.00

Find:

	Material A	Material B
1. Number of material units (pounds or square feet) needed for production of both finished products	______ lb	______ ft
2. Cost of materials needed for production	$ ______	$ ______
3. Number of material units to be purchased	______ lb	______ ft
4. Cost of materials to be purchased	$ ______	$ ______

VII Part of the organization chart of Adam Taylor Company appears below:

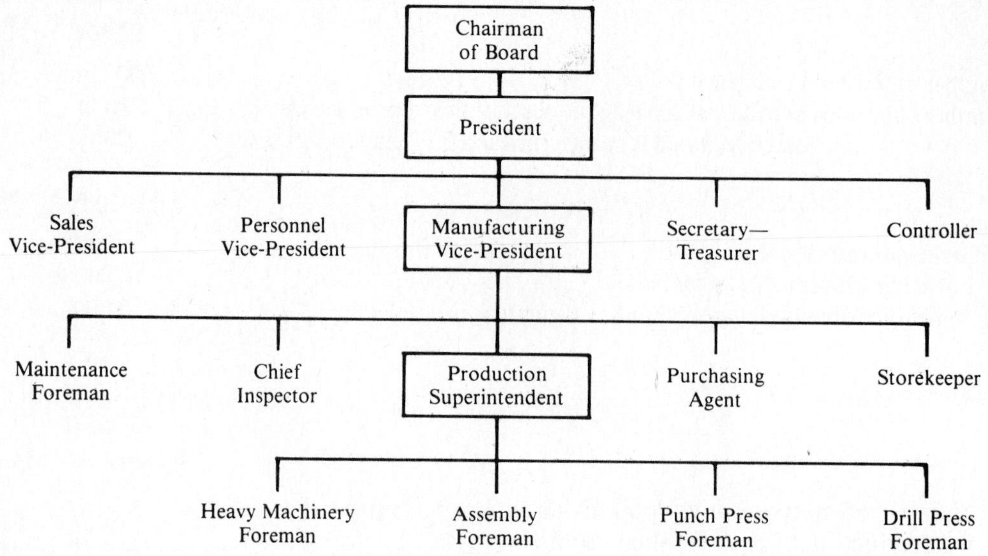

For each item listed below, indicate whether it should be classified in Adam Taylor Company as a variable cost and as a controllable cost. Enter "Yes" or "No" in each blank for each item.

		Controllable Cost			
	Variable Cost	**By Controller**	**By Punch Press Foreman**	**By Production Superintendent**	**By Manufacturing Vice-President**
1. Direct material used in drill press department	______	______	______	______	______
2. Salary of personnel vice-president	______	______	______	______	______
3. Supplies used by purchasing agent	______	______	______	______	______
4. Straight-line depreciation in punch press department	______	______	______	______	______
5. Secretary's salary in controller's department	______	______	______	______	______
6. Direct labor used in punch press department	______	______	______	______	______

Flexible Budgets and 6 Standards: Part I

BUILDING ON THE IDEAS of the preceding chapter, this chapter describes methods for analyzing differences between actual performance and budgeted operations. Paramount here is the **flexible budget**, which is a master budget adjusted to the actual level of activity volume.

The bulk of the chapter deals with **standard costs**, which are predetermined measures of what costs should be under specified conditions. The analysis of the variances of actual costs from standard costs can aid managers in judging and improving performance. The basic analysis is illustrated for the price and efficiency variances of direct-material costs and direct-labor costs.

REVIEW SUMMARY

A. For planning and controlling purposes, the comparison of actual results with a *static budget* has little value for managers.

  1. See the textbook Exhibit 6–1.

  2. Analysis Levels Zero and One are not sufficiently informative.

  3. The deficiencies of these analyses are due mainly to the limitations of a static budget:

    a. Such a budget shows forecasts at only one level of activity volume.

    b. To compare this budget with actual results at a different volume level can actually produce misleading information.

B. To remedy the inadequacies of a static budget approach, one should use a *flexible budget,* also called a variable budget.

  1. This is simply a master budget adjusted to fit the actual volume level of operations.

  2. The key textbook Exhibits 6–2 and 6–3 illustrate the flexible budget. Study these exhibits carefully.

  3. The flexible budget can be used for a more discriminating Level Two Analysis of budget variances, as illustrated by Exhibit 6–4:

    a. *Flexible-budget variances* are the differences between the figures for flexible budget and actual operations.

    b. *Sales-volume variances* are the differences between the figures for flexible budget and static budget.

c. Note that the algebraic sum of these two variances is equal to the operating income variance of the Level One Analysis.
d. Observe also how the flexible-budget variances can be explained more completely in the cost control performance report of Exhibit 6–5.
4. The flexible budget also permits a Level Three Analysis, as indicated by Exhibit 6–6:
a. A breakdown of the flexible-budget variances into price and efficiency variances (explained in the remainder of the chapter).
b. A breakdown of the sales-volume variances into sales-quantity and sales-mix variances (explained in Chapter 25).

C. Standard costs are *predetermined costs* representing target costs that should be attained; they are part of carefully prepared sets of criteria for accomplishing specific tasks.
1. Standard costs assist management in improving performance.
a. Variances are determined by comparing actual costs incurred with standard costs.
b. Such feedback helps management plan and control operations.
2. If standards are *currently attainable,* as we assume in this book, they are conceptually the same as budgets, except that we will view *standards* in terms of *unit costs* and *budgets* in terms of *total costs.*
3. The flexible-budget totals are sometimes expressed as *total standard costs allowed:*

$$\left(\begin{array}{c}\text{Good}\\\text{Output}\end{array}\right) \times \left(\begin{array}{c}\text{Inputs Allowed}\\\text{per Unit of}\\\text{Output}\end{array}\right) \times \left(\begin{array}{c}\text{Standard}\\\text{Unit Price}\\\text{of Inputs}\end{array}\right)$$

4. The general approach to cost-variance analysis is first to compute the flexible-budget variance and then to divide it into two elements:
a. *Flexible-budget variance:*

$$\left(\begin{array}{c}\text{Total}\\\text{Actual}\\\text{Cost}\end{array}\right) \text{ minus } \left(\begin{array}{c}\text{Total}\\\text{Standard Cost}\\\text{Allowed}\end{array}\right)$$

b. *Price (or rate) variance:*

$$\left(\begin{array}{c}\text{Difference}\\\text{in Unit Price}\\\text{of Inputs}\end{array}\right) \times \left(\begin{array}{c}\text{Actual}\\\text{Inputs}\\\text{Used}\end{array}\right)$$

c. *Efficiency (or usage or quantity) variance:*

$$\left(\begin{array}{c}\text{Difference}\\\text{in Quantity}\\\text{of Inputs}\end{array}\right) \times \left(\begin{array}{c}\text{Standard}\\\text{Unit Price}\\\text{of Inputs}\end{array}\right)$$

5. Textbook Exhibit 6–7 shows a graphical analysis of direct-labor cost variance. Note that the relationships are linear and that the total variance (flexible-budget variance) is equal to the algebraic sum of the price and efficiency variances.

D. When entries are made in the general-ledger accounts for monthly summaries of standard-cost transactions, as is usually the case, these entries may be made for direct-material costs in different ways:
1. When current control of purchasing activity is important, variances should be isolated as early as feasible.
a. Price variances are recorded at the time of material *purchases* on the basis of price differences for the total material quantities actually purchased.
b. Efficiency variances are recorded at the time of material *issuances* on the basis of the quantities shown by the *excess-material requisitions* at standard material prices.

2. Another general-ledger procedure for materials is often used in practice:
   a. Price variances are recorded at the time of material *issuances* on the basis of price differences for the total material quantities actually issued.
   b. Efficiency variances may be recorded at the time of material *issuances,* as in the method described above in 1b.
3. Recordkeeping costs can be saved by adopting a standard-cost system.
   a. Actual costs of materials, work in process, and finished goods need not be traced to batches of product on a daily basis; only records of physical counts would be kept.
   b. Monthly consumption of material and labor can be totaled by operation or department without tracing the consumption to individual jobs.

E. Standard costs are of two main types:
   1. *Perfection, ideal, maximum-efficiency, or theoretical standard costs* are absolute minimum costs under the best possible operating conditions with existing product specifications and manufacturing facilities. Although rarely attainable, such standards might be productive because of their motivational effects.
   2. *Currently attainable standards* are the costs that should be incurred under near-term efficient operating conditions.
      a. These standards make allowance for normal spoilage, lost time, and ordinary breakdowns in machinery.
      b. Because currently attainable standards are difficult to reach but possible to achieve, variances are more likely to be slightly unfavorable than favorable.
      c. Such standards may be used simultaneously for product costing, master budgets, and motivation.
   3. Basically, line personnel have the responsibility for setting standards and budgets, but the accounting department performs the functions of translating physical standards into monetary terms and reporting operating performance in comparison with standards.
   4. Because interdependencies among manufacturing materials and methods may permit desirable tradeoffs between price and efficiency variances, one should interpret individual variances with caution.

F. Controllability of operations depends on the particular type of cost variance.
   1. Material variances:
      a. Responsibility for price variances is usually linked to the purchasing officer.
      b. However, such variances are often viewed primarily as measures of forecasting ability.
      c. Responsibility for efficiency variances usually rests with the production manager or sales manager.
      d. The measurement of such variances is facilitated by using a *standard bill of materials* as the basic stores requisition (Exhibit 6–8) and using a separate *excess-materials requisition* when additional materials are needed.
   2. Labor variances:
      a. Price variances tend to be minor because of union contracts.
      b. Price variances are usually the responsibility of the same manager who is responsible for labor usage, because the acquisition and use of labor occur simultaneously.
      c. Standard labor times are specified by a *master operations list* (Exhibit 6–10).
      d. *Work tickets* show the actual time used, as well as causes of variances and responsibility for variances.
   3. Combined or joint price-efficiency variances:
      a. This variance is usually relatively small.
      b. It is customarily included in the price variance without separate identification (Exhibit 6–9).

I For each of the following multiple-choice and true-false statements select the most appropriate answer and enter its identification letter in the space provided:

_a_ 1. In the construction of a flexible budget, if the direct-material cost is $140,000 at the 8,000-unit level of volume, such cost would be $157,500 at the 9,000-unit level: (a) true, (b) false.

_a_ 2. Assume that a static budget showed $40,000 of direct-labor cost for the production of 8,000 units, but that the actual direct-labor cost was $48,000 when 10,000 units were produced. If only a static-budget analysis were used, the variance would be: (a) $8,000 unfavorable, (b) $2,000 favorable, (c) $10,000 unfavorable, (d) $10,000 favorable.

_b_ 3. See the above item. If a flexible-budget analysis were used, the flexible-budget variance would be: (a) $3,000 unfavorable, (b) $2,000 favorable, (c) $10,000 unfavorable, (d) $8,000 unfavorable.

_a_ 4. Trew Company's static budget shows $180,000 of direct-labor cost for the production of 20,000 units, but the actual direct-labor cost was $170,000 for the production of 18,000 units. Under a flexible-budget approach, the flexible-budget variance would be: (a) $10,000 favorable, (b) $18,000 favorable, (c) $8,000 unfavorable, (d) none of the above.

_b_ 5. When a flexible-budget analysis is used, there would never be any difference between the flexible-budget volume and the actual volume achieved: (a) true, (b) false.

___ 6. A favorable sales-volume variance for direct-material cost would be: (a) excess of the flexible-budget cost over the actual cost, (b) excess of the static-budget cost over the flexible-budget cost, (c) excess of the static-budget cost over the actual cost, (d) none of the above.

___ 7. Direct-labor cost was budgeted a $210,000 for a 6,000-unit level, but th actual cost was $185,000 for a 5,000-uni level. These data reflect: (a) a favorabl flexible-budget variance of $25,000, (b an unfavorable sales-volume variance o $25,000, (c) a favorable sales-volume variance of $35,000, (d) an unfavorabl flexible-budget variance of $10,000.

___ 8. Direct-material cost was budgeted a $240,000 for a 6,000-unit level, but the actual cost was $190,000 for a 5,000-uni level. These data reflect: (a) a favorable flexible-budget variance of $50,000, (b an unfavorable sales-volume variance o $10,000, (c) a favorable sales-volume variance of $40,000, (d) an unfavorabl flexible-budget variance of $10,000.

___ 9. Total standard cost allowed is standard unit price, times inputs allowed per uni of output, times: (a) actual outputs, (b standard outputs, (c) good outputs, (d none of the above.

___ 10. Courtney Corporation's standards fo producing a certain product included 10 pounds of material at $4 per pound for each product unit. Planned production was 2,000 product units. Actually, 1,800 product units were produced, each using 11 pounds of material purchased at $5 per pound. The standard cost allowed was: (a) $80,000, (b) $72,000, (c) $90,000, (d) some other amount.

___ 11. See the preceding item. The price variance was: (a) $19,800 unfavorable, (b) $18,000 unfavorable, (c) $27,000 unfavorable, (d) some other answer.

___ 12. See item 10 above. The efficiency variance was: (a) $7,200 favorable, (b) $27,000 unfavorable, (c) $8,000 unfavorable, (d) some other answer.

___ 13. In general, a price variance is the difference between actual and standard unit prices multiplied by the actual inputs: (a) true, (b) false.

___ 14. Effectiveness is defined as the relationship between inputs and outputs: (a) true, (b) false.

___ 15. Perfection or ideal standards are the most widely used standards: (a) true, (b) false.

___ 16. When currently attainable standards are used, variances are more likely to be: (a) favorable rather than unfavorable, (b) unfavorable rather than favorable.

___ 17. The simultaneous use of standard costs for control, product costing, master budgets, and motivation is a major benefit to be derived from the use of: (a) basic standards, (b) maximum-efficiency standards, (c) currently attainable standards, (d) ideal standards.

___ 18. In general, an efficiency variance is the standard unit price of inputs multiplied by the difference between actual inputs used and inputs that should have been used: (a) true, (b) false.

___ 19. Under a standard-cost system, when the monthly summary general-ledger entry is made for direct-labor cost incurred, Work in Process is debited: (a) at actual wage rates, (b) at standard wage rates.

___ 20. Variance accounts with debit balances generally reflect cost variances that are: (a) favorable, (b) unfavorable.

___ 21. In practice, the theoretical, combined, or joint variance for price and quantity is usually: (a) recognized separately, (b) excluded from variance calculations, (c) included as part of the efficiency variance, (d) included as part of the price variance.

___ 22. An unfavorable material-efficiency variance would be calculated by multiplying the quantity of excess materials used by: (a) standard material unit prices, (b) actual material unit prices, (c) neither of the above, (d) either of the above.

___ 23. If material-price variances are recorded in the ledger accounts at the time of material purchases, the book inventory of materials would be maintained on the basis of (a) actual costs, (b) standard costs.

___ 24. No corrective action to an existing process need be made for a random variance: (a) true, (b) false.

___ 25. A standard bill of materials is expressed in terms of: (a) money, (b) physical quantities, (c) both money and physical quantities, (d) neither money nor physical quantities.

II Complete each of the following statements:

1. The sales-volume variance is the difference between the ______________________________ ______________________ and the ______________________ ______________________. Unit prices are held constant.

2. Total standard cost allowed is the product of three amounts:

(a) ______________________________

(b) ______________________________

(c) ______________________________

3. Effectiveness is defined as ______________ ______________________________

4. Substitute terms for efficiency variance are:

(a) ______________________________

(b) ______________________________

5. A substitute term for price variance is ______________________________

6. The two main causes of differences between actual and standard costs are:

(a) ______________________________

(b) ______________________________

7. When currently attainable standards are used, it is helpful to view standards in terms of ______________________ costs and budgets in terms of ______________________ costs.

8. It is usually more feasible to recognize material-price variances at the time materials are ______________ and material-quantity variances when materials are ______________

9. Standard material prices are useful in judging the performance of the ______________ officer.

10. If book inventories of materials are maintained on the basis of ______________ costs, it would not be necessary to assume a cost-flow sequence such as ______________ ______________

11. Labor ______________ are usually more subject to managerial control than are labor ______________ ______________

III Complete this schedule for Neato Corporation, using F for favorable variances and U for unfavorable variances:

	Actual	Flexible Budget Variances	Flexible Budget	Sales Volume Variances	Static Budget
Physical units of output	12,000				10,000
Revenue (sales)	$735,000	$	$	$	$600,000
Variable costs	496,000				420,000
Contribution margin					
Fixed costs	153,000		150,000		
Operating income	$	$	$	$	$

Computations:

IV The Mustang Leather Corporation, which uses a standard cost accounting system, provides the following data concerning its operations during last week for one of its products:

Finished units produced	200 units
Standard labor-hours allowed per product unit	2.5 hours
Standard wage rate per hour	$12.00
Actual wage rate per hour	$11.00
Total direct-labor hours actually used	550 hours

1. Show calculations of costs and variances in the spaces provided in the Analysis Framework given below. Ignore payroll taxes and all other payroll deductions and fringe labor costs. Use F for favorable variances and U for unfavorable variances.
2. Using the Journal provided, prepare one compound journal entry to record direct-labor costs and variances for the week.

1. Analysis Framework

Actual Inputs at Actual Prices	Actual Inputs at Standard Prices	Standard Inputs Allowed for Actual Outputs at Standard Prices

Price Variance | Efficiency Variance

Flexible-Budget Variance

2. Journal

V Peruna Medicinal Products, Inc., which uses a standard-cost accounting system, provides the following data concerning its operations during last week for one of its products:

Finished units produced	300 units
Standard material pounds allowed per product unit	10 pounds
Standard material price per pound	$2.00
Actual material purchase price per pound	$1.80
Actual quantity of materials purchased	4,000 pounds
Actual quantity of materials used in production	3,500 pounds

1. Show calculations of costs and variances in the spaces provided in the Analysis Framework shown below. Assume that the stores account is to be carried on a *standard* price basis. Use F for favorable variances and U for unfavorable variances.
2. Using the journal provided, prepare journal entries for direct-material costs and variances:
   (a) Purchase of direct materials.
   (b) Usage of direct materials.

1. Analysis Framework

Actual Inputs at Actual Prices	Actual Inputs at Standard Prices (Purchases)	Actual Inputs at Standard Prices (Usage)	Standard Inputs Allowed for Actual Outputs at Standard Prices

Price Variance

Efficiency Variance

2. Journal

(a)		
(b)		

7 Flexible Budgets and Standards: Part II

THIS CHAPTER DEALS with factory overhead costs. To facilitate understanding, the author has divided this broad topic into two main segments: **variable factory overhead** and **fixed factory overhead.** The treatment of these distinctly different types of costs is then explained for each of two practical applications: the **budgetary control purpose** and the **product costing purpose.**

Included here are the analyses of overhead cost variances and the effects of overhead costs on the accounts and financial statements of manufacturing companies. Particular emphasis is given to the peculiarities of fixed factory overhead, the role of the **denominator volume,** and the meaning of the **production-volume variance.**

REVIEW SUMMARY

A. For *variable factory overhead costs,* the variance analysis and accounting treatment are similar in many respects to the analysis and accounting for *direct labor cost,* which was explained in the preceding chapter.

1. However, variable overhead consists of numerous different types of costs.
   a. Examples are indirect materials, indirect labor, repairs, power, and idle time.
   b. Therefore, the most practical way to investigate the difference between actual and budgeted costs is to examine the individual costs, item by item.
2. The predetermined variable-overhead rate can be calculated from data included in the flexible budget for variable factory overhead.
   a. This variable-overhead rate is computed by dividing the total variable factory overhead at a given level of activity by the standard activity at that level (often expressed in terms of direct-labor hours allowed).
3. The flexible-budget variance is the difference between the actual overhead incurred and the flexible-budget overhead. This variance has two elements:
   a. *Efficiency variance:*

$$\left(\begin{matrix}\text{Actual}\\ \text{direct-labor}\\ \text{hours used}\end{matrix} - \begin{matrix}\text{Standard}\\ \text{hours}\\ \text{allowed}\end{matrix}\right) \times \left(\begin{matrix}\text{Standard}\\ \text{price per}\\ \text{hour}\end{matrix}\right)$$

b. *Price variance* (or spending variance):

$$\begin{pmatrix}\text{Flexible-}\\\text{budget}\\\text{variance}\end{pmatrix} - \begin{pmatrix}\text{Efficiency}\\\text{variance}\end{pmatrix}$$

4. A separate set of general-ledger accounts is maintained for variable factory-overhead cost: Variable Factory Overhead Control (debit) and Variable Factory Overhead Applied (credit).
   a. The difference between the balances of these two accounts is the under- or overapplied overhead, *which is equal to the flexible-budget variance for variable overhead.*
   b. Although the variable-overhead variances may be computed and reported on a monthly basis, they need not be isolated formally in individual ledger accounts.

B. *Fixed factory overhead costs* do not change *in total* over a wide range of activity volume.
1. However, *unit costs* do change.
2. This causes a difficulty in determining standard costs per product unit at different levels of production volume, a difficulty that does not arise with variable overhead.
   a. In order to obtain a single standard product cost per unit for pricing and inventory uses, it is necessary to select in advance an appropriate annual activity or volume level for division into the budgeted fixed factory overhead for the year.
   b. The activity level preselected for this purpose, which is called the *denominator level* (often expressed in terms of direct-labor hours allowed), can have a significant effect on the fixed-overhead rates and standard unit costs.
   c. The usual denominator level chosen is the budgeted volume level for the year.
   d. However, fixed-overhead rates based upon a single denominator level have only limited significance for management control purposes, and would be used primarily for product costing and long-run pricing.
3. As in the case of variable-overhead costs a separate set of general-ledger accounts is also maintained for fixed factory-overhead cost: Fixed Factory Overhead Control (debit), and Fixed Factory Overhead Applied (credit).
   a. The difference between the balances of these two accounts is the under- or overapplied overhead, which can be divided into two parts:
   b. The *budget variance for fixed overhead* is the difference between the actual fixed-overhead cost incurred and the budgeted fixed-overhead cost.
   c. The *production-volume variance for fixed overhead* is the difference between budgeted fixed-overhead cost and applied fixed-overhead cost (the actual production on the basis of the standard hours allowed at the standard fixed-overhead rate per hour). See textbook Exhibit 7–1.
   d. Again, as in the case of variable overhead, the fixed-overhead variances may also be calculated and reported each month, but they need not be carried in individual ledger accounts.

SELF-TEST AND PRACTICE EXERCISES

I For each of the following multiple-choice and true-false statements, select the most appropriate answer and enter its identification letter in the space provided:

___ 1. The most convincing way to find out why actual variable overhead does not agree with the budgeted amount is to compute the price and efficiency variances: (a) true, (b) false.

___ 2. The variable-overhead price variance is: (a) actual price per hour times the difference between actual hours used and standard hours allowed, (b) standard price per hour times the difference between actual hours used and standard hours allowed, (c) production volume variance minus efficiency variance, (d) budget variance minus efficiency variance.

___ 3. The variable-overhead efficiency variance is: (a) actual price per hour times difference between actual hours used and standard hours allowed, (b) standard price per hour times difference between actual hours used and standard hours allowed, (c) production volume variance minus efficiency variance, (d) budget variance minus efficiency variance.

___ 4. The variable factory-overhead rate may be computed by dividing the total variable factory overhead at a given level of activity by: (a) the actual hours at that level, (b) the standard hours allowed at that level, (c) either of the above, (d) neither of the above.

___ 5. Mountain-Craft Company uses a $5 per direct-labor hour rate for applying variable factory overhead. Operating results included 8,000 standard hours allowed, 8,500 hours worked, and $44,500 variable factory overhead cost. The efficiency variance was: (a) $4,500 unfavorable, (b) $2,500 unfavorable, (c) $4,500 favorable, (d) $2,500 favorable.

___ 6. See the preceding item. The price variance was: (a) $2,000 unfavorable, (b) $2,000 favorable, (c) $4,500 unfavorable, (d) $4,500 favorable.

___ 7. The actual amount of variable factory-overhead cost incurred should be: (a) debited to Work-in-Process Control, (b) credited to Variable Factory Overhead Applied, (c) credited to Variable Factory Overhead Control, (d) debited to Variable Factory Overhead Control, (e) none of the above.

___ 8. When a standard cost system is used, the variable factory-overhead variances that are computed and reported at regular intervals must be entered in individual general-ledger accounts: (a) true, (b) false.

___ 9. For variable factory-overhead costs, the flexible budget variance is the difference between the standard hours allowed times the standard variable-overhead rate for products produced and: (a) actual outputs times the actual variable-overhead rate, (b) actual inputs times the standard variable-overhead rate, (c) actual inputs times the actual prices, (d) none of the above.

___ 10. An unfavorable spending variance for variable factory-overhead cost would be the excess of actual variable overhead incurred over: (a) variable overhead applied, (b) actual inputs times the standard variable-overhead rate, (c) standard hours allowed times the standard variable-overhead rate, (d) actual inputs times the actual prices, (e) none of the above.

___ 11. An unfavorable efficiency variance for variable factory-overhead costs would be: (a) the excess of variable overhead applied over actual inputs times standard rates, (b) the excess of actual inputs times standard rates over actual inputs times actual rates, (c) the excess of actual inputs times standard rates over flexible budget based on actual outputs, (d) the excess of actual inputs times actual rates over actual inputs times standard rates, (e) none of the above.

___ 12. Given for Forehand Corporation's variable-overhead costs: $2,500 favorable flexible-budget variance, $2,500 unfavorable efficiency variance. Compute the price variance: (a) zero, (b) $5,000 favorable, (c) $5,000 unfavorable, (d) none of the above.

___ 13. The standard-cost sheets for manufactured products should include fixed factory-overhead cost: (a) true, (b) false.

___ 14. The predetermined rates for fixed factory overhead are useful primarily for: (a) management control purposes, (b) product costing and pricing purposes.

___ 15. When the standard hours allowed for actual production are greater than the denominator level of activity used for setting the fixed-overhead rate, there is: (a) a favorable production-volume variance, (b) a favorable budget variance, (c) an unfavorable production-volume variance, (d) an unfavorable budget variance, (e) none of the above.

___ 16. The applied amount of fixed factory-overhead cost should be: (a) debited to Fixed Factory Overhead Applied, (b) credited to Fixed Factory Overhead Control, (c) debited to Fixed Factory Overhead Control, (d) credited to Work-in-Process Control, (e) none of the above.

___ 17. Given for the fixed overhead of Skillern Saws, Inc.: flexible budget $24,000, incurred $22,500, applied $20,000. What is the production-volume variance? (a) $2,500 unfavorable, (b) $4,000 unfavorable, (c) $1,500 favorable, (d) some other variance.

___ 18. See the preceding item. What is the budget variance? (a) $2,500 unfavorable, (b) $4,000 unfavorable, (c) $1,500 favorable, (d) some other variance.

___ 19. Given for Gale's Jewelry Fabricators: 2,200 standard hours allowed for work done on good units manufactured, $44,000 budgeted fixed-overhead cost, 2,000 hours of denominator activity. Compute applied fixed overhead: (a) $48,400, (b) $40,000, (c) $44,000, (d) some other amount.

___ 20. See the preceding item. If the actual overhead incurred is $50,000, what is the production-volume variance? (a) $4,000 favorable, (b) $6,000 unfavorable, (c) $4,400 favorable, (d) some other variance.

___ 21. See item 19. If the actual overhead incurred is $46,000, what is the budget variance? (a) $2,000 favorable, (b) $2,400 unfavorable, (c) $2,400 favorable, (d) some other variance.

___ 22. See item 19. If the actual overhead incurred is $42,000, what is the amount of overhead that has been underapplied or overapplied? (a) $2,000 overapplied, (b) $2,000 underapplied, (c) $6,400 overapplied, (d) some other amount overapplied or underapplied.

___ 23. For fixed factory-overhead costs, the budget variance is the difference between the budgeted costs and: (a) applied fixed overhead, (b) actual fixed overhead, (c) neither of the above.

___ 24. The predetermined rate for applying fixed factory-overhead costs is usually based on some activity or volume level predicted for a period of one year: (a) true, (b) false.

___ 25. The fixed factory-overhead variances should be: (a) computed and reported at regular intervals, (b) entered regularly in individual general-ledger accounts, (c) both of the above, (d) neither of the above.

___ 26. The fixed-overhead budget variances are usually within immediate managerial control: (a) true, (b) false.

___ 27. Most companies consider production-volume variances to be: (a) beyond immediate management control, (b) within immediate management control.

___ 28. If the standard hours allowed for actual production are less than the denominator level of activity, this would indicate: (a) below-expected utilization of available facilities, (b) better-than-expected utilization of facilities.

II Complete each of the following statements:

1. A synonym for the variable-overhead spending variance is ______________________

2. A synonym for denominator variance is ______ ______________________________

3. The actual amount of variable-overhead cost incurred should be recorded by a ______________

entry to the ______________________ account.

4. The applied amount of variable factory-overhead cost should be debited to the ______________________ account and credited to the ______________________ account.

5. The actual amount of fixed factory-overhead cost should be debited to the ______________ account and credited to the ______________________ accounts.

6. The flexible-budget variance for variable factory-overhead costs can be broken down into the ______________________ variance and the ______________________ variance.

7. The difference between variable overhead applied and actual variable overhead incurred is always equal to the ______________ variance for variable factory overhead. If the applied amount is larger than the actual amount, the variance is ______________________

8. The activity or volume level used for the calculation of the predetermined rate for fixed factory overhead is called the ______________________

9. The under- or overapplied amount for fixed factory-overhead cost is composed of the ______ ______________________ variance and the ______________________ variance.

10. Underapplied fixed factory overhead would be the excess of the balance of the ______________ ______________ account over the balance of the ______________________ account.

III You are given the following data for N.I.K. Shaving Utensils, Inc.:

Products manufactured	400 units
Standard variable-overhead cost per unit, 1.5 direct-labor hours at $2.00	$3.00
Actual direct-labor hours used	700 hr
Actual variable-overhead cost incurred	$1,350

1. Compute the following amounts:
   (a) Actual inputs times standard prices . . . . . . $ ______

   (b) Actual product units made times standard variable-overhead cost per unit . . $ ______

   (c) Flexible-budget variance for overhead . . . . . . $ ______

(d) Price variance (spending variance) .... $ ______

(e) Efficiency variance .... $ ______

For each variance, indicate whether it is favorable (F) or unfavorable (U).

2. Make the journal entries to summarize the above facts for the general ledger:

IV The following information pertains to the operations of Stamp Pest Eradicators:

Budgeted fixed-overhead cost	$1,800
Actual fixed-overhead cost	$1,750
Denominator level of activity	300 hours
Standard hours allowed for work done on product units manufactured	280 hours

1. Compute the following amounts:
   (a) Standard rate for fixed overhead .... $ ____ per hour

   (b) Applied fixed overhead.. $ ______

(c) Under- or overapplied fixed overhead .... $ ______

(d) Budget variance .... $ ______

(e) Production-volume variance .... $ ______

For each variance, indicate whether it is favorable (F) or unfavorable (U).

2. Make the journal entries to summarize the above facts in the general ledger:

8 Income Effects of Alternative Product-Costing Methods

IN DESIGNING AND OPERATING modern planning and control systems, management must choose from some costing alternatives that can produce significantly different results. This chapter examines some of these alternatives, their effects on the measurements of product costs and income, and their impacts on some operating decisions.

The chapter contains three major topics: (1) an analytical comparison of the absorption-costing approach and the variable-costing approach to income measurement; (2) an examination of the inventory and income effects of choosing various denominator levels for absorption costing; and (3) a study of the inventory and income effects of using different year-end treatments for standard-cost variances, including prorations of the variances. The three topics are individually treated in separate sections of this student guide chapter. The two chapter appendixes extend the discussion of the third topic.

REVIEW SUMMARY

Variable and Absorption Costing

A. The variable-costing approach to income measurement differs basically from the absorption-costing approach.

- **1.** *Absorption costing* is the traditional approach to income measurement.
  - **a.** *Fixed* factory-overhead costs are treated as *product costs* and are therefore *included in product inventories* and cost of goods manufactured and sold, along with direct-material, direct-labor, and *variable* factory-overhead costs.
  - **b.** This approach is more widely used than the contribution approach, must be used for income tax purposes, and is generally accepted for making financial reports to external parties.
- **2.** The *variable-costing approach* to income measurement is sometimes called *direct costing.*
  - **a.** *Fixed* factory-overhead costs are treated as *period costs* (charged directly to expense) and are therefore *excluded from product inventories,* which include only direct-material, direct-labor, and *variable* factory-overhead costs.

   b. Variable costing is growing in use for internal performance reports to management, but it is not acceptable for income tax purposes or external reporting.
3. As you can easily see in textbook Exhibit 8–1, the two approaches differ in their primary classification of costs.
   a. Absorption costing makes a primary classification of costs according to manufacturing and non-manufacturing functions, emphasizing the *gross margin* available to cover all selling and administrative expenses.
   b. Variable costing makes a primary classification of costs into variable and fixed categories, emphasizing the *contribution margin* available to cover all fixed costs.
4. The difference between the two income-measurement approaches is essentially the difference in the *timing* of the charge to expense for fixed factory-overhead cost.
   a. In the absorption-costing method, fixed factory overhead is first charged to inventory and is therefore not charged to expense until the period in which the inventory is sold and included in cost of goods sold (an expense).
   b. However, in the variable-costing method, fixed factory overhead is charged to expense immediately, and only variable manufacturing costs are included in product inventories.
   c. Therefore, if inventories increase during a period (production exceeds sales), the variable-costing method will generally report less operating income than will the absorption-costing method; when inventories decrease, the opposite effect will occur. See the helpful textbook Exhibits 8–2 and 8–3.

Role Of Various Denominator Levels In Absorption Costing

B. When absorption costing is used, reported profits can be significantly affected by the choice of an activity level for use as a denominator in computing fixed-overhead rates.

1. The activity level that is chosen should be related to the capacity of available plant, equipment, and other resources, such as people and materials.
   a. Such a capacity, called *practical capacity,* is the maximum level at which the plant (or department or other subdivision thereof) can operate efficiently, allowing for unavoidable operating interruptions.
   b. This capacity is an upper limit specified by management for current planning and control purposes, after considering engineering factors and the economic tradeoffs that must be made in providing for upward trends in customer demand and for the seasonal and cyclical fluctuations in customer demand.
2. Two lower levels of capacity utilization are commonly used:
   a. *Normal volume* is the level of capacity utilization that will meet average customer demand over a period (often five years) that includes seasonal, cyclical, and trend factors.
   b. *Master-budget volume,* or *expected annual volume,* is the expected level of capacity utilization for the coming year.
3. The choice of the level of capacity utilization to be used would affect the *predetermined rate* for applying fixed-overhead cost to production, as demonstrated by textbook Exhibit 8–8.
   a. If *normal volume* were used to compute a normal rate, unit costs of *fixed overhead* would not be influenced by annual fluctuations in volume, and there would tend to be overapplications of overhead in some years that are offset by underapplications in other years. Thus, the use of a normal rate would provide a yearly and monthly measure of the cost of idle capacity.

   b. If *master-budget volume* were used to compute the predetermined rate for fixed overhead, product and inventory costs would tend to fluctuate merely because of annual differences in utilization of facilities.
4. For various nontheoretical reasons, master-budget volume is generally used as the activity base for computing the predetermined fixed-overhead rate.
   a. There is a widespread conviction that the year is the key time period and that overhead costs for the year should be assigned to the year's production.
   b. Using the normal rate would require long-run forecasting, and this cannot be done accurately.
   c. The accounting profession and the Internal Revenue Service do not approve of carrying forward on the balance sheet the annual amounts of under- or overapplied factory-overhead cost.
5. Reasons are given by some managements for using practical capacity as an activity base for the predetermined fixed-overhead rate.
   a. Lower unit costs and higher profits can be obtained on such a larger-volume basis.
   b. Selling prices based on such lower unit costs would be more competitive and thus would induce higher volume and profits.
   c. The use of practical capacity permits a faster tax writeoff of fixed overhead than the use of normal volume or master-budget volume.
6. However, master-budget volume is usually regarded as an appropriate overhead-rate base for the purposes of current planning and control. This is because expected annual activity is the basis for the year's master budget, which is the principal short-run planning and control tool.
7. Exhibit 8–9, accompanying the solution to the textbook self-study problem, shows that the use of different activity bases for developing product-costing overhead rates results in different inventory valuations and different net incomes.
   a. There is a striking difference in the measure of utilization of facilities, the denominator variance.
   b. Note carefully the basic reasons for the substantial differences in the reported inventories and net incomes.

Standard-Cost Variances and the Income Statement

C. When accounting entries for the transactions of a standard-cost system are made in the general-ledger accounts, how should the variance accounts be disposed of at year end?
1. If the variances are not significant, they may be treated in the income statement either as direct charges or credits to cost of goods sold or as separate charges or credits after the gross margin (or gross profit) on sales.
2. If the variances are large enough to materially distort net income and inventory figures, the variances should be prorated.
   a. The proration would be in proportion to the related standard-cost charges included in the affected accounts.
   b. Material-price variances should be prorated over five accounts: Direct Material Efficiency Variance, Stores, Work-in-Process, Finished Goods, and Cost of Goods Sold.
   c. The adjusted material-efficiency variance, the labor variances, and the overhead variances should be prorated over three accounts: Work-in-Process, Finished Goods, and Cost of Goods Sold.
   d. Study carefully the comprehensive schedule of proration in Exhibit 8–10.

SELF-TEST AND PRACTICE EXERCISES

I For each of the following multiple-choice and true-false statements, select the most appropriate answer and enter its identification letter in the space provided:

Variable and Absorption Costing

___ 1. The variable-costing approach to income measurement: (a) treats variable costs as inventoriable, (b) shows all selling and administrative expenses as deductions from contribution margin, (c) both of the above, (d) neither of the above.

___ 2. The absorption-costing approach to income measurement: (a) treats all selling and administrative expenses as period costs, (b) treats variable and fixed manufacturing costs as product costs, (c) both of the above, (d) neither of the above.

___ 3. Both the variable-costing and the absorption-costing approaches: (a) treat variable manufacturing costs as inventoriable, (b) treat variable selling expenses as period costs, (c) both of the above, (d) neither of the above.

___ 4. Variable administrative expenses are treated as: (a) period costs under the variable-costing and absorption-costing approaches, (b) product costs under the variable-costing and absorption-costing approaches, (c) period costs under variable-costing but not under absorption-costing, (d) product costs under variable-costing but not under absorption-costing.

___ 5. Under the variable-costing approach, variable and fixed selling and administrative expenses are treated as period costs: (a) true, (b) false.

___ 6. Direct-labor costs and variable selling expenses: (a) are treated as product costs by the variable-costing approach, (b) are treated as period costs by the variable-costing approach, (c) are treated as period costs by the absorption-costing approach, (d) are treated as product costs by the absorption-costing approach, (e) none of the above.

___ 7. Contribution margin minus all period costs equals operating income: (a) true, (b) false.

___ 8. Gross margin minus variable and fixed period costs equals operating income: (a) true, (b) false.

___ 9. Fixed factory overhead is treated as a period cost by the variable-costing approach: (a) true, (b) false.

___ 10. Treated as period costs by the variable-costing method are: (a) variable factory-overhead costs, (b) fixed factory-overhead costs, (c) both of the above, (d) neither of the above.

___ 11. The differences between the two income approaches is basically the difference in: (a) the total amount of fixed overhead costs charged to expense, (b) the total amount of variable overhead costs charged to expense, (c) the timing of fixed overhead costs charged to expense, (d) the timing of variable overhead costs charged to expense.

___ 12. When sales exceed production for a given period, the absorption-costing approach tends to produce: (a) more profit than the variable-costing approach, (b) less profit than the variable-costing approach, (c) the same profit as the variable-costing approach.

Role of Various Denominator Levels in Absorption Costing

___ 13. A monthly and yearly measure of the cost of idle capacity would be provided by a predetermined fixed-overhead rate based upon: (a) master-budget volume, (b) normal volume, (c) both of these, (d) neither of these.

___ 14. If normal volume were used to compute the predetermined rate for fixed overhead, product and inventory costs would tend to fluctuate merely because of annual differences in utilization of facilities: (a) true, (b) false.

___ 15. The appropriate overhead-rate basis for purposes of current planning and control is usually: (a) practical capacity, (b) theoretical capacity, (c) normal volume, (d) master-budget volume.

___ 16. Normal volume is a concept of capacity utilization that is intended to reflect average customer demand over a period of several years: (a) true, (b) false.

___ 17. In general, operating budgets that are used to judge current performance should be based upon normal volume: (a) true, (b) false.

___ 18. The activity level that can usually be predicted with greatest accuracy is: (a) master-budget volume, (b) practical capacity, (c) normal volume.

___ 19. In practice, under- or overapplied fixed-overhead costs are not carried forward from year to year: (a) for income tax purposes, (b) for external reporting purposes, (c) both of the above, (d) neither of the above.

___ 20. If the master-budget volume is used for obtaining a predetermined rate for applying fixed overhead, the overapplications in some years would conceptually be offset by underapplications in other years: (a) true, (b) false.

Standard-Cost Variances and the Income Statement

___ 21. Immaterial variances from standard costs may be written off immediately to cost of goods sold unless the cost-standards are currently attainable: (a) true, (b) false.

___ 22. Most accurate proration of cost variances would be obtained by first prorating: (a) direct-labor efficiency variance, (b) direct-material efficiency variance, (c) direct-material price variance, (d) direct-labor price variance.

___ 23. If currently attainable standards are used for product costing, it would be conceptually consistent to view unfavorable variances as: (a) adjustments to product costs, (b) expenses caused by inefficiency.

___ 24. If there are no inventories at year end, cost variances need not be prorated but can be reported in the income statement as additions to or deductions from cost of goods sold or gross margin: (a) true, (b) false.

___ 25. When standard-cost variances are to be prorated among several accounts, the prorations would be based upon the related: (a) actual costs in the accounts, (b) standard costs in the accounts.

___ 26. If all standard-cost variances are prorated among inventories and cost of goods sold, the reported operating income would be the same as under an actual historical costing procedure: (a) true, (b) false.

II Complete each of the following statements:

Variable and Absorption Costing

1. In the absorption-costing approach, the primary division of costs is into two groups:

(a) ______________________________

(b) ______________________________

2. In the variable-costing approach, the primary division of costs is into two groups:

(a) ______________________________

(b) ______________________________

3. A ______________________ margin is a measurement made by the variable-costing approach, but a ______________________ margin is a measurement made by the absorption-costing approach.

4. Three main types of cost that are treated as product costs by the variable-costing approach are:

(a) ____________________

(b) ____________________

(c) ____________________

5. Three main types of cost that are treated as period costs by the variable-costing approach are:

(a) ____________________

(b) ____________________

(c) ____________________

6. Two main uses for which the variable-costing approach is not acceptable are:

(a) ____________________

(b) ____________________

7. The variable-costing method would tend to report higher profits than would the absorption-costing method when ____________________ is greater than ____________________ for a given period.

Role of Various Denominator Levels in Absorption Costing

8. The maximum level at which the plant can operate most efficiently, allowing for unavoidable operating interruptions, is called ____________________

9. Expected annual activity is a level of ____________________ utilization that is also called ____________________

10. The activity level generally used as the base for calculating the predetermined rate for fixed-factory-overhead cost is ____________________

11. Conceptually, when ____________________ is the base, the yearly over- or underapplied fixed-overhead cost should be carried forward on the balance sheet.

Standard-Cost Variances and the Income Statement

12. When currently attainable standards are used for product costing, the entire amounts of very small cost variances may be shown in the income statement as direct charges or credits to ____________________ or as separate charges or credits appearing after the ____________________ on sales.

13. If a direct-labor price variance were allocated fully to other accounts, the titles of the accounts normally used would be:

(a) ____________________

(b) ____________________

(c) ____________________

14. If an unfavorable standard-cost variance were allocated to Cost of Goods Sold, the reported amount of Gross Margin would thus be ____________________

Variable and Absorption Costing

III The Hudson Company provided the following data pertaining to its operations for the current calendar year:

Standard costs per product unit:		
Direct material	$ 3.00	
Direct labor	4.00	
Variable overhead	1.00	$ 8.00
Fixed overhead		2.00
Total		$10.00

Product units:	
In beginning inventory	10,000 units
Produced	90,000
Sold	80,000
In ending inventory	20,000
Selling and administrative expenses:	
Variable	$200,000
Fixed	100,000
Selling price per product unit	$ 15.00

1. Construct two income statements, using standard production costs for inventories and cost of goods manufactured, and ignoring income taxes:
   (a) Follow the absorption-costing method.
   (b) Follow the variable-costing method.
2. Reconcile the difference in net incomes shown by these two methods.

1. (a)

HUDSON COMPANY

Income Statement
For the Year Ending December 31, 198 __
(Absorption-Costing Method)

1. (b)

HUDSON COMPANY

Income Statement
For the Year Ending December 31, 198 __
(Variable-Costing Method)

2. Reconciliation of Difference in Net Income:

Absorption-costing method (a)	$ ______
Direct-costing method (b)	$ ______
Difference to be accounted for	$ ______

Difference accounted for as follows:

Role of Various Denominator Levels in Absorption Costing

IV Bouchard Company furnished the following data:

Fixed factory overhead for the year:	
Budgeted	$72,000
Actual	$74,000
Practical capacity per year	20,000 hours
Normal volume per year	16,000 hours
Master-budget volume for the year	12,000 hours
Standard hours allowed for the work done in the year	13,000 hours

1. Using the master-budget volume, compute:
   (a) Fixed overhead rate per hour .... $ ______

   (b) Total fixed overhead applied.. $ ______

   (c) Under- or overapplied fixed overhead .... $ ______

2. Using a normal volume basis, compute:
   (a) Fixed overhead rate per hour .... $ ______

   (b) Total fixed overhead applied.. $ ______

   (c) Under- or overapplied fixed overhead .... $ ______

3. (a) Which volume basis would tend to cause fluctuations in product and inventory costs merely because of annual differences in the utilization of facilities? ____________

   ____

   (b) Which volume basis would tend to produce underapplications of fixed overhead in some years that are offset by overapplications in other years? ____________

   ____

Standard-Cost Variances and the Income Statement

V Stage Corporation's analysis of direct-material data for a certain year includes:

	Pounds	Percentage
Location at year-end:		
Stores	16,000	20%
Material-efficiency variance	4,000	5
Work in process	none	none
Finished goods	18,000	22.5
Cost of goods sold	42,000	52.5
Total pounds accounted for	80,000	100%

Variances from standard costs were all unfavorable at year-end:

Material-price variance	$1,600
Material-efficiency variance	320
Labor-price variance	2,000
Labor-efficiency variance	3,000
Factory overhead variance	5,000

Compute the prorations of all variances on the basis of material pounds, using the following schedule:

Type of Variance	Variance Amount	To Stores	To Material Efficiency	To Finished Goods	To Cost of Goods Sold
	$	$	$	$	$

Proration Percentages:

VI The following data are supplied by Rice Company, which uses a standard-cost accounting system:

Sales	$25,000
Standard cost of goods manufactured	$20,000
Selling and administrative expenses	$ 6,000
Unfavorable material-efficiency variance	$ 700
Favorable overhead variances	$ 500
Favorable labor-price variance	$ 300
Unfavorable labor-efficiency variance	$ 900
Product units manufactured	2,000 units
Product units sold	1,600 units

Beginning inventory of finished goods	none
Ending inventory of finished goods	400 units
Work-in-process inventories	none
Income taxes	ignore

1. Compute net income before giving effect to variances . . . . $ ______

2. Compute the net unfavorable variance . . . . $ ______

3. Assuming the net variance is treated as an expense, compute:
   (a) Net income . . . . $ ______

   (b) Cost of ending inventory of finished goods . . . . $ ______

4. Assuming the net variance is prorated between inventory and cost of goods sold, compute:
   (a) Net income . . . . $ ______

(b) Cost of ending inventory of finished goods . . . . $ ______

5. Which net income figure would seem to be more consistent with the concept of *standard costs:* (3a) or (4a)? . . . . ______
6. Which ending inventory cost would seem to be more consistent with the concept of *historical costs:* (3b) or (4b)? . . . . ______

9 Determining How Costs Behave

AS OTHER CHAPTERS have emphasized, management decisions can be significantly influenced by the predicted costs of the alternative actions being considered. Cost predictions rest in turn on the manner in which costs behave under certain conditions. Therefore, managerial accountants need to know how to determine various cost-behavior patterns, which are called **cost functions.**

This chapter describes the principal approaches to determining cost functions under various circumstances, along with certain limiting assumptions and management implications. Special attention is given to the important cost function that is widely known as **the learning curve.**

REVIEW SUMMARY

A. Some accountants and statisticians distinguish between two terms that others might use interchangeably:

1. *Cost estimation* is the measurement of historical costs to aid in determining predicted costs for decision purposes.

2. *Cost prediction* is the forecasting of expected future costs.

- **a.** Such predictions are based upon cost-behavior patterns (*cost functions*).

3. Two important assumptions are usually made concerning cost behavior:

- **a.** *Only one independent variable* (for example, labor hours or machine-hours) is needed for an adequate explanation of the behavior of a particular cost.
- **b.** *Linear approximations* to cost functions are satisfactory reflections of the actual behavior, which is more likely to be nonlinear.

4. A linear cost function can be expressed as the general formula for a straight line:

$$y = a + bx$$

- **a.** The variable to be predicted is y the *dependent variable;* for example, power cost.
- **b.** The other variable is x, the *independent variable, controllable variable, decision variable,* or *explanatory variable;* for example, machine-hours.
- **c.** The *intercept* is a, the value of y when x is zero.
- **d.** The *slope coefficient* of the line is b, the amount of increase in y for each unit of increase in x.

5. See the textbook Exhibit 9-1 for three common examples of linear cost functions:
   a. Variable costs
   b. Fixed costs
   c. Mixed costs
6. *The preferable cost function is one that facilitates the prediction of changes in costs, that accurately depicts persistent relationships, whether or not cause and effect can be linked together:*
   a. The relationships between the dependent and independent variables must be credible (*economic plausibility*).
   b. The plausible function that provides the most accurate estimations should be selected (*goodness of fit*).

B. Some costs are called *mixed costs* (or *semivariable costs*) because they contain both a fixed element and a variable element.
   1. Examples are:
      a. Repairs
      b. Power
      c. Rental of a delivery truck for a fixed cost per month plus a variable cost based on mileage.
   2. Although fixed and variable cost elements should theoretically not be included in one account, mixed costs are generally not separated in accounting practice.
   3. The textbook uses a mixed cost illustration to explain five ways of arriving at a cost function.
   4. The *industrial engineering approach:*
      a. It emphasizes the use of time and motion studies and physical measures of inputs and outputs.
      b. Although the industrial engineering approach becomes less satisfactory when costs cannot be traced to inputs and outputs, its use has increased in recent years.
   5. The *account analysis approach:*
      a. Inspect ledger accounts and classify them into categories: variable, fixed, mixed.
      b. The accrual accounting basis should be reflected by the account balances.
   6. The *visual fit approach:*
      a. Plot data on a scatter diagram, textbook Exhibit 9-2.
      b. Determine whether there is a linear correlation between cost and volume.
   7. The *regression analysis approach:*
      a. Use a statistical model to measure the relative changes between two variables.
      b. *Ordinary least squares* is the most widely used model. (See textbook Chapter 24).
   8. The *high-low method:*
      a. Plot on a graph a representative high point and a representative low point.
      b. Connect points with a line to (crudely) represent the cost behavior.

C. Not all cost functions are linear.
   1. Outside the relevant range, there may be curvilinear relationships, Exhibit 9-4.
   2. Exhibit 9-5 shows the function of an upward-sloping supply curve for a scarce raw material that increases in price as demand increases.
   3. Exhibit 9-6 shows the effects of quantity discounts on material costs.
   4. Exhibit 9-7 shows the step-like cost behavior of labor services that cannot be obtained in the small fractional quantities needed for use.
      a. The cost steps may be so narrow that they approach a proportionately variable cost-behavior pattern, such as the cost of part-time employees.
      b. In other cases, the costs steps could be so wide that they approach costs classified as step-fixed costs or fixed costs (Exhibit 9-8).

D. *Learning curves* aid in predicting costs and setting standards for new production processes.

1. During a learning phase, the time needed per product unit becomes progressively smaller at some constant rate.
2. Typical items for which standard costs should be adjusted during this phase are labor, power, and other related overhead.
3. Important applications of the learning curve include competitive bidding for defense contracts.
4. Suggested steps for gaining a working knowledge of the learning-curve model:
   - **a.** See the graph in textbook Exhibit 9–9.
   - **b.** Study the textbook example very carefully.
   - **c.** Solve Problem V in this student guide.
   - **d.** Solve one or more textbook problems 9–22, 9–23, and 9–24.

E. In many cases, the selection of the independent variable, a measure of production volume or activity, would not be easy, and several helpful selection criteria should be used:

1. The activity measure should have a *causal relationship* to the variable cost.
2. The activity unit should not be significantly affected by variable factors other than volume.
3. Measurement units should be easily understandable and inexpensively obtainable.
4. The measure of budgeted activity must be under adequate control and not be subject to the influence of inefficient operations.
   - **a.** Therefore, a better measure for this purpose would be the *standard* labor or machine-hours allowed for units produced, rather than the *actual* labor or machine-hours used.

SELF-TEST AND PRACTICE EXERCISES

I For each of the following multiple-choice and true-false statements, select the most appropriate answer and enter its identification letter in the space provided:

___ 1. In developing a cost function for a certain manufacturing expense, the analyst would be more likely to use as a basis for explaining the cost behavior either direct-labor hours only or machine hours only rather than using a combination of these two bases: (a) true, (b) false.

___ 2. Accountants and managers usually assume cost behavior to be: (a) variable, (b) curvilinear, (c) nonlinear, (d) linear.

___ 3. Cost behavior is generally assumed by accountants and managers to be: (a) approximately linear rather than nonlinear, (b) dependent on a single variable rather than several, (c) both of the above, (d) none of these.

___ 4. The term *cost function* refers to: (a) the objective of costs, (b) the role of costs, (c) the behavior of costs, (d) none of the above.

___ 5. The main purpose for determining cost functions is to: (a) prove the validity of management decisions, (b) improve the accuracy of cost predictions, (c) correct errors in recording historical costs, (d) develop precise mathematical equations.

___ 6. In the general formula for a straight line, $y = a + bx$, y is: (a) the dependent variable, (b) the independent variable, (c) the intercept, (d) the slope coefficient of the line.

___ 7. In the general formula for a straight line, $y = a + bx$, a is: (a) the dependent variable, (b) the independent variable, (c) the intercept, (d) the slope coefficient of the line.

___ 8. The dependent variable in a cost function is typically some kind of: (a) input, (b) output.

___ 9. Linear cost functions can be used to represent: (a) fixed costs, (b) variable costs, (c) mixed costs, (d) all of these.

___ 10. Managerial accountants commonly assume that an adequate explanation of cost behavior requires: (a) only one independent variable, (b) two or more independent variables.

___ 11. In general, managerial accountants assume that cost behavior can be reflected satisfactorily: (a) by linear cost functions, (b) only by nonlinear cost functions.

___ 12. In determining cost functions, the cost analyst aims at predicting persistent relationships between actions and the cost incurred: (a) true, (b) false.

___ 13. In general, our search for appropriate cost functions places primary emphasis on the establishment of cause-and-effect relationships between actions and the cost incurred: (a) true, (b) false.

___ 14. Mixed costs are defined as those costs that contain both manufacturing and nonmanufacturing elements: (a) true, (b) false.

___ 15. The inclusion of fixed- and variable-cost elements in one account is: (a) theoretically proper, (b) generally done in practice, (c) both of the above, (d) neither of the above.

___ 16. The industrial engineering approach is inapplicable to nonmanufacturing activities: (a) true, (b) false.

___ 17. The industrial engineering approach: (a) traces costs to inputs and outputs, (b) deemphasizes dependence on historical cost functions, (c) both of the above, (d) neither of the above.

___ 18. A necessary first step in a serious approach to determining the behavior of costs is: (a) regression analysis, (b) the industrial engineering approach, (c) examination of the ledger accounts, (d) none of the above.

___ 19. When the account-analysis approach is used, the balances of the ledger accounts should reflect both the accrual accounting basis and adjustments for the effects of price changes: (a) true, (b) false.

___ 20. The regression line determined by the least squares method is: (a) always curved, (b) always straight, (c) usually but not always curved, (d) usually but not always straight.

___ 21. The high-low method is not recommended, but it is used to separate a mixed cost into a fixed-cost component and a variable-cost component: (a) true, (b) false.

___ 22. Step-variable costs are more often represented by: (a) material costs, (b) labor costs.

___ 23. In step-function costs, as the cost steps become wider, the cost behavior approaches the behavior of: (a) fixed costs, (b) variable costs, (c) mixed costs.

___ 24. A learning curve is appropriate for setting standards only after the start-up phase of production when "steady-state" conditions are reached: (a) true, (b) false.

II Complete each of the following statements:

1. Cost behavior patterns are called ___________

2. The ___________ variable may be expressed as a function of the ___________ variable.

3. One method for approximating cost functions is to analyze each ledger account and classify it into one of three categories:

(a) ___________

(b) ___________

(c) ___________

4. The method of approximating cost functions by simply drawing a straight line through the points on a ___________ is called the ___________ method.

5. A mathematical technique that measures the average amount of change in one variable that is associated with unit increases in another variable is called ___________

6. In the formula for a straight line, $y = a + bx$, b measures ______

7. A mathematical model for determining the equation for a particular regression line is called ______

8. A regression line is not necessarily valid when extended beyond ______

III Provost Corporation uses a least-squares equation for predicting its direct labor costs for different batch sizes in its Searing Process: $y = \$200 + \$50x$.

1. Identify or determine the symbol or amount that represents each of the following ideas or amounts:
   (a) The dependent variable ...... ______
   (b) The independent variable...... ______
   (c) The slope coefficient of the regression line...... ______
   (d) The total labor cost for a batch size of 30...... $ ______

   (e) The mathematical value of the dependent variable when the independent variable is zero ...... $ ______

2. See (e) above.
   (a) Is this the expected cost at zero activity?...... ______ Why?
   (b) Is this a valid estimate of fixed cost?...... ______ Why?

IV Given for a certain factory-overhead cost of Vee-Lee Company:

	Jan.	Feb.
Volume of activity in direct-labor hours for the month	30,000	40,000
Total cost for the month	$ 9,500	$12,000

Find:

1. The variable cost rate per direct-labor hour ...... $ ______

2. The fixed cost per month ...... $ ______

V Airpoint Corporation needs to forecast its direct-labor costs for use in making a competitive bid on a production contract. Experience shows that an 80 percent learning curve is applicable. Recently, the company produced 200 units requiring 4,000 labor hours at $15 per hour (Lot A). Compute the total forecasted labor cost for a contract of 600 units:

	Lots Produced		
	A	**B**	**C**
Quantity (in units):			
Per lot	____	____	____
Cumulative	____	____	____
Cumulative average labor costs per unit:			
A: ______________________	$ ____		
B: ______________________		$ ____	
C: ______________________			$ ____
Cumulative total labor costs:			
A: ______________________	$ ____		
B: ______________________		$ ____	
C: ______________________			$ ____
Additional total labor cost of each lot:			
A: ______________________	$ ____		
B: ______________________		$ ____	
C: ______________________			$ ____
Answer: ______________________			$ ____

10 Systems Choice, Discretionary and Nonmanufacturing Costs

THE HUMAN BEHAVIORAL ASPECTS of a management accounting system are crucial to its success. This chapter explains how motivation, goal congruence, and effective effort are related to the design, operation, and evaluation of a control system.

In addition, the chapter describes some important types of costs not previously introduced: **committed, engineered,** and **discretionary.** Methods for controlling these costs are presented, including **zero-base budgets** and **work measurement.**

REVIEW SUMMARY

A. The broad purpose of a management control system is to improve the decisions and operations within an organization toward attainment of the organizational goals.

1. The primary criterion for judging control systems is *cost-benefit,* because the systems are economic goods or services.
2. Two secondary criteria are important:
    - **a.** *Goal congruence:* alignment of individual and group objectives with those of the organization.
    - **b.** *Effort:* actions toward goals.
    - **c.** *Motivation* consists of these two elements.

B. There are three main types of control on human behavior (textbook Exhibit 10–1):

1. The *formal organization controls,* such as budgets, may impose quantitative standards of performance that motivate employees toward organizational goals.
2. *Informal group controls* tend to confine employee behavior close to accepted behavior norms.
3. *Individual controls* imposed by personal aspirations and expectations tend to keep employee behavior directed toward personal goals.
    - **a.** *Effective goal congruence* means that, in addition to the harmony of top-management goals with the subgoals specified by the control system, individual managers must *accept* the subgoals as their own personal goals.

b. However, the influence of accounting measurements on *acceptance* of subgoals as personal goals may be outweighed by other influences, such as family, religion, and opinions of colleagues.

4. In some cases, the formal control system may be dominated by an *informal system* ("little black books and special memorandums").
   a. However, as companies grow and executives become more mobile, the formal systems become more necessary.
   b. In addition, features of an informal system can often be adopted as part of a formal system.
5. *Behavior congruence* is the alignment of actions taken with the actions aimed at by the control system.
   a. This is similar to *risk congruence,* which means that *uncertainty* is not supposed to affect the congruence of actions.
   b. Achieving behavior congruence can be encouraged by using subsidies to shift risks from subordinate to superior or by modifying performance measures.
6. Motivation can be strongly influenced by constructing a formal control system that clearly specifies:
   a. *Responsibility centers:* cost centers, profit centers, and other types of accountability units.
   b. *Performance evaluation:* measures, standards, and timing.
   c. *Extrinsic rewards:* bonuses, salary increases, and promotions.

C. Three types of cost are discussed to illustrate other management approaches to control:
1. *Committed costs* are fixed costs arising from a company's basic organization or the ownership of such long-term assets as land, buildings, machinery, and equipment.
   a. Examples include certain administrative salaries, insurance, property taxes, rent, and depreciation of fixed assets.
   b. These are the least responsive of costs to short-term decisions, and they cannot be decreased without jeopardizing a company's ability to meet its long-range goals.
   c. The key to managing committed costs is careful planning through capital budgets, plus a follow-up audit.
2. *Engineered costs* are costs having explicit, specified relationships with selected measures of activity.
   a. Examples include direct materials, direct labor, and fuel.
   b. Major control techniques include the standard cost systems and flexible budgets described in previous chapters.
3. *Discretionary costs,* also called *managed costs* or *programmed costs,* are fixed costs that originate from periodic budget-appropriation decisions to implement top-management policies.
   a. Examples include costs of advertising, sales promotion, employee training programs, and research and development.
   b. Such costs, unlike committed costs, could be substantially reduced for any year, if necessary.
   c. You should especially note that discretionary fixed costs, unlike most other costs, are not subject to ordinary engineering input-output analysis.
   d. Thus, managers rarely know if they are spending proper amounts for such functions as public relations, industrial relations, legal advice, accounting services, and management training.
   e. An illuminating comparison of discretionary and engineered costs is presented by textbook Exhibit 10-2.

D. The major control technique for discretionary costs is the *negotiated static budget.*
1. Such a budget typically specifies lump-sum ceilings for expenditures.

2. These are arrived at after a negotiating and bargaining process.
3. Different types of negotiated static budgets are recognized:
   a. *Ordinary incremental budget* is essentially last year's budget plus specified increases or other changes for next year.
   b. *Priority incremental budget* is essentially last year's budget plus justifications of certain activities that might be added or dropped if the old budget were expanded or reduced by a given percentage or amount.
   c. *Zero-base budget (ZBB)* is a budget for activities that are to be justified as though they were being conducted for the first time (covered in greater depth by the textbook Appendix 10 A).

E. Measurement is needed for management control of costs.
   1. *Work measurement* is a careful analysis of a task, its size, the methods used in its performance, and its efficiency. This can also be called an engineered variable-cost approach.
      a. By using such techniques as time and motion study, one can set standard unit costs that can indicate in advance the number of *control-factor units* needed for a given quantity of some specified work (for example, the number of pieces mailed per hour).
      b. These standards also permit analyses of the efficiency and effectiveness with which the resources are being used to do the work.
      c. Advocates of work measurement contend that this is the only satisfactory way to control the costs of some nonmanufacturing types of activities, the most prominent being such high-volume, repetitive tasks as billing, mailing, and payroll operations.
   2. However, most organizations do not use work-measurement techniques for controlling their nonmanufacturing costs.
      a. Instead, they treat such costs in their budgets as discretionary fixed costs.
      b. The actual expenditures are then periodically evaluated in the light of the desired objectives.

SELF-TEST AND PRACTICE EXERCISES

I For each of the following multiple-choice and true-false statements, select the most appropriate answer and enter its identification letter in the space provided:

___ 1. Neither of the two sub-parts of motivation, congruence and effort, can exist without the other: (a) true, (b) false.

___ 2. The three types of control of human behavior (organization, informal group, and individual) are: (a) independent of each other, (b) interdependent.

___ 3. Compared with formal control systems, informal systems are seldom satisfactory: (a) true, (b) false.

___ 4. Behavior congruence pertains to alignment or synchronization of: (a) goals, (b) risks, (c) actions, (d) events.

___ 5. The top management of a public accounting firm awarded its San Antonio branch office a subsidy of full billing rates to certain new clients, whose actual rates would probably be much less because of competitive bidding. This procedure is aimed most specifically at achieving: (a) goal congruence, (b) maximum effort, (c) risk congruence, (d) maximum goodwill.

___ 6. Examples of "intrinsic rewards" include: (a) salary increases, (b) promotions, (c) both of these, (d) neither of these.

___ 7. Examples of committed costs include: (a) advertising, (b) executive training, (c) both of the above, (d) neither of the above.

___ 8. Examples of discretionary costs include: (a) property taxes, (b) research, (c) both of the above, (d) neither of the above.

___ 9. The most likely type of costs that could be substantially reduced or completely eliminated in a given year without serious injury to an organization's long-term goals is: (a) engineered costs, (b) committed costs, (c) discretionary costs, (d) variable costs.

___ 10. Examples of engineered costs include: (a) handlebars for a manufacturer of bicycles, (b) fuel for an airline, (c) both of the above, (d) neither of the above.

___ 11. The relationship between costs and results is most likely to be a "black box" for: (a) discretionary costs, (b) committed costs, (c) engineered costs, (d) direct-material costs.

___ 12. Compared with engineered costs, discretionary costs are more likely to: (a) represent intangible outputs, (b) relate to repetitive human activities of a routine nature, (c) both of the above, (d) neither of the above.

___ 13. Fixed costs that arise from periodic budget appropriation decisions that directly reflect top-management policies are called: (a) fixed asset-ownership costs, (b) fluctuating fixed costs, (c) committed costs, (d) discretionary costs.

___ 14. It is likely that the committed cost classification would include: (a) sales promotion costs, (b) the cost of employee training programs, (c) both of the above, (d) neither of the above.

___ 15. In contrast to committed costs, discretionary costs are: (a) more easily influenced by management on a short-term basis, (b) more difficult to measure and evaluate in terms of their outputs, (c) both of the above, (d) neither of the above.

___ 16. The bulk of discretionary costs is composed of: (a) materials and salaries, (b) salaries and professional fees, (c) professional fees and materials, (d) direct labor and factory overhead.

___ 17. Discretionary costs are basically: (a) fixed, (b) variable, (c) mixed.

___ 18. If ZBB is adopted by an organization, ZBB should be used by all of its departments annually: (a) true, (b) false.

___ 19. The major contribution of ZBB is in the area of: (a) variable costs, (b) committed costs, (c) engineered costs, (d) none of the above.

___ 20. In the application of work-measurement techniques, examples of control-factor units would include: (a) postings of entries per hour to customers' accounts, (b) cases of beer loaded per day, (c) both of the above, (d) neither of the above.

___ 21. Work-measurement techniques are applicable to: (a) manufacturing activities alone, (b) both manufacturing and nonmanufacturing activities.

___ 22. Work measurement is an engineered variable-cost approach to cost control: (a) true, (b) false.

___ 23. In general, the application of work-measurement techniques to certain types of nonmanufacturing costs assumes that such costs are discretionary fixed costs: (a) true, (b) false.

II Complete each of the following statements:

1. The most basic criterion for comparing one management control system with another is ___

___

2. The two sub-parts of motivation are:

(a) ___

(b) ___

3. The three types of control of human behavior are:

(a) ___

(b) ___

(c) ___

4. The performance criteria for informal group control of human behavior consists of ___

___

5. An example of an "intrinsic reward" is ____
____

6. Three important elements of an effective management control system are:

(a) ______________________________

(b) ______________________________

(c) ______________________________

7. Discretionary costs may be called

(a) ______________________________

(b) ______________________________

8. The most common technique for controlling discretionary costs is the use of ______________
____

9. Fixed costs that arise from the possession of plant and equipment or from the existence of a certain basic organization are known as ______________ costs.

10. In controlling manufacturing costs, most organizations treat such costs as ____________ costs.

11. Incremental budgets are definitely contrasted to (dissimilar to) ________________ budgets.

12. Last year's budget plus justifications of certain activities that might be added or dropped if the old budget were expanded or reduced by a given percentage or amount are referred to as __________
______________________________ budgets.

13. In the application of work-measurement techniques, the work load is expressed as ____________
____

14. PPB means ______________________
____

III The Umbrella Insurance Company processes each month thousands of casualty claims from policy holders. Thirty claims adjusters work a five-day week at a salary of $600 per week. Automobile expenses are reimbursed at $20 per working day per adjuster. An average of four claims per day has been set as an appropriate work quota. Last week, 580 claims were processed by the adjusters.

1. Analyze the week's results by a discretionary-cost approach. How much is the cost variance? Use F for favorable, U for unfavorable.

2. Analyze the week's results by a work-measurement approach. What is the cost variance?

3. Should one adjuster be fired? Why?

11 Relevance, Pricing, and the Decision Process

PREVIOUS CHAPTERS DEALT primarily with product costing and the control of **routine operations.** One of the main concepts used in these studies was the **contribution approach,** which is also one of the two keys to **special decisions.** The other key is **relevant costs,** which are defined as the expected future costs that will differ for alternative actions. This is the major conceptual lesson of this chapter.

The basic function of the management accountant in decision making for special purposes is to select, measure, and analyze the costs that pertain to the available courses of action. These actions involve such decisions as the acceptance or rejection of special orders, the manufacture or purchase of direct materials (make or buy), and the replacement of equipment.

REVIEW SUMMARY

A. Cost accountants process and report information for use by management in making decisions.
   1. Such information should be *relevant* to the decisions.
   2. *Qualitative factors* may be decisive in many cases.
      a. For example, impact of decisions on employee morale or on the local environment.
      b. However, accountants usually try to express as many decision factors as possible in *quantitative terms,* in order to reduce the number of qualitative factors to be judged.

B. We must clearly understand the meaning of *relevance* as it pertains to costs used in management decision processes.
   1. Because the function of management decision making is to choose objectives and select appropriate courses of action for the future, decisions always involve *prediction.*
   2. For this reason, the costs that are relevant to managerial decision making are the predicted costs that must be compared under available alternatives.
      a. *These costs include only the expected future costs that will differ under alternatives.*
      b. Although *historical costs* are often helpful in predicting future costs, *they are not relevant to the management decision itself.*

C. The *relevant-cost approach* is well suited to the choosing of appropriate activity levels for evaluating special orders.
   1. Idle capacity often permits the filling of special reduced-price sales orders that would not affect regular sales.
      a. Average overall unit costs do not necessarily serve as the proper basis for evaluating such orders.
      b. The only costs that would usually be relevant to these situations are the variable costs that would be affected by accepting the special sales orders, not the variable costs that are unaffected. See textbook Exhibit 11-3.
      c. Because fixed costs would usually not be affected by the decision, they would usually be irrelevant.
      d. However, if the decision would affect certain fixed costs immediately or in the future, they should of course be given appropriate consideration.
      e. On the basis of a relevant-cost approach, it is possible that some special orders should be accepted at selling prices below the *average* unit costs that include all fixed and variable costs—as in the textbook example.
   2. The important point is that such decisions should depend primarily on the revenues and costs expected to be *different* among alternatives.
      a. This is true whether or not accountants' reports to management also include any revenues and costs expected to be the same among alternatives.

D. For pricing decisions, the *contribution approach* can be quite useful to management.
   1. Compared to the conventional or *absorption-costing approach,* the contribution approach has certain advantages:
      a. The delineation of variable- and fixed-cost behavior patterns facilitates the development of pricing formulas for various activity levels in addition to the normal level.
      b. The contribution approach provides insights that help in weighing the short-run benefits of cutting prices on special orders against the long-run benefits of not cutting such prices.
   2. On the other hand, it has been claimed that the use of full manufacturing costs is better than the contribution approach to pricing decisions:
      a. It has been argued that using the contribution approach in pricing decisions will result in underpricing and ultimate losses, whereas full manufacturing cost is a safer guide because it does not ignore fixed factory-overhead costs.
      b. However, pricing decisions can be quite complex, and either method can lead to unprofitable pricing if used without understanding and judgment.
   3. The contribution-margin approach reveals some factors more clearly than does the conventional approach and can help to avoid some unwise decisions:
      a. To sell products at less than out-of-pocket costs.
      b. To refuse contracts that could make contributions to fixed costs in an idle-capacity situation.
   4. Another major influence sometimes affecting pricing decisions is the Robinson-Patman Act and other laws in the United States that prohibit unreasonably low prices aimed at lessening or eliminating competition.

E. Other important types of management decisions can be assisted by the relevant-cost and contribution approaches:
   1. When a multi-product plant is being operated at capacity, the orders that are accepted should maximize profits.
      a. The criterion for maximum profits for a given capacity is the greatest possible contribution to profit per unit of the *constraining factor or resource.*
      b. Constraining factors may include such resource measures as machine-hours, labor-

hours, or cubic feet of space, but not necessarily the contribution-margin ratio per product unit. See Exhibit 11-4.

2. When manufacturers are confronted with the question of whether to make or buy a product, the decision may be based on qualitative factors, such as the quality of the products or long-run business relationships.
   a. However, the decision may depend partly on the quantitative measurement of the difference in future costs among the alternatives, especially if idle productive facilities are involved.
   b. Such relevant costs would not necessarily be restricted to variable costs, but could include fixed costs that may be avoided in the future.
3. The essence of the make-or-buy decision is how best to utilize available facilities after considering such alternatives as:
   a. Leaving facilities idle
   b. Buying products and renting out unused facilities
   c. Buying products and using facilities for other products
4. In arriving at make-or-buy decisions, managers and accountants should be aware of several pitfalls:
   a. Distorted unit costs could be produced by irrelevant allocations of a fixed cost that would not be affected by the decision.
   b. Improper comparisons of *unit costs* not computed on the same basis could lead to the wrong decision. This error can be avoided by comparing *total costs* for alternatives.

F. Our definition of *relevant costs*—expected future costs that will differ among alternatives—excludes historical costs.

1. Although past costs may be of aid in predicting future costs, they are irrelevant to the decision itself.
2. The historical cost of materials or finished inventories (whether obsolete or not) would be common to all future alternatives and therefore would not affect the differences in expected profits from such alternatives as:
   a. Scrapping the inventory
   b. Selling it at reduced prices
   c. Remaking the inventory into other products and selling them at certain prices
3. For convenience in analyzing the alternatives under consideration, one can use as an *opportunity cost* the benefits promised by the best of the excluded alternatives (the copper example in the textbook).
   a. Opportunity cost is the maximum contribution or value that is sacrificed or given up by using limited resources for a certain purpose.
   b. Because opportunity costs are derived from transactions that do not actually take place, they are not ordinarily entered in the accounting records.
4. The book value of old equipment is a past or historical cost.
   a. Therefore, it is irrelevant to *making decisions.*
   b. However, book value might be relevant to *developing predictions* of future cash flows that are partly dependent on the income tax effects of the depreciation or sale of equipment.
   c. Exhibits 11-5 and 11-6 are particularly helpful models for comparing costs in a machine-replacement situation.
   d. An important motivational aspect should be recognized in such situations: the somewhat natural reluctance of a manager to replace a machine because of adverse effects on his perceived profit performance in the year of replacement.

SELF-TEST AND PRACTICE EXERCISES

I For each of the following multiple-choice and true-false statements, select the most appropriate answer and enter its identification letter in the space provided.

___ 1. A comparative analysis schedule of costs for two alternative courses of action: (a) must include both relevant costs and irrelevant costs, (b) must exclude irrelevant costs, (c) may include irrelevant costs if they are not misleading to the decision maker.

___ 2. The total fixed costs of each of two alternatives: (a) are irrelevant to the choice of the alternatives, (b) are relevant if they are different in amount.

___ 3. A taxicab company is comparing two kinds of cars to add to its fleet of cabs. Qualitative decision factors could include differences in: (a) miles per gallon of fuel consumption, (b) comfort and satisfaction of customers, (c) both of the above, (d) neither of the above.

___ 4. "Full cost" per unit usually means: (a) absorption manufacturing cost, (b) variable manufacturing cost, (c) absorption manufacturing cost plus an allocation of selling and administrative cost, (d) variable manufacturing cost plus an allocation of variable selling and administrative cost.

___ 5. In general, all variable costs are relevant to decisions, but all fixed costs are not: (a) true, (b) false.

___ 6. Fixed costs need not be considered in making a decision unless they are expected to be altered by that decision, either immediately or in the future: (a) true, (b) false.

___ 7. Historical costs may be: (a) relevant to decisions about the future, (b) helpful in predicting future costs, (c) both of the above, (d) neither of the above.

___ 8. Costs that are relevant to management decision making usually include all expected future costs: (a) true, (b) false.

___ 9. Costs that are relevant to decisions about the future might include: (a) an expected future fixed cost, (b) a past variable cost, (c) both of the above, (d) neither of the above.

___ 10. Big Falls Company's average "full cost" of making 9,000 units of its product for regular sale is $20 per unit. If it manufactures 1,000 additional units to fill a special order, the average "full cost" per unit of total production will be $19. If the selling price of the special order is $18 per unit, the order should be rejected: (a) true, (b) false.

___ 11. See the preceding item. What is the lowest selling price per unit of the special order that would cover the additional "full costs" of the order? (a) $20, (b) $15, (c) $10, (d) some other price.

___ 12. When there is idle plant capacity and reduced-price special orders are received, the relevant-cost approach: (a) would evaluate the orders on the basis of average overall unit costs, (b) might indicate acceptance of orders at prices below average overall unit costs, (c) both of the above, (d) neither of the above.

___ 13. The relevant-cost approach to evaluating reduced-price special orders implies that future fixed costs: (a) are irrelevant, (b) are usually relevant, (c) might be relevant.

___ 14. The approach that is more helpful in furnishing insights that help in weighing the short-run benefits of cutting prices on special orders against the long-run benefits of not cutting such prices is: (a) the absorption-costing approach, (b) the contribution approach.

___ 15. An approach to pricing decisions that can lead to unprofitable pricing if used without understanding and judgment includes: (a) the contribution approach, (b) the full-costing approach, (c) either of the above, (d) neither of the above.

___ 16. Opportunity Corporation normally produces and sells 5,000 units per year of a certain product. Its total costs are $275,000 fixed and $200,000 variable. A special order is received for 500 units at a selling price of $75 per unit. Sufficient idle capacity exists for making these additional units. Compute the overall average cost per unit of total production: (a) $100, (b) $95, (c) $90, (d) some other unit cost.

___ 17. See the preceding item. Compute the incremental cost per unit of the special order: (a) $95, (b) $90, (c) $40, (d) some other unit cost.

___ 18. See the two preceding items. Should the special order be accepted, assuming its sale would not affect regular sales? (a) yes, (b) no.

___ 19. The pricing approach that is more helpful in preventing decisions to refuse contracts that could make contributions to fixed costs in an idle-capacity situation is: (a) the contribution-margin approach, (b) the absorption-costing approach.

___ 20. When a multi-product plant is being operated at capacity, orders that are accepted should maximize: (a) available machine-hours, (b) total profits, (c) contribution-margin ratio per product unit, (d) available labor hours, (e) cubic feet of factory space.

___ 21. Rambling Company has a limited number of machine hours that it can use for two products: Product A or Product B. Each product has a selling price of $80 per unit, but A has a 40 percent contribution margin and B has a 70 percent contribution margin. One unit of Product B takes twice as long to make as a unit of A. Which product or products should the entire capacity be used for? (a) A, (b) B, (c) both A and B.

___ 22. See the preceding item. Suppose all data are the same except that the selling price of A is $50, and B is $60. Which product should the entire capacity be used for? (a) A, (b) B, (c) both A and B.

___ 23. In deciding among alternatives for using inventories, their historical cost is irrelevant if the inventories are: (a) obsolete, (b) not obsolete, (c) either of the above, (d) neither of the above.

___ 24. Items that can be relevant to making predictions of future costs include: (a) disposal value of old equipment, (b) gross book value of old equipment, (c) both of the above, (d) neither of the above.

___ 25. Items that can be relevant to choosing among alternative uses of certain materials on hand include: (a) their salvage value, (b) their net book value, (c) both of the above, (d) neither of the above.

___ 26. Opportunity costs: (a) are not ordinarily entered in the accounting records, (b) do not require dollar outlays, (c) both of the above, (d) neither of the above.

___ 27. The American antitrust laws expressly prohibit sales below variable costs: (a) true, (b) false.

II Complete each of the following statements:

1. Ideally, the information collected by accountants and reported to decision makers should be

____

2. Costs that are relevant to managerial decision making include only the ______________ costs that ______________ under alternative courses of action.

3. ______________ costs may be relevant to the prediction of future costs but are not relevant to

____

4. It has been contended that the use of the ______________________ in pricing decisions will result in underpricing and ultimate company disaster.

5. The American antitrust laws prohibit selling prices intended to ______________________

6. It has been argued that, in comparison with the contribution approach, the ______________ would be a safer guide in pricing decisions because it does not ignore ______________________ factory-overhead costs.

7. When a multi-product plant is being operated at capacity, the criterion for maximum profits is the largest contribution ______________________

8. The maximum contribution that is foregone by using limited resources for a particular purpose is called ______________________

III Given for Wild-Flower Products:

Plant capacity per month	25,000 units
Current production per month	20,000 units
Special order received from a mail-order house	4,000 units
Average full cost per product unit for current production	$ 24.00
Proposed selling price per unit for special order	$ 18.00
Average full cost per product unit for current production plus special order	$ 22.50

1. Compute the incremental cost per unit of the special order . . . . $ ______

2. Assuming that the special order sales would have no effect on regular current sales, compute the incremental profit (or loss) from accepting the special order. . . . . $ ______

IV Given for Belknap Products:

Normal production and sales per year:

Product units	15,000 units
Fixed costs	$720,000
Variable costs	$660,000

Special order received:

Product units	3,000 units
Selling price per unit	$ 70

Assumptions:

Idle capacity exists to cover special order.
Special order sales will not affect normal annual sales.

Compute:

1. Overall average cost per unit of normal production plus special order .... $ ______

2. Incremental cost per unit of special order .... $ ______

3. Incremental profit (or loss) if the special order is accepted................. $ ______

V Cody Corporation has an annual plant capacity of 2,800 product units. Its predicted operations for the year are:

Sales (2,000 units at $40 each)	$80,000
Manufacturing costs:	
Variable	$23 per unit
Fixed	$18,000
Selling and administrative expenses:	
Variable (sales commissions)	$ 4 per unit
Fixed	$ 2,000

Should the company accept a special order for 600 units at a selling price of $30 each and subject to half the usual sales commission rate per unit, assuming no effect on regular sales at regular prices? Show supporting computations.

VI The Grimes Company has a useful machine with a book value of $102,000, a present scrap value of $15,000, and an estimated remaining life of ten years. A new machine that is available at a cost of $193,000 has the same capacity, but it would reduce power costs by $19,000 per year. It has a predicted useful life of ten years. Neither machine will have a scrap value at the end of its useful life. Ignoring income taxes and the time value of money, which of the two alternatives should the company select: keep the old machine or replace it with the new machine? Show supporting computations.

VII Redbird Corporation has 1,300 hours of plant capacity available during a certain period for manufacturing two products with the following characteristics:

	C	D
Selling price per unit	$40	$85
Variable expenses per unit	$18	$35
Units that can be manufactured in one hour (C or D)	9	5

Compute the number of its 1,300 available production hours that this company should devote to the manufacture of each product:

C ____________________ D ____________________

VIII The Houma Novelty Company has three product lines: T, L, and C. The company furnished the following operating statement for its most recent year (in thousands of dollars):

	T	L	C	Total
Sales	120	150	180	450
Variable costs and expenses	80	90	100	270
Fixed costs and expenses:				
Annual salaries of product-line supervisors	17	20	23	60
Total company-wide fixed costs allocated equally to product lines	30	30	30	90
Total costs and expenses	127	140	153	420
Operating income (loss)	(7)	10	27	30

1. Using a format similar to the above, prepare a projected operating statement on the assumption that Product T operations are discontinued with no effects on sales of the other product lines or on the total assets used by the comany.

	L	C	Total

2. On the basis of the statement you have prepared, would you advise the elimination of Product T operations? Why?

Capital Budgeting and Cost Analysis 12

THIS CHAPTER DEALS with **capital budgeting,** the making of long-term planning decisions for investments and their financing. Such decisions typically involve a nonrecurring set of specific alternatives that can have significant long-run effects on a company's profits and financial condition. Therefore, for each of the available alternatives, management should systematically quantify the expected results and measure them against the required investment.

This chapter describes and compares the principal capital-budgeting approaches (decision models) that are in general use. Of central importance is the concept of the **time value of money** and its use in measuring cash flows for decision purposes.

REVIEW SUMMARY

A. *Capital budgeting* means making-long term planning decisions for investments and their financing.

1. Such decisions typically involve special projects that require commitments over a period of several years.
2. For this reason, it is not necessarily appropriate to use the same planning and control models of traditional general-purpose accounting systems, which are designed primarily to meet the routine needs of current periods only.
3. This chapter concentrates on *discounted cash-flow (DCF) models.*
   a. These represent the conceptually superior approach.
   b. However, other models are also described:
   - Urgency and persuasion
   - Payback (or payout or payoff)
   - Accrual accounting rate of return

B. *Urgency and persuasion* do not provide a systematic approach that evaluates economic considerations on a timely and objective basis.

1. The urgency of critical situations caused by neglect and procrastination often limits management decisions to those that are not optimal.

2. Moreover, decisions based on the persuasive powers of managers who advocate different alternatives do not necessarily reflect appropriate consideration of valid evaluation data.

C. *DCF analysis* focuses on flows of cash instead of flows of revenues and expenses (net income).

1. This approach, which systematically weighs the time value of money, has two main variations:
   a. The *net-present-value (NPV)* model uses a *required rate of return (RRR),* or *hurdle rate,* for discounting cash outflows and inflows to a given present date so that their net difference may be measured at that date, as illustrated in textbook Exhibit 12–2.
   b. The *internal rate of return (IRR),* or *time-adjusted rate of return,* is the rate of return (discount rate) that equates the amount invested at a given date with the present value of the expected cash inflows from the investment as demonstrated in textbook Exhibit 12–4.
2. Note especially that DCF analysis is based upon flows of *cash* and not the *accrual* concepts of revenues and expenses.
   a. Therefore, no adjustments should be made to cash flows for the periodic allocation of asset cost called *depreciation expense.*
   b. Instead, the *initial cost* of an asset is usually treated in DCF computations as a *lump-sum cash outflow* at time zero.
3. DCF models assume a world of certainty regarding interest rates and the amounts and timing of predicted cash flows.

D. Important differences should be recognized between the two variations of the discounted cash-flow approach.

1. Different decision rules are used:
   a. If the internal rate of return equals or exceeds the hurdle rate, accept the project; if not, reject the project.
   b. If the net present value is zero or positive, accept the project; if negative, reject the project.
2. The internal rate of return usually requires more tedious manual calculations than are necessary for the net-present-value method, which can be more easily applied to situations with uneven periodic cash flows.
3. On the other hand, electronic computers can be programmed for calculation, and the internal rate of return is more widely used for two reasons:
   a. The internal rates appear to be more easily interpreted than the net-present-value amounts.
   b. The internal-rate-of-return method avoids the task of selecting a hurdle rate for discounting cash flows.
   c. Of course, in the *decision* model, a hurdle rate must be used.

E. *Sensitivity analysis* is a helpful way to cope with risk and uncertainty.

1. Actual cash flows may not be the same as expected cash flows.
2. Sensitivity analysis is a technique that measures how the basic forecasted results in a decision model will be affected by changes in the critical data inputs that influence those results.
3. By providing an immediate financial measure of the possible errors in forecasting, sensitivity analysis helps managers to concentrate attention on the most sensitive decision factors in a given case, such as amounts of cash flows and useful lives of assets.

F. The relationships of several important items to discounted cash-flow analysis should be clearly understood:

1. Errors in forecasting future disposal values are usually not crucial, because the combina-

tion of relatively small disposal values and long time periods tends to produce small present values.

2. Any additional investments that might be required for current assets (such as cash, receivables, and inventories) may be regarded as outflows at time zero, their terminal disposal values being regarded as inflows at the end of a project's useful life.
3. Current disposal values of old assets are more conveniently handled by offsetting them against the gross cash outlays for new assets.
4. Depreciation and book values are ignored, because historical costs are irrelevant.
5. Income taxes, which do affect cash flows, are ignored in this chapter but are considered in the next chapter.
6. In the relevant-cost analysis of factory overhead, the only pertinent cost is the overhead that will differ among alternatives.

G. Another model used for capital-budgeting decisions is called *payback, payout,* or *payoff.*

1. If there are uniform annual cash inflows, the initial cash investment is divided by the annual cash inflow to find the estimated number of years it will take to recoup the investment.
2. This may be useful in certain circumstances, *but it ignores the profitability of investments.*

H. Another capital-budgeting model is often used.

1. It is called the *accrual-accounting-rate-of-return model.*
2. Other names for this are:
   - **a.** Book-value method
   - **b.** Unadjusted rate-of-return method
   - **c.** Financial statement method.
3. The predicted amount of future average annual net income, or increase therein, is divided by the initial (sometimes average) amount of the required investment, or increase therein.
4. The accrual-accounting-rate-of-return method is widely used.
   - **a.** It aims at profit measurement by conventional accounting methods.
   - **b.** However, *it ignores the time value of money.*

I. In general, the best approach to long-range decisions is the discounted cash-flow method because, by explicitly and automatically weighing the time value of money, it aims at the overriding goal of maximizing long-run net cash inflows.

J. See the two textbook problems for self-study, especially the accompanying Exhibit 12–6 for the second problem.

1. Note that the same net-present-value difference between two alternative projects can be obtained by either of two approaches for discounting cash flows to a common present date:
   - **a.** Calculate the net present value *of the cash flows* of each of the two projects and determine the difference between these two amounts (*the total-project approach*).
   - **b.** Calculate the net present value *of the cash flow differences* between the two projects (*the incremental approach*).
2. Note also the helpfulness of the "sketch of cash flows," a key step in solving problems of this type.

SELF-TEST AND PRACTICE EXERCISES

I For each of the following multiple-choice and true-false statements, select the most appropriate answer and enter its identification letter in the space provided:

____ 1. The focus is on cash inflows and outflows by: (a) NPV models, (b) IRR models, (c) both NPV and IRR models, (d) neither NPV nor IRR models.

___ 2. NPV models assume a world of: (a) certainty, (b) uncertainty.

___ 3. The time value of money is systematically weighed by: (a) payback and IRR models, (b) IRR and NPV models, (c) NPV and payback models, (d) all of these three models.

___ 4. All DCF models are usually feasible to use when the predicted cash flows are: (a) uniform, (b) not uniform, (c) either uniform or not uniform.

___ 5. A required rate of return must be used in: (a) the IRR method, (b) the IRR decision model, (c) IRR method and decision model, (d) neither the IRR method nor decision model.

___ 6. The IRR used in capital budgeting approaches corresponds conceptually to the yield rates or effective rates quoted in the markets for bonds and other forms of long-term debt: (a) true, (b) false.

___ 7. The present value of one million dollars due or receivable ten years from now would be lowest if computed at a discount rate of: (a) 15 percent, (b) 10 percent, (c) zero percent.

___ 8. If the NPV of a project is zero, the IRR is equal to the RRR: (a) true, (b) false.

___ 9. A 13 percent RRR was used to compute the net present value of a project. If the NPV is negative, the IRR is: (a) more than 13 percent, (b) less than 13 percent.

___ 10. The choice of a discount rate for computing the net present value of a project depends partly upon how the project is to be financed: (a) true, (b) false.

___ 11. Errors in the predictions of cash flows beyond ten years into the future can have major impacts on net present values: (a) true, (b) false.

___ 12. The "bail-out payback time" is reached when the cumulative cash operating savings plus the salvage value at the end of a particular year equals the original investment: (a) true, (b) false.

___ 13. The internal rate of return is the discount rate that equates the amount invested at a given date with the present value of the expected cash inflows from the investment: (a) true, (b) false.

___ 14. Depreciation is a periodic flow of: (a) cash, (b) expense, (c) both of the above, (d) neither of the above.

___ 15. If the minimum desired rate of return exceeds the internal rate of return expected from a certain project, the project should be rejected: (a) true, (b) false.

___ 16. Compared with DCF approaches to capital budgeting, the emergency-persuasion approach is inferior both conceptually and for practical purposes: (a) true, (b) false.

___ 17. If the payback reciprocal is 20 percent, the internal rate of return would be: (a) 20 percent, (b) more than 20 percent, (c) less than 20 percent.

___ 18. When cash-flow analysis is applied to two mutually exclusive projects, the one that shows the smaller net present value should be: (a) accepted, (b) rejected.

___ 19. In DCF computations, depreciation is properly added to: (a) expected cash inflows, (b) expected cash outflows, (c) neither cash inflows nor cash outflows.

___ 20. The internal rate of return can usually be more easily applied to situations with uneven periodic cash flows than can the net-present-value method: (a) true, (b) false.

___ 21. The use of conventional accrual accounting models for evaluating performance tends to impede the adoption of DCF models for capital-budgeting decisions: (a) true, (b) false.

___ 22. Generally, in DCF analysis, we should ignore: (a) depreciation and book values, (b) income taxes, (c) both of the above, (d) neither of the above.

___ 23. In DCF analysis, the most convenient way to handle current disposal values of old assets is to: (a) treat them as cash inflows, (b) treat them as cash outflows, (c) offset them against initial cash outlays for new assets, (d) add them to the required investment in the project.

___ 24. The profitability of an investment is ignored by: (a) the net-present-value method, (b) the internal-rate-of-return method, (c) both of the above, (d) neither of the above.

___ 25. The payback model: (a) may be useful in certain circumstances, (b) ignores the profitability of investments, (c) both of the above, (d) neither of the above.

___ 26. A project requires an initial investment of $120,000 in depreciable assets having an estimated useful life of eight years and no terminal scrap value. The predicted annual savings in cash operating expenses are $45,000. Compute the accrual accounting rate of return on the initial investment: (a) 37.5 percent, (b) 30 percent, (c) 25 percent, (d) some other rate.

___ 27. The time value of money is ignored by: (a) the accounting-rate-of-return approach, (b) the internal-rate-of-return model, (c) both of the above, (d) neither of the above.

___ 28. Compared to the total-project approach for computing the net-present-value difference between two alternative projects, the incremental approach would usually produce: (a) a smaller present-value difference, (b) a larger present-value difference, (c) the same present-value difference.

II Complete each of the following statements:

1. A synonym for the required rate of return is ________________________________

2. The present value of a given amount due five years from now would be ________________ at a 12 percent discount rate than at a 15 percent discount rate.

3. The internal rate of return is also called the ________________________________ ________________________________

4. A proposed project should be rejected if its net present value is ________________

5. A technique that measures how the basic forecasted results in a decision model will be affected by changes in certain input data is called ________________ ________________________________

6. In the relevant-cost analysis of factory overhead, the only pertinent cost is the overhead that ________________________________ ________________________________

7. If there are uniform annual cash inflows, the payback reciprocal can be computed by dividing the ________________ by the ________________________________

8. Essentially, the accounting rate of return is the predicted amount of ________________, or increase therein, divided by the initial (sometimes average) amount of the ________________ ________________ or increase therein.

9. When the incremental approach is used for determining the net-present-value difference between two alternative projects, one should calculate the present value of the ________________ ________________________________

III Write out the words for each set of initials:

DCF ________________________________

NPV ________________________________

IRR ______________________________

RRR ______________________________

IV Given for Implement Manufacturing Company:

Initial cost of a special purpose machine	$80,000
Predicted useful life	12 years
Predicted residual value at end of useful life	$ 6,000
Predicted annual savings in cash operating expenses	$15,000
Minimum desired rate of return	16%
Present value of $1 due 12 years from now, using a 16% effective interest rate	$ 0.168
Present value of an annuity of $1 per year due at the end of each of 12 years from now, using a 16% effective interest rate	$ 5.197

Compute the following, ignoring income tax effects:

1. Present value of expected annual savings:

2. Present value of predicted residual value:

3. Total present value of expected cash inflows:

4. Net present value of expected cash inflows:

V Given for Good Accessories, Inc.:

Initial cost of a special purpose machine	$120,000
Predicted useful life (no terminal scrap value)	15 years
Predicted annual savings in cash operating expenses	$ 20,000
Present value of an annuity of $1 for 15 years:	
Using a 14% effective interest rate	$ 6.142
Using a 16% effective interest rate	$ 5.575

Compute the internal rate of return to the nearest tenth of a percent, ignoring income tax effects . . . . . . ______ %

VI Given for Wrangler Industries:

Initial cost of proposed new equipment	$180,000
Predicted useful life	8 years
Predicted residual value at end of useful life	$20,000
Predicted savings per year in cash operating expenses	$40,000

Compute the following, ignoring income tax effects:

1. Payback period .... ______years

2. Payback reciprocal .... ______%

3. Depreciation expense per year by straight-line method .... $______

4. Predicted increase in future average annual net income .... $______

5. Accounting rate of return based on initial investment .... ______%

6. Accounting rate of return based on average investment .... ______%

13 Capital Budgeting: A Closer Look

CAPITAL BUDGETING was introduced in the preceding chapter without the complications of income taxes. However, income taxes almost always play a basic role in decision making, because they usually require relatively large cash outflows that depend for their amounts and timing upon the choices among alternative projects. This chapter describes the treatment of income taxes and the function of depreciation in capital budgeting.

In addition, several other important aspects of capital budgeting are examined: effects of inflation, cost of capital, conflict of techniques for ranking projects, and the rationing of capital within a total capital-budgeting constraint.

REVIEW SUMMARY

A. The combined federal and state income tax rate may easily exceed 50 percent of corporate earnings.

1. Thus, the income tax effects on cash and net income should not be ignored in capital budgeting.

2. Income taxes affect both the amount and the timing of cash flows.

3. Depreciation is a *noncash expense* used in computing periodic net income.

a. The basic relationships of depreciation to net income and cash flows are clearly shown in the key textbook Exhibit 13–1, which should be studied very carefully.

b. Depreciation expense is subtracted in arriving at the amount of periodic net income, but it is not a periodic cash disbursement.

c. Therefore, it may be *added back* to the net-income figure to arrive at current net cash inflow from all revenue-producing operations.

4. Although depreciation itself is not a cash inflow, the deductibility of depreciation from revenues in determining net income subject to taxes reduces income tax payments and thus serves as a *tax shield.*

a. The tax-savings effect of depreciation has a *present value* that is partially dependent upon the depreciation method chosen, as shown by the textbook Exhibit 13–2.

b. The double-declining-balance method (DDB) and the sum-of-years'-digits method (SYD), which are two widely used accelerated-depreciation methods, produce higher present values for the tax savings than does the straight-line method.

5. Although consideration must be given to income tax effects in making capital-budgeting decisions, this does not require a change in the general approach described in the preceding chapter. See textbook Exhibits 13–3 and 13–4, and note carefully the following main points:
   a. The same net-present-value difference between two alternative projects may be computed either by the total-project approach or by the incremental approach.
   b. The *after-tax basis* is used to compute the present values of cash flows: cash operating costs, cash revenues, and the amounts expected to be received on disposals of assets.
   c. The present value of the tax savings from depreciation is computed separately from other cash flows.

B. Do not confuse the role of depreciation in capital budgeting.
   1. Book values and depreciation of old equipment can provide helpful information for the *prediction method.*
   2. However, these amounts, by themselves, are not relevant to the *decision model.*
   3. Depreciation and book values do affect income taxes, of course.
   4. But it is the *future cash flows of the income taxes* that are relevant to the decision model.

C. Discounted cash flow models should be adjusted for the effects of inflation (the decline in the general purchasing power of money).
   1. The discount rate should be increased to include an element representing the rate of inflation.
   2. The expected after-tax cash operating inflows should be adjusted upward by this same rate.
   3. However, the expected cash flows caused by income tax savings from depreciation should not be adjusted by the rate of inflation. (Do you know why?)
   4. See the very helpful textbook Exhibit 13–5:
      a. Note that the 22 percent discount rate includes a 12 percent inflation rate.
      b. Note also how Table 1 at the end of the book is used to adjust the expected cash flows by the 12 percent inflation rate.

D. The basic discount rate we use in capital budgeting is called the required rate of return (RRR).
   1. For our purposes, a synonym for RRR is the *cost of capital.*
      a. This rate varies with *risk* from project to project.
      b. The higher the risk, the higher must be the RRR.
   2. Thus, the divisions or other subunits within an organization should not necessarily use the same discount rates.

E. Occasionally, the net-present-value and internal-rate-of-return techniques produce *conflicting rankings* of mutually exclusive investment proposals, as indicated by Exhibit 13–6.
   1. When alternative projects have unequal lives, differences in ranking by the two methods can occur because of different implicit assumptions as to the rate of return on the reinvestment of cash proceeds at the end of the shorter project life.
   2. The two approaches can be reconciled:
      a. By using a common terminal date for alternative projects.
      b. By making explicit assumptions as to the appropriate rates for reinvestment of funds.

F. Theoretically, a general rule for evaluating capital projects would be to undertake any project with a *positive net present value* after discounting cash inflows at the minimum desired rate of return.

1. However, in practice, this rule is subject to some important qualifications:
   a. It may be necessary to practice *capital rationing* because of an overall capital-spending budget limit influenced by such factors as management philosophy and the feasibility of obtaining funds from operations and security issues.
   b. In the absence of capital rationing, the *excess-present-value index* would indicate the acceptance of the same projects indicated by the net-present value approach.
2. But capital-spending constraints are quite common, and the *net-present-value method* is the best general guide for choosing among investments of different sizes, as illustrated by Exhibit 13–7:
   a. Optimal decisions would not always result from the use of the excess-present-value index.
   b. If there are *investment indivisibilities* within a budget constraint, total returns in some instances would be maximized by accepting smaller, though less attractive, projects.

SELF-TEST AND PRACTICE EXERCISES

I For each of the following multiple-choice and true-false statements, select the most appropriate answer and enter its identification letter in the space provided:

___ 1. Assume, as in the key textbook Exhibit 13–1, that all transactions involve cash except depreciation. If the income tax rate is 60 percent, depreciation in the amount of $5,000 would produce a cash tax savings of $3,000: (a) true, (b) false.

___ 2. See the preceding item. Assume also $60,000 of sales and $40,000 of cash expenses. Net income is: (a) $15,000, (b) $9,000, (c) $6,000, (d) some other amount.

___ 3. See the two preceding items. The total after-tax effect on cash inflow from operations is: (a) $9,000, (b) $11,000, (c) $8,000, (d) some other amount.

___ 4. The current net cash inflow from all revenue-producing operations may be measured by adding net income and: (a) depreciation expense, (b) the income tax effect of depreciation expense, (c) depreciation expense less its income tax effect.

___ 5. Depreciation is: (a) a periodic cash inflow, (b) a periodic operating expense, (c) both of the above, (d) neither of the above.

___ 6. Cash sales minus cash operating expenses minus income tax equals the total after-tax effect on cash inflow from operations: (a) true, (b) false.

___ 7. If depreciation expense is the only non-cash item in an income statement, the total after-tax effect on cash inflow from operations is equal to net income plus: (a) depreciation expense, (b) the cash tax savings from depreciation expense, (c) depreciation expense less its tax effect, (d) none of the above.

___ 8. The total after-tax effect on cash inflow from operations is equal to the income tax savings from depreciation expense plus the after-tax effects of operations (excluding depreciation expense): (a) true, (b) false.

___ 9. Assume two expenses of a business: cash advertising $10,000 and depreciation $10,000. If the income tax rate is 40%, the after-tax effects on cash would be: (a) inflow $4,000 for advertising and inflow $4,000 for depreciation, (b) inflow $6,000 for advertising and inflow $6,000 for depreciation, (c) outflow $4,000 for advertising and inflow $6,000 for depreciation, (d) outflow $6,000 for advertising and inflow $4,000 for depreciation.

___ 10. The after-tax effect of depreciation expense on the measurement of periodic net income is the periodic: (a) depreciation expense, (b) income tax effect of depreciation expense, (c) depreciation expense less its income tax effect.

____ 11. In contrast to the use of the double-declining-balance depreciation method, the use of the straight-line depreciation method would produce for the tax savings: (a) a larger present value, (b) a smaller present value, (c) about the same present value.

____ 12. Fractionating Company acquired a depreciable asset for $72,000. It has an estimated life of eight years with no terminal salvage value. Depreciation expense for the first year by the sum-of-years'-digits (SYD) method would be: (a) $18,000, (b) $2,000, (c) $9,000, (d) some other amount.

____ 13. See the preceding item. First-year depreciation expense by the DDB method would be: (a) $36,000, (b) $16,000, (c) $18,000, (d) some other amount.

____ 14. See the two preceding items. If the income tax rate is 60%, what is the tax-saving effect of using the DDB method instead of SYD for the first year? (a) $800 less tax, (b) $800 more tax, (c) $1,200 less tax, (d) $1,200 more tax.

____ 15. Because it is appropriate to consider income tax effects in making capital-budgeting decisions: (a) the general approach of the preceding chapter must be changed, (b) the difference in the net present values of two alternatives computed by the incremental approach will not be the same as the difference computed by the total-project approach, (c) both of the above, (d) neither of the above.

____ 16. Determinator Corporation sold for $44,000 cash an old piece of equipment. It was purchased 8 years ago for $130,000 and was being depreciated on a straight-line basis over a useful life of 10 years with an expected terminal scrap value of $10,000. What was the gain or loss on the sale before income taxes? (a) $20,000 gain, (b) $18,000 loss, (c) $10,000 gain, (d) some other gain or loss.

____ 17. See the preceding item. Compute the after-tax cash increase from the sale transaction only, assuming a 40 percent income tax rate: (a) $40,000, (b) $17,600, (c) $26,400, (d) some other amount.

____ 18. Book values and depreciation can, by themselves, be relevant to: (a) the decision model, (b) the prediction method, (c) both the decision model and the prediction method, (d) neither the decision model nor the prediction method.

____ 19. The expected future cash flows caused by income tax savings from depreciation should be adjusted by the rate of inflation before being discounted to the present: (a) true, (b) false.

____ 20. To compensate for the effects of inflation, one should adjust the discounted cash flow model by: (a) increasing the discount rate and reducing the cash operating inflows, (b) reducing the discount rate and reducing the cash operating inflows, (c) reducing the discount rate and increasing the cash operating inflows, (d) increasing the discount rate and increasing the cash operating inflows.

____ 21. In the absence of capital rationing, all projects should be undertaken that have: (a) positive net present values using the required rate of return, (b) excess-present-value indexes above 100 percent using the required rate of return, (c) either of the above, (d) neither of the above.

____ 22. The best general guide for choosing among investments of different sizes is the excess-present-value index: (a) true, (b) false.

II Complete each of the following statements:

1. If the "nominal rate" or "money rate" is used for the RRR or hurdle rate, the three elements of this rate are called:

(a) ____________________

(b) ____________________

(c) ____________________

2. For our purposes, the cost of capital is a synonym for ______________________

3. Two depreciation methods that produce larger after-tax net present values than produced by straight-line depreciation are:

(a) ______________________

(b) ______________________

4. When differences in ranking of alternative projects with unequal lives are produced by the net-present-value and internal-rate-of-return techniques, this is caused by different implicit assumptions as to the rate of return on ______________________

____

5. The selection of projects when there is an overall budget limit for capital expenditures is called ______________________

6. The required rate of return used in capital budgeting is frequently called ______________________

____

III Given for Mrs. Brady's Bread Company for 19__4:

Sales	$800,000
Depreciation expenses	$ 40,000
All other expenses	$700,000
Income tax rate	45%

1. Compute net income:

2. Compute the total after-tax effect on cash inflow from operations. Use three different numerical approaches.

IV For each case, compute the after-tax cash effect of the sale transaction only:

	Case A	Case B
Original cost of machinery	$300,000	$270,000
Life used for straight-line depreciation	8 years	10 years
Residual scrap value used for depreciation purposes	$ 20,000	$ 30,000
Age of machinery when sold	6 years	7 years
Cash sales price	$120,000	$ 82,000
Income tax rate	60%	40%
Answer:	$ ______	$ ______

V Shield Corporation has asked you to compare two of its expenses:

	Salaries	Depreciation
Total expense	$100,000	$100,000
Income tax rate	55%	55%

Compute the after-tax effect on cash for each expense, indicating whether the amount is an inflow or an outflow $ ______ $ ______

VI Fractionating Company acquired a depreciable asset for $72,000. It has an estimated life of eight years with no terminal salvage value.

1. Compute the *second* full year's depreciation, using the:
   (a) straight-line method:

   (b) sum-of-year's-digits method (SYD):

   (c) double-declining-balance method (DBB):

2. Assume a 60 percent income tax rate and compute the second year's income tax saving effects of:
   (a) SYD compared with straight-line:

   (b) DDB compared with straight-line:

VII Flex-Tex Company's discount rate of 20 percent for capital budgeting includes a 10 percent inflation element. Assume a 60 percent income tax rate and compute the present value of:

1. A $50,000 pretax cash operating inflow expected one year from now.

2. A $50,000 depreciation expense one year from now.

VIII The Centre Company provides the following data:

Purchase price of special equipment	$100,000
Predicted useful life	10 years
Predicted annual savings in cash operating costs	$ 30,000
Predicted residual value (terminal scrap value)	none
Depreciation method: straight line	
Required *after-tax* rate of return	10%
Income tax rate	60%
Present value of $1 at 10%:	
Due at the end of 5 years	$ 0.62
Due at the end of 10 years	$ 0.39
Present value of an annuity of $1 for 10 years:	
At 10%	$ 6.15
At 12%	$ 5.65
At 14%	$ 5.22

Compute the following on an *after-tax* basis:

1. The payback period .... ____ years

2. The internal rate of return to the nearest tenth of one percent .... ____ %

3. The net present value of the investment .... $ ____

IX The following projects of similar risk are available to Optional Corporation:

Project	Total Cost	Present Value	Net Present Value	Excess-Present-Value Index
A	$15,000	$21,000	$	%
B	8,000	12,000		
C	5,000	7,500		
D	4,000	6,400		
E	2,000	3,500		
F	1,000	1,900		

1. For each project, compute and make entries in the above schedule for the net present value and the excess-present-value index.

2. Assuming a total budget constraint of $25,000, which projects would you advise Optional to accept? List them below:

Project	Total Cost	Present Value	Net Present Value	Excess-Present-Value Index
	$	$	$	%
Totals	$	$	$	%

3. Assuming a total budget constraint of $24,000, which projects would you advise Optional to accept? List them below:

Project	Total Cost	Present Value	Net Present Value	Excess-Present-Value Index
	$	$	$	%
Totals	$	$	$	%

14 Cost Allocation: An Introduction

COSTS MUST OFTEN be assigned to such cost objectives as periods, processes, programs, products, departments, and divisions. This is an identification or tracing procedure that may be called cost allocation, apportionment, assignment, or distribution. Important purposes of cost allocation include making economic decisions, obtaining desired motivation, measuring income and assets for external parties, and justifying prices charged to customers for products and services.

This chapter describes the general process of allocation and explains how the basic guidelines can be applied. More specifically, illustrations demonstrate how production costs can be allocated to final outputs by different techniques.

REVIEW SUMMARY

A. Let's look at the general approach to cost allocation.

1. There are three main facets to cost allocation:

a. Determining the *cost objective;* for example, products, services, processes, or departments, all of which represent *actions.*

b. Identifying and accumulating (*pooling*) the costs that pertain to the cost objective; for example, selected manufacturing and nonmanufacturing costs.

c. Choosing an *allocation base* for linking costs to objectives; for example, direct-labor hours or machine hours.

2. It is often not practicable to use the ideal cost-allocation base that would relate cost to its most causal factor.

a. The preferable cost-allocation base is one that *facilitates the prediction of changes* in total costs.

B. You should become familiar with some important cost-allocation terminology:

1. *Indirect cost pools* are groupings of various cost items that are not individually identified with a cost objective.

a. Examples include: pools of factory service or producing-department costs, pools of fixed or variable costs, and pools of costs related to materials or people.

2. Cost objectives may be either:
    a. *Intermediate,* such as a manufacturing department
    b. *Final,* such as the finished product
3. Costs may have a *direct relationship* to an intermediate cost objective but an *indirect relationship* to the final cost objectives in the allocation process.
    a. For example, a stores clerk's salary is directly related to the stores department, but indirectly related to the product.
4. The key to cost allocation is the *cost-allocation base,* such as direct-labor hours or machine-hours.
    a. An average plant-wide rate for applying factory-overhead costs to jobs could be quite inaccurate compared to the departmental overhead rates, as demonstrated in textbook Exhibit 14–1.

C. Two of the most important purposes for allocating costs are making economic decisions and obtaining desired motivation.
1. General guidelines are:
    a. Use *flexible* budgets, not *static* budgets.
    b. Allocate *variable* and *fixed* costs separately.
    c. Use *budgeted or standard* prices or hours, not actual prices or hours.
2. The variable cost pool should be allocated by multiplying two factors:
    a. *Predetermined rate* per hour or other measure.
    b. *Actual usage* of hours or other measure.
3. Allocate fixed costs by assigning *lump-sum amounts of budgeted costs of long-term capacity to serve,* not portions of *actual* costs on the basis of actual consumption of services.

D. For all four purposes of allocation, costs eventually must be allocated to outputs of goods and services.
1. This requires the allocation of service-department costs to production departments.
    a. Then the production-department costs are applied by predetermined rates to the units of goods and services produced.
2. The most widely used allocation method is the *direct method.*
    a. This allocates each service department's total costs directly to production departments. See textbook Exhibit 14–2.
    b. Note that the direct method ignores services rendered to other service departments.
3. Another widely used allocation method is the *step-down method.*
    a. This method allocates costs of service departments to both production and service departments. See Exhibit 14–3.
    b. The sequence of allocation usually begins with the one rendering service to the greatest number of other service departments and progresses in descending order to the one rendering service to the least number of other departments.
    c. Once a service department's costs have been allocated, no subsequent service-department costs are recirculated back to it.
    d. The textbook illustration shows the scheduling and computation techniques.
    e. This exhibit also shows the computation of predetermined rates for applying overhead costs from production departments to products.
4. The most accurate allocation method for service-department costs would recognize reciprocal services among service departments. See Exhibit 14–4.

SELF-TEST AND PRACTICE EXERCISES

I For each of the following multiple-choice and true-false statements, select the most appropriate answer and enter its identification letter in the space provided:

___ 1. It is generally more practical to use plant-wide rates instead of departmental rates for allocating overhead costs to individual jobs: (a) true, (b) false.

___ 2. An example of a cost objective would include: (a) direct materials purchased, (b) finished products manufactured, (c) both of the above, (d) neither of the above.

___ 3. A cost pool is a collection of: (a) cost objectives, (b) costs that have been allocated to a cost objective, (c) costs that are to be allocated to several cost objectives, (d) none of the above.

___ 4. The preferable cost-allocation base is one that facilitates the accurate measurement of output costs: (a) true, (b) false.

___ 5. The salary of the foreman of a manufacturing department serves as an example of a cost directly related to: (a) the department, (b) the product being manufactured in the department, (c) both of the above, (d) neither of the above.

___ 6. The key to cost allocation is: (a) determining cost objectives, (b) pooling costs, (c) selecting the cost-allocation base, (d) none of the above.

___ 7. Variable costs of service departments are best allocated to production departments on the basis of: (a) actual short-term usage based on *predetermined* rates, (b) actual short-term usage based on *actual* rates, (c) the service department's *budgeted costs* of long-term capacity to serve, (d) the service department's *actual costs* on the basis of actual consumption of services.

___ 8. Fixed costs of service departments are best allocated to production departments on the basis of: (a) actual short-term usage based on *predetermined* rates, (b) actual short-term usage based on *actual* rates, (c) the service department's *budgeted costs* of long-term capacity to serve, (d) the service department's *actual costs* on the basis of actual consumption of services.

___ 9. If all of a service department's actual costs were allocated to production departments: (a) the charges to a particular production department could be affected by the quantity of services consumed by other production departments, (b) the charges could be affected by factors not directly subject to the control of the production-department managers, (c) both of the above, (d) neither of the above.

___ 10. The most widely used method for allocating service-department costs to production departments is: (a) the reciprocal method, (b) the step-down method, (c) the direct method.

___ 11. The step-down method allocates costs of service departments to: (a) other service departments, (b) production departments, (c) both service and production departments.

___ 12. Once a service department's costs have been allocated by the step-down method, no other service-department costs are to be charged back to it: (a) true, (b) false.

___ 13. The most accurate allocation method for service-department costs is: (a) the direct method, (b) the step-down method, (c) the reciprocal method.

II Complete each of the following statements:

1. The preferable cost-allocation base is one that accurately ______________________________

____

____

2. Costs may have a direct relationship to ______ ______________________ cost objective, but an indirect relationship to ______________ ______________________ cost objective.

3. A systematic means for connecting costs with cost objectives is called ______________

____

4. In allocating the costs of such services as repairs and computers to production departments, it would be more accurate to use, instead of a single basis, one basis for the ______________ cost element and another basis for the ______________ cost element.

5. In order to prevent the charges to a specific production department from depending on the quantity of services consumed by other production departments, a ______________ rate should be used for charging service-department costs.

6. In the step-down method of cost allocation, the sequence usually begins with the service department that renders service to the ______________ number of other service departments and progresses in descending order to the one rendering service to the ______________ number of other service departments.

III From the following data for Innovation Emanators, Inc., use the step-down method to prepare a budget schedule showing the allocation of factory-overhead costs to production departments and the computation of predetermined direct-labor hour rates for applying overhead to products:

	Service Departments			Production Departments		
	A	B	C	X	Y	Z
Overhead costs before allocation (in thousands of dollars)	300	210	240	160	110	105
Proportions of service to be furnished by:						
Department A to other departments	–	10%	20%	30%	15%	25%
Department B to other departments	20%	–	10%	30%	10%	30%
Department C to other departments	–	10%	–	30%	30%	30%
Total direct-labor hours	–	–	–	300	100	190

	Service Departments			Production Departments		
	A	B	C	X	Y	Z
Overhead costs before allocation (in thousands of dollars)						

IV All-Energy Company's power plant provides electricity for its two producing departments, A and B. The 19__6 budget for the power plant shows:

Budgeted fixed costs	$80,000
Budgeted variable costs per kilowatt-hour (KWH)	$ .05

Additional data for 19__6:

	Long-Run Demand (KWH)	Budgeted for 19__6 (KWH)	Actual for 19__6 (KWH)
Producing Dept. A	300,000	250,000	230,000
Producing Dept. B	200,000	180,000	190,000

Actual power-plant costs for 19__6 are:

Fixed costs	$81,000
Variable costs	$22,000

Compute the 19__6 allocation of power-plant costs to A and B:

	Dept. A	Dept. B
1. Fixed costs	$	$
2. Variable costs	$	$

V Given for OK Products:

	Service Depts.		Production Depts.	
	J	K	1	2
Overhead costs before allocation	$50,000	$90,000	$34,000	$43,000
Proportions of service by J	–	10%	40%	50%
Proportions of service by K	25%	–	50%	25%
Machine hours used			2,500	4,000

Use the reciprocal method to compute:

1. Allocation of service-department costs to Departments 1 and 2.

2. Predetermined overhead rates for Departments 1 and 2.

Cost Allocation: A Closer look 15

THIS CHAPTER continues our study of cost allocation introduced in the preceding chapter. Here we examine some important practical applications that illustrate how cost allocation can be used to help management evaluate the performance of the individual segments of an organization and to produce better-informed decisions for planning and controlling all operations.

Of the several topics included here, the first is probably the most basic and the most important: the **contribution approach to cost allocation.** The key illustration is the very helpful textbook Exhibit 15–1. It deserves your thorough study.

REVIEW SUMMARY

A. A useful framework for understanding and applying cost-allocation principles is provided by the *contribution approach.*

1. See the key example in the textbook, Exhibit 15–1, a model income statement by segments.
2. In addition to responsibility centers and products, cost objectives can include *segments* or *sub-units* of the organization such as divisions, sections or product lines.
3. A cost-contribution approach by segments can be valuable because it emphasizes the cost behavior patterns that are generally useful for evaluating performance and making decisions.
4. Suppose a cost cannot be allocated to segments on a meaningful basis.
   - **a.** It should be included in the income statement and be clearly identified as unallocated with respect to those segments.
5. The *segmented contribution margins* (excess of revenues over allocable variable costs) are helpful in predicting the impact on segment income of short-run changes in volume.
6. The *contribution controllable by segment managers* may be computed as the excess of the segment contribution margins over the fixed costs controllable by segment managers (discretionary fixed costs).
   - **a.** However, the performance of a division (or other segment) as an economic investment is measured only after a further deduction for allocable fixed costs controlled by others.

7. Although the nonsegmented figure for income before income taxes may be helpful in estimating the long-run earning power of the entire company, it could be quite misleading in many cases to use some arbitrary basis for breaking it down into segment figures.

B. In many corporations, there is a group of expenses and costs pertaining to the entire organization.

1. These are sometimes called the *costs of central services.*
2. Some of these services may be feasible to allocate to segments on the basis of actual usage.
    a. Examples are electronic data processing, advertising, and operations research.
3. Other services have very little discernible connection with individual segments.
    a. Examples include top corporate management overhead, public relations, and corporate planning.
    b. An "ability-to-bear" allocation base may be chosen, such as sales revenues or total costs.
    c. If sales is used as the base, it should be *budgeted sales* instead of *actual sales.*
    d. The use of budgeted sales avoids the distortion of short-run costs of an individual user department by fluctuations in the actual sales of other user departments.
    e. Of course, it may be preferable to make *no allocation,* if no logical basis is determinable.

C. Two closely related objectives of cost allocation are motivation and economic decisions.

1. Generally, it may be thought that cost allocations that reflect causal relationships are most likely to produce information leading to optimum decisions.
2. However, there is much controversy concerning the ways to apply this concept and the motivational effects of various cost-allocation ideas and methods.
3. For example, some accountants and managers favor the use of "full costs."
    a. This is the total of "incremental" or variable costs and the allocation of fixed costs.
    b. Managers can thus become more aware of the real long-run costs incurred.
4. But others maintain that such costs as central corporate costs *should not be allocated at all,* because there is no measurable cause-and-effect relationship and managers would have no direct influence over the amounts allocated to their departments.

D. Cost allocations are often used to justify selling prices, especially for the prices of government contracts.

1. In the United States, there exists a body of rules, regulations, and standards for making such allocations.
    a. These were developed by the Cost Accounting Standards Board (CASB), now terminated.
    b. The general purpose of the standards set by the CASB is to reach a "fair price" for buyers and sellers.
2. Our textbook emphasizes cause-and-effect as the preferable criterion for cost allocation.
3. However, other criteria are frequently advocated, such as "equity," "fairness," and "benefits received."
    a. These seem so broad and nebulous as to be impractical to apply in most cases.

E. Because it is often not feasible to allocate individual cost items directly to cost objectives, they are usually aggregated or pooled to produce a cost-allocation rate.

1. If this rate achieves the same cost allocations that would be obtained by the individual rates, the rate is said to be *homogeneous.*
2. General guidelines regarding homogeneity include:
    a. Begin with the most detailed cost data that are economically feasible to collect.
    b. To increase homogeneity, establish additional cost pools.

c. Form the pools by responsibility centers, cost behavior patterns, or natural category.

F. In practice, attempts are made to apply each pool of factory-overhead costs to products by using an appropriate allocation base.

1. The choice of bases for allocating pools of factory-overhead costs should depend on the factors obviously associated with individual jobs or products, related clerical costs, and the differences in final results.
2. Four bases are widely used as denominators in calculating rates for applying factory-overhead costs to products.
   - **a.** *Direct-labor hours* result in the application of overhead on a time-expiration basis, the factor to which most overhead costs are most closely related.
   - **b.** *Machine-hours* may be a more accurate base than direct-labor hours if overhead costs result largely from the use of machines instead of people.
   - **c.** *Direct-labor cost* rates would produce about the same results as direct-labor hour rates when wage rates are fairly uniform for each type of labor.
   - **d.** *Direct-material cost or quantity* would not usually be valid for rate bases except for factory-overhead costs associated with material storage and handling.

SELF-TEST AND PRACTICE EXERCISES

I For each of the following multiple-choice and true-false statements, select the most appropriate answer and enter its identification letter in the space provided:

___ 1. The contribution margin by segments is the excess of net sales over: (a) variable cost of goods sold and variable selling and administrative expenses by segments, (b) allocable fixed costs controllable by segment managers, (c) both of the above, (d) neither of the above.

___ 2. If a cost cannot be allocated to certain segments on a meaningful basis, it should be: (a) excluded from the income statement, (b) allocated to segments on the basis of segment sales, (c) clearly identified as unallocated with respect to those segments.

___ 3. Most helpful in predicting the impact on segment income of short-run changes in volume is: (a) contribution margin, (b) contribution controllable by segment managers, (c) contribution by segments, (d) income before income taxes.

___ 4. The performance of a segment as an economic investment is best measured by: (a) income before income taxes, (b) income after income taxes, (c) contribution margin, (d) contribution margin less fixed costs controllable by segment managers, (e) contribution controllable by segment managers less allocable fixed costs controllable by others.

___ 5. It is usually quite helpful for management planning and control purposes to show in a segmented income statement the income of each segment before income taxes: (a) true, (b) false.

___ 6. Discretionary fixed costs controllable by segment managers would ordinarily include: (a) sales promotion, (b) management consulting, (c) both of the above, (d) neither of the above.

___ 7. Central-services costs that are most likely to be feasibly allocable to segments on the basis of usage would probably include: (a) public relations, (b) product advertising, (c) both public relations and product advertising, (d) neither public relations nor product advertising.

___ 8. In general, if some central-services costs are allocated to segments by an organization, all central-services costs of the organization should be allocated: (a) true, (b) false.

___ 9. The distortion of the short-run costs of an individual user department may be caused by fluctuations in the sales of other user departments if the cost-allocation base is budgeted sales: (a) true, (b) false.

___ 10. The inexorable "creep effects" of costs can be compensated for by allocating to specific batches of goods or services: (a) incremental or variable costs, (b) fixed costs, (c) full costs.

___ 11. Managers of segments can be made aware of the real long-run costs involved by charging their segments with incremental or variable costs: (a) true, (b) false.

___ 12. It is usually feasible and reasonable to allocate most costs to segments of an organization on the basis of actual dollar sales: (a) true, (b) false.

___ 13. The preferable general criterion for cost allocation is: (a) fairness, (b) equity, (c) benefits received, (d) cause-and-effect.

___ 14. Fairness and equity are usually: (a) broad ethical standards, (b) operational guidelines for allocating costs, (c) both of the above, (d) neither of the above.

___ 15. Relative benefits received are usually of practical value as a basis for allocating indirect costs to operations and products: (a) true, (b) false.

___ 16. Some accountants and managers feel that: (a) full allocation of costs will help all managers become more aware of the costs incurred and benefits offered by other segments of an organization, (b) some central costs should not be allocated at all, (c) both of the above, (d) neither of the above.

___ 17. The major criterion in designing systems for cost allocations should be: (a) accuracy, (b) expediency, (c) motivation, (d) income tax effects.

___ 18. Higher homogeneity of cost-allocation rates may be achieved by: (a) increasing the number of cost pools, (b) decreasing the number of cost pools.

___ 19. In the application of factory-overhead costs to products, the two rate bases that are most fundamentally related to the cause of most overhead costs are: (a) direct-labor cost and direct-material cost, (b) direct-labor hours and direct-material quantity, (c) machine-hours and physical units produced, (d) physical units produced and direct-material quantity, (e) direct-labor hours and machine-hours.

II Complete each of the following statements:

1. The contribution controllable by division managers is the excess of the ________________ margin over the fixed ________________ ________________________________

2. The contribution by segments is the excess of the contribution ________________ ________________ over the allocable fixed costs ________________________________

3. Most companies allocate their central-services costs on the basis of ________________

4. When General Motors uses national television for central advertising, it is better to allocate such costs to its divisions on the basis of ____________ sales rather than ________________ sales.

5. "Full costs" equal ____________ costs plus ____________ costs.

6. CASB stands for ________________ ________________________________

7. The use of sales dollars as a basis for allocating central-services costs to segments ignores ________ ____________ relationships and could lead to ____________ reports of segment operations.

8. If an average rate for applying cost pools to cost objects produces the same cost allocations as produced by separate rates for individual cost items, the average rate is said to be ______________

____

9. In the application of factory-overhead costs to products, the two bases that would produce about the same results are ______________

and ______________________________

III From the following data for General Omnibus Company, prepare a contribution-approach income statement by segments:

(In thousands)	Company Total	Alpha Division	Omega Division
Net revenues	$900	$500	$400
Fixed costs:			
Controllable by segment managers	140	60	80
Controllable by others	70	30	40
Variable costs:			
Manufacturing cost of goods sold	450	300	150
Selling and administrative expenses	130	60	70
Unallocated costs	75	–	–

COST ALLOCATION: JOINT PRODUCTS AND BYPRODUCTS 16

THIS CONTINUATION OF cost allocation focuses on a major area: costs of manufactured products. Many manufacturing processes produce two or more products from a single raw material, for example, petroleum refining. Such outputs are called joint-products or byproducts. We deal here with the problem of allocating to the various individual products the direct-material costs and the other manufacturing costs incurred prior to the point at which the separate products are individually indentifiable, the **split-off point.**

Methods for allocating such joint costs to the different products are examined in this chapter. However, the idea emphasized here is that any method for assigning these costs to joint-products and byproducts is useful **only for purposes of product costing.** Such cost assignments are **useless** for management decision, planning, or control purposes.

REVIEW SUMMARY

A. When two or more individual products are simultaneously produced, with each product having significant relative sales values, the outputs are usually called *joint-products.*

1. The *split-off point* is the stage of production at which the different individual products can be identified.
2. *Joint costs* include all manufacturing costs incurred prior to the split-off point.

B. For the purposes of product costing, several methods are used for allocating joint costs to the different units produced.

1. Joint costs may be allocated to products on the basis of *physical measures* at the split-off point; for example: pounds, gallons, yards.
   - **a.** However, this basis ignores the revenue-producing properties of the separate products, which could vary widely in unit values at the split-off point.
   - **b.** As a result, the physical-measures method of allocation could show unrealistically large profits for some joint products while showing unrealistically large losses for others.

2. Joint costs may be allocated to products on the basis of their *net realizable values.*
   a. If there are zero costs of completion and disposal because all products are sold upon split-off at no incremental costs, the net realizable values would simply be their sales values: the quantities multiplied by unit selling prices at the split-off point.
   b. If there is no market for joint products at the split-off point and they must be further processed individually before they are salable, their sales values at the split-off point may be *approximated* by deducting costs beyond that point from their respective expected sales values on a fully processed basis.
   c. The allocation of joint costs on the basis of net realizable values implicitly recognizes the different abilities of joint products to generate revenue.
   d. In effect, this method allocates costs in proportion to a product's ability to absorb the costs, and as a result, all end products usually show some profit margin under typical marketing conditions.
   e. However, such allocated costs are useful *only for product-costing purposes* and should not be used for sell-or-process-further decisions, for judging the performance of either the joint or the separable processes, or for product-pricing decisions.
3. Some companies ignore the joint-cost allocation approach and carry their joint-product inventories on a *noncost basis.*
   a. The use of *net realizable values* (ultimate sales values less estimated separable costs to complete and sell) results in the recognition of profit before sales are made, which is not a generally acceptable accounting concept.
   b. The use of *net realizable values less normal profit margins* avoids the criticism of profit recognition before the goods are sold.

C. The allocation of joint costs to different products is useful *only for purposes of product costing.*
   1. When a product is an inherent result of a joint process, the decision to process further should not be influenced by either the size of the total joint costs or the portions of the joint costs assigned to particular products.
   2. The only costs that are relevant to further processing decisions are the costs *beyond* the split-off point.
      a. Such costs are the incremental costs, including implicit costs (opportunity costs) as well as explicit costs.
      b. *It is profitable to process beyond the split-off point if these incremental costs are exceeded by the incremental revenue produced by such processing.*
   3. Product-pricing decisions should not be influenced by allocation of joint costs.
      a. Circular reasoning would be involved: prices used to set costs, and costs used to set prices.
      b. As an example, the textbook pointed out the distorting effects on natural gas prices.

D. *Byproducts* are products with relatively minor sales value that are simultaneously produced in the manufacture of the main product(s).
   1. In general, byproducts have relatively more sales value than *scrap materials* and are often processed beyond the split-off point.
   2. The basic accounting for both byproducts and scrap materials is the same; two leading methods are described.
   3. As illustrated by textbook Exhibit 16–3, both methods recognize that byproducts reduce the cost of the major products—and they show the same net income over a period that has no beginning or ending inventories.
   4. In the first method, the net revenue from *sale* of byproduct is deducted from the cost of the major product(s) *sold.*
      a. Unsold byproduct is inventoried at zero value.

   b. This method has practical appeal, but conceptually it fails to match the value of the byproduct with the cost of the major related products.
5. In the second method, the net realizable value of the byproduct *produced* is deducted from the cost of the major product(s) *produced.*
   a. The byproduct inventory is carried forward at net realizable value (plus separable manufacturing costs incurred, if any).
   b. This method is more precise about the timing of the cost reductions from the major related products.
6. When byproducts are used internally as fuel or materials, they are frequently accounted for at net realizable values or replacement values, the cost of the main product being reduced by such values.
7. In the petroleum industry, many products are produced.
   a. Gasoline is viewed as the sole major product for product-mix decisions even though a byproduct method may not be followed for costing the inventories of all the other products.
   b. Linear programming models are used to determine the optimal product mix between the byproducts and gasoline.

SELF-TEST AND PRACTICE EXERCISES

I For each of the following multiple-choice and true-false statements, select the most appropriate answer and enter its identification letter in the space provided:

___ 1. Depreciation accounting by a merchandiser of sports supplies is an example of cost allocation: (a) true, (b) false.

___ 2. Joint products are defined as: (a) two or more products that are combined to make one finished product, (b) finished products that are made from two or more products, (c) products that can be used for more than one purpose, (d) none of the above.

___ 3. Ordinarily, joint costs include: (a) direct-material costs, (b) direct-labor costs, (c) indirect manufacturing costs, (d) all of the above, (e) none of the above.

___ 4. The allocation of joint costs to products is useless for: (a) cost-planning and control purposes, (b) product-costing purposes, (c) both of the above, (d) neither of the above.

___ 5. For cost-planning and control purposes, it is useful to identify processing costs after the split-off point with units produced: (a) true, (b) false.

___ 6. Unrealistically large profits for some joint products and unrealistically large losses for others would most likely be shown by: (a) the use of net realizable values for joint products, (b) allocating joint costs on the basis of relative sales values at the split-off point, (c) allocating joint costs on the basis of physical measures at the split-off point.

___ 7. The different abilities of joint products to produce revenue would be recognized by allocating joint costs on the basis of: (a) physical measures, (b) net realizable values, (c) both of the above, (d) neither of the above.

___ 8. The most widely used basis for allocating joint costs to products is relative to: (a) physical measures, (b) net realizable values, (c) further processing costs, (d) gross profit, (e) net profit.

___ 9. The recognition of profit before the goods are sold result from carrying joint-product inventories on the basis of: (a) net realizable values, (b) net realizable values less normal profit margins, (c) both of the above, (d) neither of the above.

___ 10. Using selling prices or variations thereof as bases for inventory valuation would have a greater degree of justification when: (a) inventory turnover is high, (b) differences between costs and selling prices are small, (c) both of the above, (d) neither of the above.

___ 11. When a product is an inherent result of a joint process, the decision to process further should be influenced partly by: (a) the size of the total joint costs, (b) the portions of the joint costs allocated to particular products, (c) both of the above, (d) neither of the above.

___ 12. The costs beyond the split-off point that are relevant to further processing decisions could include: (a) opportunity costs (implicit costs), (b) explicit costs, (c) both of the above, (d) neither of the above.

___ 13. In making managerial decisions regarding whether a joint product should be sold or processed further, one should compare the incremental costs of further processing with: (a) the incremental revenue derived from such processing, (b) the net sales value at split-off point, (c) the net sales value after further processing, (d) none of the above.

___ 14. The allocations of joint costs to products can generally be useful in making valid product-pricing decisions: (a) true, (b) false.

___ 15. In general, byproducts: (a) are often processed beyond the split-off point, (b) have relatively less sales value than scrap materials, (c) both of the above, (d) neither of the above.

___ 16. The accounting for scrap materials and byproducts is basically the same: (a) true, (b) false.

___ 17. When the net revenue from byproduct sold is deducted from the cost of the major product sold, the unsold byproduct is inventoried at: (a) cost, (b) net realizable value, (c) no value, (d) some other value.

___ 18. Conceptually, the better of the two leading methods of accounting for byproducts is to treat the net realizable values of byproducts produced as deductions from production costs: (a) true, (b) false.

___ 19. Expediency is usually a major factor influencing the selection of the byproduct accounting method: (a) true, (b) false.

II Complete each of the following statements:

1. When two or more individual products are simultaneously produced, with each product having significant relative sales values, the outputs are usually called ______________________________

____

2. The split-off point is defined as ______________

____

____

3. When joint costs are allocated to products on the basis of physical measures at the split-off point, this basis ignores ______________________

____

4. A uniform gross-margin percentage would tend to be produced for joint products if the

____

____

approach for allocation of joint costs were used.

5. If there is no market for joint products at the split-off point and they must be further processed individually before they are salable, their approximate sales values at the split-off point may be estimated by deducting ______________________

____

from the ______________________________

____

6. The allocation of joint costs to different products is useful only for purposes of ______________

____

7. The only costs that are relevant to further processing decisions are ______________________

____

8. Products with relatively minor sales value that are simultaneously produced in the manufacture of the main product(s) are called ______________

____

III The Steer Wheeling Corporation produced the following two products from a joint process at a joint cost of $4,000:

	Product REV	Product ROL
Quantities produced and processed beyond split-off point	150 yd	300 yd
Total processing costs beyond split-off point	$1,500	$1,500
Unit selling prices of completely processed products	$ 40	$ 10

1. Compute the amount of joint costs allocated to each of the products by using selling prices and processing costs beyond the split-off point and working back to find approximate sales values at split-off for use in allocating joint costs.

2. On the basis of your allocation of joint costs, determine the gross profit that would be realized from Product REV sales, Product ROL sales, and total sales.

3. If the selling prices *at the split-off point* were known to be $32 per yard for Product REV and $4 per yard for Product ROL, what would your decisions be regarding further processing of each product? Show supporting calculations.

4. On the basis of your further processing decisions, determine the total gross profit that would be realized from *total* sales.

5. Would the allocation of joint costs be relevant to your further processing decisions? Why?

IV The N.C. Dental Products Company presents the following data:

Gross production costs of main product and byproduct	$50,000
Total sales of main product	$75,000
Net realizable value of byproduct produced (including ending inventory of byproduct)	$ 2,000
Beginning inventories	none

Ending inventory of main product is 10% of production.

Determine the gross margin on sales of main product by using Method Two of accounting for byproducts.

17 Process Costing and Operation Costing

WHEN THERE IS a continuous mass production of like product units, **process-costing methods** are appropriate for product-costing purposes. This chapter covers three process-costing techniques: the weighted-average method; the first-in, first-out method; and the standard-cost approach. Also covered is **operation costing,** a combination of process and job costing. The key to all of these methods is the idea of **equivalent units produced,** which is the measure of the amount of work done in a manufacturing process.

To gain a working knowledge of these concepts and methods, one must solve problems. The chapter exhibits provide helpful models to be followed, step by step, before you attack the problems in this student guide and the assigned textbook problems.

REVIEW SUMMARY

A. Process costing, like all product costing, is an *averaging process.*

1. Basically, average unit costs for each process are calculated by dividing cost totals by the number of units processed.
2. The key concept is *equivalent units produced.*
   - **a.** This measures the amount of work done by each process in terms of units fully processed by it during a given period.
   - **b.** Equivalent units are divided into the appropriate cost totals of each process to arrive at unit costs within the process for a given period.
   - **c.** Textbook Exhibits 17–2, 17–7, and 17–8 illustrate the computation of equivalent units when there is a beginning inventory in process.
   - **d.** You should study these exhibits very carefully, because a thorough understanding of them is absolutely essential to your success in applying the main concepts presented in this chapter.
3. A systematic approach that is helpful in making process-cost calculations involves five steps:
   - **a.** Summarize in terms of units the *physical quantities* of production inflows and outflows.
   - **b.** Compute equivalent units of production.

c. Summarize the total costs to be accounted for.
d. Compute the appropriate unit costs.
e. Use these unit costs to allocate and reconcile the total costs of goods completed and work in process.

4. When goods are transferred out of a manufacturing process, their total cost is credited to that process (a departmental work-in-process control account).
   a. The debit is to the next process or to the finished-goods control account.

B. Two alternative *cost-flow assumptions* are available for computing unit costs: first-in, first-out (FIFO), and weighted-average.
1. The *first-in, first-out method* treats the beginning inventory of work in process as though it were a batch of goods separate and distinct from goods started and finished by a process within the same period, as illustrated in Exhibit 17–2.
   a. Thus, beginning-inventory costs are *not* mingled with current costs.
   b. Therefore, the *divisor* for computing unit costs includes *only the equivalent units for the current period* and *not* the equivalent units of work done on the beginning inventory in previous periods.
   c. As a result, monthly unit costs represent only the work that was actually done during the *current period.*
   d. However, when costs are transferred out of one process to the next process or to finished-goods inventory, a *single unit cost* is used that is a weighted average of beginning-inventory costs and currently incurred costs.
2. The *weighted-average method* treats the beginning inventory of work in process as though it were begun and finished during the current period, as illustrated in Exhibit 17–7.
   a. Beginning-inventory costs for each type of cost are mingled with the respective current costs.
   b. These costs include *transferred-in costs* (or *previous-department costs*), as well as the present department's costs of material, labor, and overhead.
   c. Therefore, the *divisor* for computing unit costs is the *total work done;* that is, the equivalent units that include the previous work on the beginning inventory as well as the current work.
   d. Thus, monthly unit costs actually represent *weighted averages* of beginning-inventory costs and current costs.
3. Generally, the weighted-average and FIFO methods arrive at about the same product costs.
   a. However, if material prices are volatile, there may be significant differences in results between these two methods.
   b. For purposes of cost control, neither of the methods is as effective as standard process costing.

C. A popular hybrid costing system is called *operation costing* (or *specification costing*).
1. This method is a blend of ideas from the systems of job-order costing and process costing.
2. An *operation* is defined as a standardized method or technique.
   a. Examples include milling, cleaning, and grinding.
   b. Such procedures are applied in like manner to batches of *different products.*
3. *Direct material costs* are identified with specific product batches (the job-cost idea).
4. *Conversion costs* (direct labor and factory overhead) are identified with the particular operation (the process-cost idea):
   a. An average conversion cost per unit is applied to the units passing through each operation.
   b. An average material cost per unit is applied to the units in a batch, which passes through one or more operations.

D. Instead of actual costs, *standard costs* may be used for process-costing purposes, as illustrated in Exhibit 17–14.

1. The standard cost is the predetermined cost per equivalent unit.
2. Thus, when standard costs are used, the process-cost calculations are relatively much simpler than those of the weighted-average and first-in, first-out methods.
   a. The standard cost of goods completed is the actual quantity completed multiplied by the standard cost per unit.
   b. The standard cost of ending goods in process is determined by multiplying the equivalent units for each cost element by the respective standard cost per unit.
3. Standard costing of production is especially useful where there are numerous combinations of materials, operations, and product sizes, as in steel mills, textile manufacturing, and paint production.
4. In addition, a standard-costing approach facilitates management control.
5. Standard costing can be used in all cost systems: job, operation, and process systems.

SELF-TEST AND PRACTICE EXERCISES

I For each of the following multiple-choice and true-false statements, select the most appropriate answer and enter its identification letter in the space provided.

___ 1. A certain process had a beginning inventory of 5,000 units that were 40 percent completed as to conversion costs and an ending inventory of 1,000 units that were 50 percent completed. Units started were 20,000 and units completed were 24,000. The equivalent units produced using the FIFO method were: (a) 24,500, (b) 22,000, (c) 22,500, (d) 20,000, (e) some other quantity.

___ 2. See the preceding item. Using the weighted-average method, the equivalent units produced were: (a) 24,500, (b) 22,000, (c) 22,500, (d) 20,000, (e) some other quantity.

___ 3. See the first item above. If materials are entered at the beginning of the process, the equivalent units produced for materials, using the FIFO method, were: (a) 24,500, (b) 22,000, (c) 22,500, (d) 20,000, (e) some other quantity.

___ 4. See the preceding item. The equivalent units produced for materials, using the weighted-average method, were: (a) 24,500, (b) 22,000, (c) 22,500, (d) 20,000, (e) some other quantity.

___ 5. The process-cost method that treats the beginning inventory of work in process as though it were begun and finished during the current period is: (a) weighted average, (b) first-in, first-out, (c) both of the above, (d) neither of the above.

___ 6. Beginning inventory costs are mingled with current costs in making unit-cost calculations by the weighted-average method: (a) true, (b) false.

___ 7. When the FIFO process-cost method is used, the divisor for computing unit costs for a period should exclude the equivalent units for work done on the beginning inventory of work in process during previous periods: (a) true, (b) false.

___ 8. Monthly unit costs represent only the work that was actually done during the current period, if the unit costs are calculated by: (a) the weighted-average method, (b) the first-in, first-out method, (c) both of the above, (d) neither of the above.

___ 9. When costs are transferred into a process from the preceding process, a single unit cost is used if unit costs are computed by: (a) the weighted-average method, (b) the first-in, first-out method, (c) either of the above, (d) neither of the above.

___ 10. In general, about the same product costs are determined by the weighted-average and first-in, first-out methods: (a) true, (b) false.

____ 11. In comparison with process costing, the operation costing method treats these costs in a similar way: (a) direct material and direct labor, (b) direct labor and factory overhead, (c) factory overhead and direct material, (d) none of the above.

____ 12. Standard costing procedures can be used in process and operation systems but not in job-order systems: (a) true, (b) false.

____ 13. Seldom used in practice is the FIFO process costing system: (a) true, (b) false.

____ 14. When work is transferred out from a final process, the general ledger entry would include: (a) a debit to the final process, (b) a credit to the final process, (c) a credit to the finished goods account, (d) a debit to the final process and a credit to the finished goods account.

____ 15. In general, additions are *always* made at the beginning of any process subsequent to the first process: (a) for any new material costs and for previous-department costs, (b) for any new material costs but not for previous-department costs, (c) for neither new material costs nor for previous-department costs, (d) for previous-department costs but not for any new material costs.

____ 16. Transferred-in costs for Process D cannot include labor and other costs that are incurred by other processes in the same accounting period as the labor and other costs of Process D: (a) true, (b) false.

____ 17. For cost-control purposes, the standard process-costing method is generally superior to: (a) the weighted-average method using actual costs, (b) the first-in, first-out method using actual costs, (c) both of the above, (d) neither of the above.

____ 18. When standard costs are used in process-type operations, product costing is relatively more complex than when actual costs are used with the weighted-average method or the first-in, first-out method: (a) true, (b) false.

____ 19. When standard costs are used in process-type operations, equivalent units need not be used: (a) true, (b) false.

II Complete each of the following statements:

1. When there is a mass production of product units requiring similar conversion costs and procedures but different costs and kinds of materials, the appropriate cost method is ____________

____

2. The key concept in process-costing calculations is ____________________

____

3. For goods that are transferred out of the final manufacturing process or production step, an entry should be made to:

Debit: ____________________

Credit: ____________________

4. When there are beginning inventories in a process and actual costs are to be used instead of standard costs, the two alternative process-cost methods that are available are:

(a) ____________________

(b) ____________________

5. The process-cost method that is conceptually closer to the job-order costing method is ________

____

6. Where there are numerous combinations of materials, operations, and product sizes, a process-costing method that is especially useful is ______

____

III Given for the EQ manufacturing process for November:

	Units
Inventory in process, November 1, 70% completed	200
Transferred into process in November	700
Completed and transferred out of process in November	600
Inventory in process, November 30, 60% completed	300

Materials are added at the beginning of the process.

1. Find the equivalent units for computing unit costs by the *first-in, first-out* method:

	Material Costs	Conversion Costs

2. Find the equivalent units for computing unit costs by the *weighted-average* method:

	Material Costs	Conversion Costs

IV Given for the WA manufacturing process for January:

Inventory in process, January 1, 40% completed	300 units
Transferred into process in January	600 units
Completed and transferred out of process in January	700 units
Inventory in process, January 31, 50% completed	200 units

January 1 inventory costs:	
Transferred-in costs	$3,000
Conversion costs	$2,000
Current costs charged in January:	
Transferred-in costs	$5,100
Conversion costs	$3,600

No materials are added in this process.

Using the *weighted-average* unit-cost method, calculate the cost of work transferred out in January and the cost of the January 31 inventory of work in process:

Step 1—Summarize Physical Units

Step 2—Compute Output in Equivalent Units

	Transferred-in Costs	Conversion Costs

Step 3—Summarize Total Costs to Account for

	Transferred-in Costs	Conversion Costs	Total Costs

Step 4—Compute Unit Costs

	Transferred-in Costs	Conversion Costs	Total Costs

Step 5—Compute Total Costs of Work Completed and in Process

V Given for the FI manufacturing process for February:

Inventory in process, February 1, 75% completed	200 units
Transferred into process in February	600 units
Completed and transferred out of process in February	500 units
Inventory in process, February 28, 50% completed	300 units

February 1 inventory costs:	
Transferred-in costs	$2,200
Conversion costs	$1,300
Current costs charged in February:	
Transferred-in costs	$6,000
Conversion costs	$4,000

No materials are added in this process.

Using the *first-in, first-out* unit-cost method, calculate the cost of work transferred out in February and the cost of the February 28 inventory of work in process:

Step 1—Summarize Physical Units

Step 2—Compute Output in Equivalent Units	Transferred-in Costs	Conversion Costs

Step 3—Summarize Total Costs to Account for	Transferred-in Costs	Conversion Costs	Total Costs

Step 4—Compute Unit Costs

	Transferred-in Costs	Conversion Costs	Total Costs

Step 5—Compute Total Costs of Work Completed and in Process

18 Spoilage, Waste, Defective Units, and Scrap

IN ALMOST EVERY manufacturing operation, there are some outputs that either do not meet established production standards or otherwise appear in some undesirable form or state. Such outputs are called spoilage, waste, defective units, or scrap. This chapter describes them, emphasizing the accounting implications of the distinction between the normal and the abnormal causes of these outputs.

Accounting for spoilage aims at both the management-control purpose and the product-costing purpose. The chapter demonstrates techniques for handling spoilage in job-order, process, and standard cost systems. Particularly helpful in quickly gaining a useful perspective of some key relationships are textbook Exhibit 18–1 and the summary of job-order journal entries on page 610.

REVIEW SUMMARY

A. Although some of the terms and accounting procedures in this area are often vague and inconsistent, we recognize certain basic definitions:

1. *Spoilage* is production that falls below quality or dimensional standards and is sold for *disposal value,* or *salvage value.*
2. *Net spoilage cost* is the excess of costs accumulated to the point of rejection over the disposal value of the spoiled goods.
3. *Defective units* are substandard outputs that are feasible to rework and sell as firsts or seconds.
4. *Waste* is manufacturing residue that has no measurable recovery value.
5. *Scrap* is manufacturing residue that has measurable but relatively minor recovery value.

B. The most economical production method or process usually includes some allowance for spoilage.

1. *Normal spoilage* occurs under *efficient* processing conditions that *are* inherent parts of planned operations.
   - **a.** Thus, such spoilage is *uncontrollable* in the short run.
   - **b.** In general, the net cost of normal spoilage should be *included* as a necessary part of the cost of good (unspoiled) production.

2. *Abnormal spoilage* is due to *inefficient* processing conditions that are *not* inherent parts of planned operations.
   a. Thus, such spoilage is usually regarded as *controllable.*
   b. In general, the net cost of abnormal spoilage should be *excluded* from the cost of good production and should be charged to a special loss account for abnormal spoilage because it is not an inventoriable cost of good production.
   c. Thus, the net cost of abnormal spoilage would be appropriately isolated for management control purposes.
3. Textbook Exhibit 18–1 provides a helpful summary of the general accounting for spoilage.
   a. Note the distinction between normal and abnormal spoilage.
   b. Compare the conceptual and practical accounting approaches.

C. Exhibits 18–2 through 18–4 demonstrate the accurate methods for dealing with spoilage in process-cost computations.
1. You should study these helpful exhibits very carefully.
2. Note especially that both normally spoiled units and abnormally spoiled units are *included* in the computation of equivalent units used for finding unit processing costs.
3. Costs applicable to spoiled units may then be easily determined and accounted for.
   a. The cost of abnormally spoiled units would be charged to a special loss account for abnormal spoilage.
   b. No normal spoilage costs of the current process would be allocated to the ending inventory of work in process, if—as in the textbook example—these units have not yet reached the inspection point.
   c. Thus, if the ending inventory of work in process has not reached the inspection point, *all* of the cost of normally spoiled units would be included in the cost of good units completed—as in the textbook examples.

D. The accounting treatment of *net spoilage costs* in a *job-costing system* depends upon the general cause of the spoilage.
1. If the spoilage is *normal and is common to all jobs,* the net cost of spoilage may be applied to production through a predetermined overhead rate that anticipates this net cost.
   a. The net cost of such normal spoilage actually incurred would therefore be charged to Factory Overhead, Stores being debited with disposal value and Work in Process being credited with the gross spoilage cost.
2. If the spoilage is *normal but is directly attributable to the nature of a particular job,* Stores may be debited and Work in Process credited only with the disposal value of the spoiled goods.
   a. This entry will leave in Work in Process the net cost of such normal spoilage actually incurred as part of the cost of the particular job.
3. If the spoilage is *abnormal,* its net cost actually incurred should be charged to a special loss account for abnormal spoilage.
   a. Stores is debited with disposal value.
   b. Work in Process is credited with the gross spoilage cost.

E. The accounting treatment of the material, labor, and overhead costs of reworking *defective units in a job-costing system* depends upon the same set of general causes described above for spoilage and therefore parallels that accounting treatment.
1. In each case, of course, credits would be made to the usual cost-originating accounts:
   a. Stores
   b. Accrued Payroll
   c. Factory Overhead Applied

2. The cost of normal defective work common to all jobs would be charged to *Factory Overhead.*
3. The cost of normal defective work due to the nature of particular jobs would be charged to *Work in Process.*
4. The cost of abnormal defective work would be charged to *a special loss account for abnormal defective work.*

F. The accounting treatment of *scrap* value recovered in a *job-costing system* depends upon certain circumstances in addition to the general causes of the scrap.

1. When the dollar value of scrap is significant and there is a prolonged time lag between the recovery and sale of scrap, a *debit* to Stores should be made for the value of the scrap at the time of recovery.
   a. Otherwise, the accounting recognition of scrap value may be postponed to the time of sale, when a *debit* would be made to Cash or Accounts Receivable.
2. The account to be *credited* when scrap value is recognized depends on the general cause of the scrap.
   a. The value of *normal scrap common to all jobs* may be used to reduce the cost of all jobs through a predetermined overhead rate that anticipates this value. The actual value of such scrap recovered or sold would therefore be credited to Factory Overhead.
   b. The value of *abnormal scrap due to the nature of particular jobs* may be used to reduce the cost of those jobs. The actual value of such scrap recovered or sold would therefore be credited to Work in Process.
3. Summarizing the job-order accounting entries for spoilage, defective work, and scrap is the helpful set of examples on textbook page 610.

G. When a *standard-costing system* is used, allowances for shrinkage, waste, scrap, and spoilage are often included in the standard costs for direct material, direct labor, and factory overhead.

1. Shrinkage and waste in excess of standard cause a material efficiency, usage, or quantity variance.
2. The excess is usually revealed through excess-materials requisitions or by comparing actual-yield percentages with standard-yield percentages.
3. Normally spoiled units are credited to Work in Process at standard costs and charged to Factory Overhead.
4. Periodic comparisons of budget allowances with actual spoilage provide summary information for managerial control.

SELF-TEST AND PRACTICE EXERCISES

I For each of the following multiple-choice and true-false statements, select the most appropriate answer and enter its identification letter in the space provided.

___ 1. Generally, it is desirable to eliminate spoilage entirely: (a) true, (b) false.

___ 2. There is very little distinction between normal spoilage and abnormal spoilage: (a) on a conceptual basis, (b) for management control purposes, (c) both of the above, (d) neither of the above.

___ 3. Substandard outputs that are feasible to rework and sell as firsts or seconds are known as: (a) scrap, (b) waste, (c) spoiled units, (d) defective units, (e) all of the above, (f) none of the above.

___ 4. Manufacturing residue that has no measurable recovery value is called: (a) waste, (b) scrap, (c) either of the above, (d) neither of the above.

___ 5. The most economical combination of production factors usually results in some spoilage: (a) true, (b) false.

____ 6. Normal spoilage is: (a) controllable in the short run, (b) uncontrollable in the short run.

____ 7. Normal spoilage occurs under efficient processing conditions that are inherent parts of planned operations: (a) true, (b) false.

____ 8. Generally, abnormal spoilage: (a) is uncontrollable, (b) should be excluded from cost of good production, (c) both of the above, (d) neither of the above.

____ 9. Spoilage that is due to inefficient processing conditions includes: (a) normal spoilage, (b) abnormal spoilage, (c) both of the above, (d) neither of the above.

____ 10. When spoilage is actually incurred that is normal and is common to all jobs, Work in Process should be credited with: (a) nothing, (b) the disposal value of the spoiled goods, (c) the net spoilage cost, (d) the gross spoilage cost.

____ 11. The predetermined overhead rate used in a job-costing system should include an element for the anticipated net cost of: (a) normal spoilage, (b) abnormal spoilage, (c) both of the above, (d) neither of the above.

____ 12. When abnormal spoilage occurs in a job-costing system, the Work-in-Process account should be credited with: (a) nothing, (b) the disposal value of the spoiled goods, (c) the net spoilage cost, (d) the gross spoilage cost.

____ 13. In a job-costing system, Work in Process would ordinarily be charged with the cost of defective work that is: (a) abnormal, (b) normal and common to all jobs, (c) normal and due to the nature of particular jobs.

____ 14. In a job-costing system, a special loss account should be charged for: (a) the net cost of abnormal spoilage, (b) the cost of remedying abnormal defective work, (c) each of the above, (d) neither of the above.

____ 15. When the dollar value of scrap is significant and there is a prolonged time lag between the recovery and sale of scrap, the accounting recognition of scrap value should be made: (a) at the time of scrap recovery, (b) at the time of scrap sale on account, (c) at the time of cash collection from scrap sale.

____ 16. The value of normal scrap common to all jobs would be: (a) debited to Work in Process, (b) credited to Work in Process, (c) debited to Factory Overhead, (d) credited to Factory Overhead.

____ 17. When a standard-costing system is used, allowances for shrinkage, waste, scrap, and spoilage are included in the standard costs for direct material, direct labor, and factory overhead: (a) often, (b) seldom, (c) never.

II Complete each of the following statements:

1. ____________________ is defined as production that does not meet dimensional or ________________ standards and that is sold for ____________________

2. Net spoilage cost is defined as the excess of ____________________ ____________________ over the ____________________

3. Scrap is defined as manufacturing residue that has ____________________ recovery value.

4. The ____________________ spoilage should be included as part of the costs of good production.

5. The net cost of normal spoilage expected to be common to all jobs would usually be budgeted as part of ____________________

6. When spoilage is normal but is directly attributable to the nature of a particular job, the Work-in-Process amount should be credited with __________ ____________________

7. The cost of normal defective work common to all jobs would ordinarily be charged to the ______ ______________________ account.

8. The value of abnormal scrap attributable to the nature of particular jobs would be credited to the ______________________ account.

9. When a standard costing system is used, normally spoiled production may be charged to ______ ______________________ at standard costs and credited to ______________________

10. Appendix 18B:

A ______________________ account may be used as an accounting device to permit the recognition of abnormal spoilage only when actual spoilage ______________________ a normal range.

III Given for Coronado & Cunningham, Inc., which uses a job-costing system:

Spoiled work:	
Gross cost incurred	$900
Disposal value	$200
Cost incurred to remedy defective work	$600
Scrap material value recovered	$150

Enter selected dollar amounts in the following table to indicate the appropriate journal entries for each of the listed items. Use the dollar amounts above for both normal and abnormal items listed below.

Item	Entry	Stores	Work in Process	Factory Overhead	Special Loss
1. Normal spoilage common to all jobs:	Debit				
	Credit				
2. Normal spoilage due to the nature of particular jobs:	Debit				
	Credit				
3. Abnormal spoilage:	Debit				
	Credit				
4. Normal defective work common to all jobs:	Debit				
	Credit*	–	–	–	–
5. Normal defective work due to the nature of particular jobs:	Debit				
	Credit*	–	–	–	–
6. Abnormal defective work:	Debit				
	Credit*	–	–	–	–
7. Normal scrap common to all jobs:	Debit				
	Credit				
8. Abnormal scrap due to the nature of particular jobs:	Debit				
	Credit				

*Credit Stores, Accrued Payroll, and Factory Overhead Applied, Total $600

IV Given for the Melding Process of Amorphous Products, Inc., which uses the weighted-average method of process costing:

Beginning work in process, 3/5 completed	100 units
Transferred in	620 units
Lost from normal spoilage	40 units
Lost from abnormal spoilage	60 units
Good units transferred out	540 units
Ending work in process, 3/4 completed	80 units
Conversion costs in beginning inventory	$2,000
Current conversion costs	$9,200

Spoilage is detected upon completion of the process, when the units are inspected.

Find by the weighted-average method:

1. Equivalent units for conversion costs .... ____ units

2. Unit conversion cost .... $ ______

3. Total conversion costs of normal spoilage .... $ ______

4. Total conversion costs of abnormal spoilage .... $ ______

5. Total conversion costs transferred out to the following process .... $ ______

6. Total conversion costs in the ending inventory of work in process .... $ ______

19 Decentralization and Transfer Pricing

AS ORGANIZATIONS GROW, they tend to develop more segments such as departments, cost centers, profit centers, and divisions. The freedom to make decisions may be distributed more widely among managers (**decentralization**).

Decentralized operations often involve exchanges of goods and services among the subunits of an organization. **Transfer prices** are the monetary values assigned to these exchanges. Ideally, transfer prices should motivate managers to make decisions that maximize the profits of the organization as a whole. However, there is rarely a single type of transfer price that will accomplish this goal. In this chapter, we examine the main types of transfer prices and their impacts on three major problems involved in designing or judging accounting control systems: **goal congruence, managerial effort,** and **subunit autonomy.**

REVIEW SUMMARY

A. The decentralization of an organization's management is a matter of degree.

1. The essence of decentralization is the *freedom of managers to make decisions.*
2. Certain claimed advantages of decentralization are supposed to benefit the company through increased profits.
   - **a.** Decisions are better and more timely because of the manager's proximity to local conditions.
   - **b.** Top managers have more time for strategic planning.
   - **c.** Managers' motivation increases because they have more control over results.
   - **d.** Greater latitude of managerial action develops more frequent comparison of outside market prices with prices used for internal transfers.
   - **e.** Increased decision making provides better training for managers.
   - **f.** The profit-center structure has a more desirable motivational effect.
3. The largest cost of decentralization is probably *dysfunctional decision making,* which produces a net negative benefit to the subunits affected (and to the organization as a whole).
   - **a.** This can be caused by lack of goal congruence, insufficient information, or increased costs of obtaining sufficient information.

b. Dysfunctional decision making is most likely when there is a high degree of *interdependence* among subunits.

4. It is difficult to determine the optimal degree of decentralization, the maximization of the *net benefit* (excess of benefits over costs).
   a. When the organizational subunits are *independent* (self-contained), decentralization is likely to be most beneficial and least costly.
5. A *profit center* is any subunit of an organization that is assigned both revenues and expenses.
   a. The profit center is normally the major organizational device used to maximize decentralization.
   b. However, various segment labels used by different companies (for example, "cost center" and "profit center") are sometimes deceptive indicators of the actual degrees of decentralization.
   c. The degree of decentralization within a given company (General Electric, for example) depends not only on the number of subunits and their size, but also on the way they are managed.

B. In designing or judging accounting control systems, one should consider how they relate to three major problems:
1. Inducing *goal congruence,* the harmonizing of managers' goals with organization goals.
2. Maintaining an appropriate level of *managerial effort* toward goals.
3. Preserving *autonomy,* the freedom of managers to operate their subunits as decentralized entities.

C. Transfer pricing necessarily results from interactions among decentralized subunits, typically a profit center supplying a product or service to another profit center.
1. The transfer price will affect not only the reported profit of each center, but will also affect the allocation of an organization's resources.
2. The basic purpose of transfer pricing is to induce *optimal decision making* in a decentralized organization; i.e., to maximize the profit of the organization as a whole.
3. Transfer-pricing methods should be evaluated in the light of the same three major problems identified above: goal congruence, managerial effort, and autonomy.

D. Under some conditions, *market prices* are the most appropriate transfer prices because they help solve the three major problems.
1. Favorable conditions for using market prices include:
   a. *Minimal interdependencies of subunits.*
   b. Existence of a *competitive intermediate market* with dependable market-price quotations.
2. There are three principal guidelines for using market prices for transfer prices:
   a. Use a market price or a negotiated market price.
   b. The selling subunit should have the option of not selling internally.
   c. An arbitration procedure should be available for settling disputes among subunit managers.
3. Generally, the outside market price would be a *ceiling* not to be exceeded by the internal transfer price.
4. The main difficulty with the use of market prices for transfer prices is the frequent lack of a market that is perfectly competitive or that contains the exact product or service subject to transfer.
5. If there is idle capacity in a supplying division and no market for the intermediate product, the extent of top management's interference in a transfer-pricing dispute between independent divisions can create a dilemma.
   a. To benefit the organization as a whole, the supplying division should transfer the intermediate product at a price equal to its variable cost only.

b. However, if the manager of the supplying division were forced by top management to forego a profit by accepting such a low price, there would be a natural lessening of both managerial effort and subunit autonomy.

6. If there are only some isolated price quotations reflecting temporary distress or dumping prices, they may be appropriate in general for monitoring short-term performance but not for making long-range plans.

E. There is no general rule for transfer pricing that will lead toward optimal economic decisions.

1. However, there is a general rule that serves as a helpful first step in reaching an optimal economic decision in a particular situation. This rule is that the minimum transfer price should be the sum of two elements:

a. One element is composed of the *additional outlay costs* incurred to the point of transfer: cash outflows that are directly associated with the production and transfer of the goods or services (sometimes approximated by variable costs).

b. The other element consists of *opportunity costs* for the firm as a whole: the maximum contribution to profits foregone by the firm as a whole if the goods are transferred internally (often quite difficult to measure).

2. Transfer pricing is often complicated by imperfect, ill-structured, or nonexistent intermediate markets.

a. *Imperfect competition* occurs when a single buyer or seller can influence the market price.

b. If imperfect competition exists in the intermediate market, additional volume can be obtained only if selling prices are lowered, thus causing transfer-price analyses to be exceedingly complex.

3. Again, when heavy interdependencies exist among organization subunits and intermediate markets, transfer-pricing analyses can become quite complex.

a. An economic analysis might dictate variable cost to be used for the transfer price, but this would seldom be appropriate for solving all three problems: goal congruence, managerial effort, and autonomy.

b. Therefore, as a practical solution, different kinds of transfer prices (for example, market prices and cost prices) may be assigned to different classes of transactions.

F. Although nearly every version of a transfer price has some drawbacks, there are several useful bases other than market prices for setting transfer prices.

1. There is a widespread use of *full cost* as a transfer price.

a. Because full *actual* costs can include inefficiencies, this basis for transfer pricing often fails to provide an incentive to control such inefficiencies.

b. Although the use of full *standard* costs may minimize the inefficiencies mentioned above, suboptimal decisions can result from the natural inclination of the manager of an autonomous buying division to view such *mixed costs* of a selling division as *variable costs* of his buying division.

c. Despite the above defects of the full-cost basis, it is commonly used for transfer prices because of its clarity and convenience and because it is often viewed as a satisfactory approximation of outside market prices.

2. Top management may want buying-division managers to make purchasing decisions based on the variable costs of supplying divisions.

a. In such cases, the transfer could be made at standard variable cost for the purpose of motivating buying-division managers toward the desired purchasing decisions.

b. However, the buying divisions would be charged periodically with lump-sum amounts to cover the supplying divisions' related fixed costs and to provide them with a profit margin.

3. Managers can negotiate a single transfer price so that the overall contribution to cor-

porate profit from a given internal transfer would be *prorated* between the buying and selling divisions on some mutually agreeable basis (for example, variable cost).

4. *Dual transfer prices* can be devised.
   a. For the purpose of motivating the manager of the buying division to make the *optimal economic decision,* the transfer price would be *variable cost.*
   b. For the purpose of fairly *evaluating performance* of the supplying division, the transfer price would be a *synthetic market price* allowing for a normal profit margin to the supplying division.
   c. However, a disadvantage of this scheme is that both managers may tend to relax cost controls within their divisions.

G. A given company may well use different transfer prices for different purposes.
1. Various purposes related to *internal* problems could include:
   a. To induce goal congruence
   b. To maintain managerial effort
   c. To preserve subunit autonomy
2. Various purposes related to *external* problems could include:
   a. To minimize tariffs and income taxes
   b. To observe certain legal restrictions on selling prices

H. Despite the weaknesses of profit centers and control systems in improving goal congruence and incentive in an economically feasible way, profit centers provide the formal device that is so often the most persuasive means of communicating top management's goals and improving effort.

I. If intracompany transfers are accounted for at prices in excess of cost, appropriate elimination entries should be made for external reporting purposes. When consolidated financial statements are prepared, items to be eliminated include:
1. Intracompany receivables and payables
2. Intracompany sales and cost of goods sold, and
3. Intracompany gross profit in inventories

SELF-TEST AND PRACTICE EXERCISES

I For each of the following multiple-choice and true-false statements, select the most appropriate answer and enter its identification letter in the space provided.

___ 1. The degree of decentralization in a business depends primarily on: (a) the number of profit centers, (b) the size of profit centers, (c) the responsibility of profit center managers for their subunit operating performance, (d) none of the above.

___ 2. The claimed advantages of decentralization include: (a) improved management motivation, (b) decreased costs of gathering and processing information, (c) both of the above, (d) neither of the above.

___ 3. The costs of decentralization can include: (a) poorer training for managers, (b) dysfunctional decision making, (c) both of the above, (d) neither of the above.

___ 4. Included among the causes of dysfunctional decision making are: (a) lack of goal congruence, (b) insufficient information, (c) both of the above, (d) neither of the above.

___ 5. Decentralization is likely to be most beneficial and least costly when the organization's subunits are: (a) independent, (b) interdependent.

___ 6. A profit center is: (a) an organization subunit that is assigned both revenues and expenses, (b) normally the prime organizational device for maximizing decentralization, (c) both of the above, (d) neither of the above.

___ 7. The three major problems of goal congruence, managerial effort, and subunit autonomy should be considered in designing or judging: (a) accounting control systems, (b) transfer-pricing methods, (c) both of the above, (d) neither of the above.

___ 8. Subunit autonomy means the freedom of each individual member of the organization to define his own job or function: (a) true, (b) false.

___ 9. Transfer pricing deals primarily with the problems of determining appropriate transportation charges for goods exchanged or traded between two companies: (a) true, (b) false.

___ 10. The fundamental objective of a transfer-pricing system is to: (a) minimize income taxes, (b) minimize clerical and bookkeeping costs, (c) maximize a company's assets, (d) maximize a company's profits.

___ 11. The dominant idea behind the use of transfer prices is: (a) income taxation, (b) customer satisfaction, (c) stockholder information, (d) management motivation.

___ 12. The transfer-pricing problem is most difficult in organizations that are: (a) *highly centralized* with *many interdependencies* among subunits, (b) *highly decentralized* with *many interdependencies* among subunits, (c) *highly centralized* with *few interdependencies* among subunits, (d) *highly decentralized* with *few interdependencies* among subunits.

___ 13. A floor for transfer prices is typically established when market prices are used for transfer prices: (a) true, (b) false.

___ 14. A principal difficulty with the use of market prices for transfer prices is the frequent lack of a perfectly competitive intermediate market: (a) true, (b) false.

___ 15. If there is idle capacity in a supplying division and no intermediate market, a transfer price dictated by top management would tend to cause: (a) decreased managerial effort, (b) decreased subunit autonomy, (c) both of the above, (d) neither of the above.

___ 16. There is no general rule for transfer pricing that will lead toward optimal economic decisions: (a) true, (b) false.

___ 17. A helpful general way to determine a transfer price that will lead toward optimal economic decisions is to determine the relevant opportunity costs for the firm as a whole and to add: (a) fixed costs incurred to the point of transfer, (b) market prices in the intermediate market, (c) additional outlay costs incurred to the point of transfer, (d) all of the above.

___ 18. When many interdependencies exist among organizational subunits and markets, the use of dependable market prices alone would often fail to indicate directly the optimum buying decision: (a) true, (b) false.

___ 19. Transfer prices based upon full cost are widely used: (a) true, (b) false.

___ 20. When full costs are used as transfer prices, an incentive to control the inefficiencies that might increase such costs would be provided by using: (a) full actual costs, (b) full standard costs.

II Complete each of the following statements:

1. Dysfunctional decision making is most likely to occur in an organization with a high degree of

____

____

2. The three major problems to be considered in judging the effectiveness of transfer prices are:

(a) ______________________________

(b) ______________________________

(c) ______________________________

3. For routine use where the intermediate market is ______________________________, the most desirable transfer price is market price if the interdependencies of subunits are ______________________________

____

4. The use of transfer prices based only on some simple rule such as a price to cover the full costs of a

supplier division would tend to cause ______________ ______________ decision making.

5. When there is no intermediate market and when marginal or variable cost is used as a transfer price, this would tend to please the manager of the ______________ division.

6. Although total decentralization implies complete freedom for organizational subunits to make decisions in their best interests as though they were ______________, a major cost of such decentralization would be ______________ ______________

7. If intracompany transfers are accounted for at prices in excess of ______________, appropriate elimination entries must be made when consolidated financial statements are prepared for ______________ reporting purposes. Items to be eliminated include intracompany: receivables and ______________, sales and ______________, and ______________

III Given for the Quotient Division of Abacus Calculator Equipment, Inc:

Costs of manufacturing 5,000 units of a certain part:

	Total	Per Unit
Variable costs	$200,000	$40
Fixed costs	$ 40,000	$ 8

1. Find the total benefit (or detriment) to the company if there *are no alternative uses* for Quotient Division's facilities, and if the Subtrahend Division of the same company purchases 5,000 units of this part from an outside supplier at a market price of:
   (a) $43 per unit . . . . $______
   (b) $36 per unit . . . . $______

2. Find the total benefit (or detriment) to the company if there *is an alternative use* for Quotient Division's facilities by other Abacus operations that would otherwise require an additional outlay of $26,000, and if Subtrahend Division of the same company purchases 5,000 units of this part from an outside supplier at a market price of:
   (a) $43 per unit . . . . $______
   (b) $36 per unit . . . . $______

IV Among the many divisions in Manifold Company are J, K, and L. Division J needs to buy one thousand units of a certain component for its final product. The uniform outside market price for this is $98 per unit. Division K is working at full capacity and can provide this component to Division J or to an outside buyer at this same market price. The outlay costs of filling either of these orders amounts to $70 per unit. An outside supplier has bid the market price for selling the component to Division J. This supplier would in turn buy some raw materials from Division L for $15,000. Division L, which has spare capacity, would have outlay costs of providing such raw materials of $6,000.

1. Compute the net advantage or disadvantage to the company of Division J buying from the outside at the market price instead of from Division K at the market price.

2. What should be the minimum transfer price, using the "general rule" described in the textbook?

Hint: Use a diagram of cost flows and revenue flows.

Systems Choice: Division Performance Measurement 20

IN THE PRECEDING CHAPTER, we saw how decentralization highlights the problems of goal congruence, managerial effort, and subunit autonomy. Here we consider the measurement of segment performance in developing management motivation toward the achievement of organizational goals.

Earlier chapters have shown how responsibility accounting helps measure the performance of managers of cost centers by focusing on the cost objects subject to an individual's control. This chapter extends the basic ideas of responsibility accounting beyond cost centers to investment centers. We examine the nature of these business segments and the principal problems of measuring both segment performance and managerial performance. Special emphasis is placed upon the widely used measure called **rate of return on investment (ROI).**

REVIEW SUMMARY

A. Large business organizations may have at least three kinds of subunits or segments:

1. A *cost center,* typically a department, is the smallest segment of activity or area of responsibility for which costs are accumulated.

2. A *profit center,* often called a division, is a segment responsible for both revenues and expenses.

3. An *investment center* is a segment responsible for its invested capital and the related income.

a. "Investment center," not a widely used term, is usually also designated by the terms "profit center" and "division."

B. Basic matters to be considered by control system designers include:

1. Making some critical choices concerning performance measures:

a. Measures of accomplishment that reflect top-management goals.

b. Definitions of key terms such as "income" and "investment."

c. Bases for measuring various items: historical cost, replacement cost, realizable value.

d. Standards of performance to be required.

e. Timing of feedback on performance.

2. Assessing the feasibility of the system in solving certain broad problems (detailed in preceding chapter):
   a. Goal congruence
   b. Managerial effort
   c. Subunit autonomy

C. The measures of accomplishment that best represent the objectives of top management usually relate profits to invested capital.
   1. One widely used measure is the *rate of return on investment (ROI).*
      a. ROI is the ratio of *net income* to *invested capital.*
      b. ROI can also be computed by multiplying *capital turnover* by the *net income percentage of sales:*

$$\frac{\text{Sales}}{\text{Invested Capital}} \times \frac{\text{Net Income}}{\text{Sales}} = \frac{\text{Net Income}}{\text{Invested Capital}} = \text{ROI}$$

      c. Management's understanding and use of ROI can be aided by thus breaking it down into its basic components.
   2. *Residual income* is another measure of accomplishment that relates profit to invested capital.
      a. This is the excess of an investment center's *net income over the imputed interest on the invested capital used by the center.*
      b. This approach induces a desirable expansion of an investment center as long as it earns a rate in excess of the charge for invested capital (the minimum desired rate of return).
      c. In contrast to the results of the residual-income approach, using the maximization of ROI as an investment criterion would sometimes result in the rejection by division managers of projects that, from the viewpoint of the organization, should be accepted because they promise an ROI in excess of the minimum desired rate of return.

D. In measuring performance by whatever means, one should make a distinction between the performance of the *division manager* and the performance of the *division* as an investment by the corporation.
   1. To measure divisional performance, division income would be compared with the total division investment.
   2. Because operating conditions vary so widely, performances should be compared only with extreme caution among divisions or among managers.
      a. Actual performances of both divisions and managers are more appropriately judged against *budget targets,* rather than against competing divisions or managers.
   3. Different bases are available for measuring invested capital.
      a. In general, for evaluating the operating performance of managers, it is appropriate to use as a base an asset total *not* reduced by any long-term debt, such as *total assets available, total assets employed,* and *working capital plus other assets.*
      b. On the other hand, the use of *stockholders' equity* as an investment base is more appropriate for evaluating owners' returns under a particular capital structure, which might involve a significant degree of *financial leverage,* or *trading on the equity.*

E. In designing performance measures, one should be aware of different definitions of key elements and their implications for appraising performance and motivating managers.
   1. The definitions of income, investment, etc., should be agreed on within an organization.
   2. Helpful in distinguishing between the performances of divisions and managers is the *contribution approach* of Chapter 15.
   3. The method of allocating assets to divisions can significantly affect the motivation of managers.

a. The aim, of course, should be to allocate a way that induces the desired management behavior.
b. In general, if managers perceive that they are being treated *uniformly,* they tend to accept asset allocations as fair.
c. However, many managers feel it is better not to allocate assets to divisions than to use an arbitrary basis for allocation.

F. Of crucial importance in evaluating performance and making decisions is the selection of appropriate alternatives for the measurement of investments and the related performance of managers and divisions.
1. For the routine measurement of assets included in the investment base, the most frequently used valuation is *net book value,* but this is not necessarily conceptually correct.
2. If expansion of assets is an available alternative, one should compare the additional asset's *total present value* with its *acquisition cost* (*the required investment*).
3. Valid productivity comparisons among executives as managers and among divisions as economic investments should be made.
   a. Therefore, a performance measurement model should be used that is consistent with the decision model.
   b. If not, dysfunctional decisions could be induced, for example, by combining a DCF decision model, with an accrual-accounting performance model.
4. In choosing between the disposal of an asset and its continuance, one should compare the asset's highest *current disposal value* with its *total present value* (present value of expected cash inflows).

G. To compare the performances of subunits as economic investments, one should use a uniform basis for measuring assets.
1. Using *historical cost* of assets would usually involve different acquisition dates and therefore would not provide an appropriate common denominator.
2. Although many theorists claim that *total present value* is the ideal investment measure for the evaluation of performance, its use is rarely feasible because of its *high degree of subjectivity:*
   a. Uncertain cash flows must be estimated.
   b. Discount rates must often be changed.
3. A practical substitute for the "ideal" present value is *replacement cost,* for which it is often quite feasible to obtain objective approximations at given dates.
4. Although historical cost has defects as an investment measure, it is often used.
   a. The reason: because it is generally believed that its routine use for this purpose may be more economical on a regular basis than the use of replacement cost and current disposal values, which are often viewed as feasible to obtain only for special decisions.
   b. Some companies are experimenting with the use of historical cost adjusted for general price-level changes.
   c. When historical cost is used as an investment measure, some users prefer *gross cost* (undepreciated cost) because it facilitates comparisons among divisions.
   d. Others prefer *net cost* (net book value) because it is consistent with conventional external reporting of assets and net income.
5. Many observers contend that replacement cost measures are superior to historical cost measures.
6. Why then does the overwhelming majority of businesses use historical costs in valuing assets for measuring subunit performance? Possible reasons include:
   a. Ignorance of defects of historical costs.
   b. Overlooking the importance of budgets in planning and control.

c. Historical data are already being routinely accumulated as a normal feature of operations.
d. The defects of historical costs may be overcome by a practical use of budgets in measuring subunit performance.
e. Historical costs are still the main basis for external reporting.

SELF-TEST AND PRACTICE EXERCISES

I For each of the following multiple-choice and true-false statements, select the most appropriate answer and enter its identification letter in the space provided.

___ 1. Return on investment is equal to net income divided by capital turnover: (a) true, (b) false.

___ 2. Net income percentage of sales is equal to ROI divided by capital turnover: (a) true, (b) false.

___ 3. Roma Bottling Co. has an invested capital of $3,000,000, a net income percentage of sales of 4%, and an ROI of 12%. Its sales are: (a) $360,000, (b) $9,000,000, (c) $1,440,000, (d) $12,000,000, (e) none of the above.

___ 4. See the preceding item. The capital turnover is: (a) 5 times, (b) 4 times, (c) 3 times, (d) 2 times, (e) none of the above.

___ 5. A useful synonym for net income is: (a) return on investment, (b) retained income, (c) residual income, (d) none of the above.

___ 6. Howard McDonald's, Inc. has a residual income of $180,000 and a net income of $500,000. If the imputed interest rate is 16 percent, what is the amount of invested capital? (a) $320,000, (b) $3,125,000, (c) $8,000,000, (d) $2,000,000, (e) some other amount.

___ 7. See the preceding item. Compute the ROI: (a) 5%, (b) 10%, (c) 15%, (d) 20%, (e) none of the above.

___ 8. The critical test of the profitability of an organization is: (a) the absolute amount of profit, (b) the relationship of profit to sales, (c) the relationship of profit to total assets, (d) the relationship of profit to invested capital.

___ 9. ROI may be computed by dividing invested capital by net income: (a) true, (b) false.

___ 10. Capital turnover is computed by dividing invested capital into: (a) sales, (b) total assets, (c) stockholders' equity, (d) none of the above.

___ 11. A measure of accomplishment that induces a desirable expansion of an investment center as long as it earns a rate in excess of the charge for invested capital is: (a) the ROI measure, (b) the residual income measure, (c) either of the above, (d) neither of the above.

___ 12. To use the maximization of ROI as an investment criterion could result in the rejection by division managers of projects that, from the viewpoint of the organization as a whole, should be accepted: (a) true, (b) false.

___ 13. In general, it is desirable to use the same criteria in evaluating the performance of the division manager and the performance of the division as an investment by the corporation: (a) true, (b) false.

___ 14. Actual performances of divisions and managers should be judged against: (a) competing divisions or managers, (b) budget targets.

___ 15. Many managers: (a) tend to accept asset allocations as fair if they believe they are being treated uniformly, (b) think it is better not to allocate assets to divisions than to use an arbitrary basis for allocation, (c) both of the above, (d) neither of the above.

___ 16. In the evaluation of owners' returns under a particular capital structure, the most meaningful investment base to which an appropriate income figure should be related would be: (a) total assets, (b) total liabilities, (c) stockholders' equity.

___ 17. For the routine measurement of assets included in the investment base, the most frequently used valuation is: (a) total present value, (b) current disposal value, (c) net book value.

___ 18. It is generally desirable to use DCF models for making investment decisions and the traditional accrual accounting models for evaluating the performance resulting from those decisions: (a) true, (b) false.

___ 19. Practical disadvantages of using total present value as an investment measure for the evaluation of performance include: (a) volatility of discount rates, (b) uncertainties in estimating cash flows, (c) both of the above, (d) neither of the above.

___ 20. Reasons for the widespread use of historical costs instead of replacement costs in valuing assets for measuring segment performance include: (a) conceptual inferiority of replacement costs, (b) conventional use of historical costs for external reporting, (c) both of the above, (d) neither of the above.

II Complete each of the following statements:

1. ROI is equal to ______________________

multiplied by______________________

____

2. Residual income is the excess of an investment center's net income over______________________

____

3. It would be appropriate to evaluate a division manager's performance by comparing the controllable contribution of his division with ______

____

4. In choosing between the disposal of an asset and its continuance, one should compare the asset's

______________________value with its

______________________ value.

5. A practical substitute for the "ideal" present value as the investment measure for the evaluation of performance is______________________

____

III Given for three companies:

	Capover Company	Investurn Company	Marsales Company
Invested capital	$200,000	$300,000	*
Sales	$900,000	*	$600,000
Net income	$ 27,000	*	$ 24,000
Capital turnover	*	*	5 times
Net income percentage of sales	*	4%	*
Return on investment	*	10%	*

**To be computed*

1. Find for Capover Company:
   (a) Capital turnover .... ______ times
   (b) Net income percentage of sales .... ______ %
   (c) Return on investment .... ______ %

2. Find for Investurn Company:
   (a) Net income .... $ ______
   (b) Sales .... $ ______
   (c) Capital turnover .... ______ times

3. Find for Marsales Company:
   (a) Invested capital.......................... $ ______
   (b) Net income percentage of sales .... ______ %
   (c) Return on investment....................... ______ %

IV Given for Key Division of Hard Lock Company:

Invested capital	$450,000
Net income	99,000

1. What is Key Division's ROI? .... ______ %

2. If interest is imputed at 18%, what is Residual Income? .... $ ______

3. If an available project promises a 20% ROI, would it tend to be accepted if:

   (a) ROI were used to evaluate performance? __________ Why?

   (b) Residual Income were used to evaluate performance? __________ Why?

V Given for a special project of Astute Computer Company:

Investment in special equipment	$200,000
Annual net cash inflows from operations	$ 38,344
Useful life of equipment	10 years
Internal rate of return	14%

(The 14% rate was determined by dividing $200,000 by $38,344 and entering the annuity present value table with the quotient at the 10-year line, as explained in Chapter 12.)

1. Assuming that the traditional accrual accounting model is used as a basis for performance evaluation, compute the ROI as follows (use straight-line depreciation with no terminal salvage value):

	First Year	**Sixth Year**
(a) Using gross cost as the investment base	_______ %	_______ %
(b) Using net book value at the beginning of the year as the investment base	_______ %	_______ %

2. What would be the objection to using the traditional accounting model as a basis for performance evaluation in this case?

3. If the traditional accrual model is used as a basis for performance comparisons among divisions, which cost basis would be preferable, gross cost or net book value? _______ Why?

21 Decision Models, Uncertainty, and the Accountant

BUSINESS DECISIONS ARE MADE by managers, not by accountants **per se.** However, accountants participate in the management function of an organization by providing the main source of the quantitative information needed for making decisions. Thus, accountants who design and operate accounting information systems, must understand the entire managerial decision process. An important part of this process is the **decision model,** a method for systematically aiding managers to make decisions.

In this chapter, we study formal decision models expressed in mathematical form: the nature of their basic elements, the selection of appropriate models, and the relationship of information to these models. A considerable part of the chapter deals with the use of mathematical decision models under **conditions of uncertainty.**

REVIEW SUMMARY

A. Mathematical decision models typically have five principal elements:

1. A *choice criterion,* or *objective function,* which is a maximization (or minimization) of some form of profit (or cost) for the purpose of evaluating courses of action and thus assisting in the selection of the best alternative.
2. A set of *alternative courses of action* that are collectively exhaustive and mutually exclusive.
3. A set of *events,* also called *states* or *states of nature,* that are also collectively exhaustive and mutually exclusive.
4. A set of *probabilities* of occurrence of the various events.
5. A set of *outcomes* or *payoffs* that measure the predicted consequences of various possible combinations of actions and events.

B. Decisions may be classified as being made under certainty or uncertainty.

1. When decisions are made *under certainty,* this means that for each action there is only one event, and therefore *only one* outcome or payoff for each action.
   - **a.** The decision consists of choosing the action that will produce the most desirable outcome.

b. However, this could be quite difficult if there is a great number of possible actions to consider.

2. When decisions are made *under uncertainty,* for each action there are *several* events, each with its probability of occurrence.
   a. The probability may be determinable with a high degree of confidence because of mathematical proofs or actual experience.
   b. However, if mathematical proofs and actual experience are not available, probabilities can be assessed *on a subjective basis.*

C. When decisions are to be made under uncertainty, it is often helpful to make some selected computations.
   1. The *expected value* of each action is the average of the outcomes of each of its events weighted by their probabilities of occurrence (the sum of the products of payoffs and probabilities).
      a. Be sure that you understand how such calculations are made, as shown in the textbook examples for Proposals A and B on page 718.
   2. The *standard deviation* is the common measure of the *dispersion* of a probability distribution.
      a. It is the square root of the mean of the squared deviations from the expected value.
   3. The *coefficient of variation* is a relative measure of *uncertainty.*
      a. It is the standard deviation divided by the expected value.

D. The measurements of almost all accounting data are subject to uncertainty.
   1. This is true whether we are estimating historical costs or predicting future costs.
   2. Because of inadequacies in representing probability distributions by single amounts, accountants will probably begin to provide decision makers with more complete data such as the summary measures described above in C.

E. It is sometimes feasible to compute the *value of additional information* that may be available to the decision maker at some cost. Major steps are:
   1. Identify the five principal elements for a decision model in a particular case.
      a. See the textbook illustration beginning on page 720.
   2. Construct a *decision table,* textbook Exhibit 21-2.
      a. Compute *expected value with existing information.*
      b. This is the expected value of the action that would maximize payoff under conditions of uncertainty ($19,320 to buy M 2).
   3. Compute *expected value with perfect information.*
      a. This is the sum of the optimum outcome for each event multiplied by its probability ($19,800).
   4. Subtract $19,320 from $19,800 to arrive at $480.
      a. This is the *expected value of perfect information.*
      b. It is the maximum amount that should be paid for perfect advance information.
   5. A similar approach can sometimes be used to estimate the *expected value of imperfect information.*
   6. These textbook examples illustrate the *cost-benefit* aspect of getting information relevant to decision making:
      a. The *cost* of information (including alternative accounting systems for providing the information) should be compared with its *value* in arriving at management decisions.

F. The probabilistic decision models described here arrive at an expected monetary value for each of the several actions that can be chosen.
   1. However, when relatively large amounts of money are involved in such actions, expected monetary values may not be effective determinants of decisions.
   2. For psychological reasons, different people faced with the same situation may use

personal money evaluations that are quite different from the actual dollar amounts involved.

3. These different expressions of personal preference reflect different *utility values* of money that in turn may produce different decisions.
4. The main idea here is illustrated by the textbook example, which in essence is like tossing a fair coin where "heads" wins $25,000 and "tails" loses only $10,000.
   a. This would indeed be an attractive proposition to a person with sufficient cash to rely on these probabilities.
   b. However, there are many more persons who simply could not afford the 50% probability of losing $10,000 on the first toss of the coin.
5. Three basic attitudes toward risk will affect the decision maker's *utility function* (Exhibit 21-3):
   a. Risk neutrality
   b. Risk aversion
   c. Risk seeking
6. Most managers and investors are *risk averse:*
   a. They are willing to take risks only if the required investment is less than the expected monetary value of the results.

SELF-TEST AND PRACTICE EXERCISES

I For each of the following multiple-choice and true-false statements, select the most appropriate answer and enter its identification letter in the space provided.

___ 1. The sets of probabilities in mathematical decision models pertain to the likelihood of occurrence of: (a) courses of action, (b) outcomes, (c) events, (d) the objective function, (e) none of the above.

___ 2. Used as synonyms in formal decision models are: (a) outcomes and events, (b) states and payoffs, (c) events and actions, (d) payoffs and outcomes.

___ 3. Certainty exists when there is absolutely no doubt about which: (a) action will occur, (b) event will occur.

___ 4. Although the relevant probabilities can be determined with a high degree of confidence in some situations, decisions are said to be made under uncertainty: (a) true, (b) false.

___ 5. When decisions are made under certainty, there is: (a) only one event, (b) only one outcome for each action, (c) both of the above, (d) neither of the above.

___ 6. When decisions are made under uncertainty, the relevant probabilities may be determined: (a) by mathematical proofs, (b) by actual experience, (c) either of the above, (d) neither of the above.

___ 7. The coefficient of variation is a relative measure of: (a) efficiency, (b) profitability, (c) accuracy or reliability, (d) uncertainty.

___ 8. If two probability distributions have the same expected values, they would not necessarily also have the same standard deviations: (a) true, (b) false.

___ 9. Accounting-data measurements that are subject to uncertainty include: (a) historical costs, (b) future costs, (c) both of the above, (d) neither of the above.

___ 10. The expected value of perfect information is the difference between the expected value with perfect information and the expected value with existing information: (a) true, (b) false.

___ 11. Utility values of money: (a) are determined by well-known formulas, (b) are usually equal to the actual monetary amounts, (c) are the same for persons facing the same decisions, (d) reflect different personal preferences in a given situation.

II Complete each of the following statements:

1. The choice criterion of a mathematical decision model is also called the ______________________

____

2. The choice criterion of a mathematical decision model is often expressed as a maximization of ______________________ or a minimization of ______________________

3. A mathematical decision model contains a set of events, which are also called ______________________ or ______________________

4. Typically, mathematical decision models include sets of alternative courses of action that are collectively ______________________ and mutually ______________________

____

5. The payoffs in a mathematical decision model indicate the possible outcomes of ______________________

______________________ for ______________________

6. A mathematical decision model may include ______________________ costs.

7. If the relevant probabilities can be determined by subjective means, decisions are said to be made under ______________________

8. Decisions are said to be made under uncertainty when there are several ______________________

______________________, each with its ______________________ of occurrence.

9. The common measure of the dispersion of a probability distribution is called ______________________

____

10. The expected value of a particular action is the sum of ______________________, each multiplied by ______________________

____

11. The coefficient of variation is ______________________

______________________ divided by ______________________

____

III Precision Automatix predicts the following benefits and probabilities for a certain contemplated action:

Benefits	$10	$30	$40	$50
Probabilities	.2	.3	.3	.2

1. Compute the expected value of this action: $ ________

2. Compute the standard deviation: $ ________

3. Compute the coefficient of variation: $ ______

IV Given for Kismet Fortune Cookies, Inc.:

		A	B	C	D
Event or state of nature		A	B	C	D
Probability of occurrence		.1	.4	.3	.2
Outcomes or payoffs for actions:	1	$10	$ 5	-0-	– $10
	2	$15	$10	$5	– $ 5
	3	$20	$15	-0-	-0-
	4	$30	$10	-0-	– $15

1. What is the expected value of action 1? .... $ ______

2. What is the expected value of action 2? .... $ ______

3. What is the expected value of action 3? .... $ ______

4. What is the expected value of action 4? .... $ ______

5. What is total expected value with perfect information? .... $ ______

6. What is the action that would maximize the payoff? .... $ ______

7. What is the total expected value of perfect information? .... $ ______

22 Inventory Planning, Control, and Costing

INVENTORIES INCLUDE manufacturing materials held for use in production and finished products held for sale to customers. We seek to keep our inventories above the levels that would be insufficient for production and sales requirements and below the levels that would cause excessive inventory carrying costs or value deterioration. Holding inventories and other assets at appropriate levels helps to maximize long-run profits.

Inventory control means the determination and maintenance of the optimum amounts of investments in all types of inventories. The body of this chapter explains various approaches and techniques for accomplishing inventory control. The chapter appendix describes the leading inventory-costing methods and their effects on reported operating results and financial position.

REVIEW SUMMARY

A. Inventories have some important managerial aspects.

1. Inventories permit prompt service to customers and a smooth flow of production operations.
2. If inventories are sufficient, they serve as cushions to absorb fluctuations in supply and demand.
3. Inventories also help minimize the interdependence of various parts of the organization.
4. Keeping inventories at levels that maximize profits (or minimize costs) is called *inventory control.*
   - **a.** This is not achieved merely by maintaining a high level of clerical accuracy in inventory records and documents.

B. Two main types of costs are relevant to inventory decisions:

1. *Ordering costs* are the clerical costs of preparing purchase or production orders and the special processing and receiving costs affected by the number of orders made.
2. *Carrying costs* include the desired rate of return on inventory investment and the costs of storage, breakage, obsolescence, deterioration, insurance, and personal property taxes.

3. These two types of costs are affected in opposite ways as the average size of the inventory increases because of larger orders at less frequent intervals: carrying costs increase, but ordering costs decrease.

C. One of the two key factors in applying inventory policy is the determination of the *economic order quantity (EOQ)*, the optimum size of a normal purchase order for replenishing materials or a shop order for a production run.

1. The EOQ may be estimated by computing the annual carrying cost and the annual purchase-order cost (or setup cost) for each of several selected order sizes.
   a. The order size with the least total cost would be the approximate economic order quantity.
   b. This is illustrated by the key textbook Exhibit 22–1.
2. The EOQ may be computed more quickly and more accurately by a well-known formula:

$$E = \sqrt{\frac{2AP}{S}}$$

where E = Order size in units
A = Annual quantity used in units
P = Cost per purchase order
S = Annual cost of carrying one unit in stock one year

3. Total relevant costs may be easily computed by another widely used formula:

$$C = \sqrt{2APS}$$

   a. This is the minimum total relevant costs at the EOQ level.

D. The EOQ model for inventory decisions contains some important implications for accountants.

1. By studying the graph of relevant costs in Exhibit 22–2, you can easily see that the EOQ falls at the lowest point in a range where the total-cost curve tends to flatten.
   a. In other words, the total costs are affected very little by errors in the approximations of unit costs; for example, the carrying cost per unit.
   b. Thus, an important feature of inventory decisions is that they are usually not affected by small variations in cost predictions.
2. Inventory control for the benefit of the entire organization can often be complex and difficult because of the natural conflicts among the management objectives generally associated with the main functions of the business: sales, production, purchasing, and financing.
   a. For example, a production manager would usually like to have longer (and less frequent) production runs, because they tend to produce lower annual costs chargeable to him, although larger inventories must be carried.
   b. Thus, the performance-evaluation system must be designed so that the carrying costs are charged to the appropriate manager, even though not all such costs are recorded by the usual accounting system.
3. Some inventory costs are difficult to identify and to measure because they are *opportunity costs,* which ordinarily are not entered in conventional accounting records, for example:
   a. Foregone quantity discounts,
   b. Foregone contributions to profit from sales lost due to inventory shortages, and
   c. Foregone fortuitous purchases because existing stock inhibits additional purchases.
4. Some inventory costs are not relevant to inventory planning and control decisions because they would be unchanged under different alternatives (for example, fixed rent or depreciation of warehouse).

E. Another key factor in applying inventory policy is the determination of the *reorder point,* the quantity level that automatically triggers a new order.

1. The inventory reorder point depends on several factors, which are graphed in Exhibit 22–3:
   a. The *economic order quantity* was described above.
   b. The *lead time* is the time interval between placing an order and receiving delivery.
   c. The *demand during lead time* is the expected average usage during lead time.
   d. The *safety stock* is the estimated minimum inventory quantity needed as a buffer or cushion against reasonable expected maximum usage.
2. The inventory reorder point is commonly computed as the safety stock plus expected average usage during lead time.
3. The optimum safety-stock level would minimize the total of two types of cost that are difficult to measure:
   a. *Inventory carrying costs* include interest on investment, warehousing costs, and losses due to deterioration and obsolescence.
   b. *Stockout costs* are costs of not carrying the inventory: expediting expenses and the costs of losing orders because of lack of inventory (loss of contribution margins and customer good will).
4. Exhibit 22–4 shows how the optimum safety stock can be estimated with the aid of probability measures of expected inventory usage.

F. When a huge number of different inventory items must be stocked, certain control techniques may be appropriate.

1. *The ABC approach* divides all inventory items into three classes based upon their *total consumption costs* (average usage for each item multiplied by the purchase price per unit).
   a. Class A items have the highest consumption costs and therefore justify the closest control: frequent ordering, low safety stocks, and special attention in placing and following up orders.
   b. Class C items have the lowest consumption costs and therefore justify less frequent ordering, higher safety stocks, and less paper work.
2. See the textbook Exhibit 22–5.

G. Inventory control is interdependent with production planning and requires systematic procedures for division of duties and handling of documents.

1. Although inventory control systems are being increasingly automated, human judgment is always needed when models must be revised to accommodate changing conditions.
2. The basic rules for internal control systems should always be observed; for example, the separation of recordkeeping duties from material-handling duties.

H. When identical material units are acquired at different times and prices, alternative methods are available for costing inventories (the textbook chapter appendix).

1. Essentially, these methods rest upon assumptions concerning the *sequence of cost flows;* that is, the method chosen directly affects the *timing* of the transfer of costs from inventory to expenses (costs of goods used or sold).
2. The *first-in, first-out method (FIFO)* assumes that the cost of the earliest-acquired stock is used first, whereas the *last-in, first-out method (LIFO)* makes the opposite assumption.
3. As a result, FIFO leaves the inventory valuation nearer current replacement costs, but LIFO tends to match current costs more closely with current sales.
4. By the same token, FIFO tends to match old costs with current sales, whereas LIFO values the inventory on an old-cost basis.

5. Therefore, compared to LIFO, the use of FIFO tends to show higher inventory and net-income measurements during periods of rising prices and lower figures for these when prices are falling.
   a. If prices are rising, LIFO shows less income than FIFO, and thus it tends to postpone the payment of income taxes.
   b. The use of LIFO also permits management to influence net-income measurement by deciding on the timing of purchases.
6. The average-inventory methods tend to produce figures for inventories and net income that fall between those for FIFO and LIFO.
7. The use of currently attainable standard costs produces variances that isolate the effects of price changes for managerial use (unlike FIFO, LIFO, and the average methods).
   a. This prevents price fluctuations from distorting management appraisals of efficiency.
   b. The use of standard costs also emphasizes and measures the impact of some price changes on overall company results.

SELF-TEST AND PRACTICE EXERCISES

I For each of the following multiple-choice and true-false statements, select the most appropriate answer and enter its identification letter in the space provided:

___ 1. Inventory control means: (a) minimizing errors in inventory measurements, (b) maximizing clerical accuracy in inventory documents and records, (c) minimizing inventory losses from fire and theft, (d) decreasing the chances for improper use of inventory, (e) determining and maintaining inventory investment at the optimum level.

___ 2. Inventories can serve as cushions: (a) to absorb planning errors and unforeseen fluctuations in supply and demand, (b) to facilitate smooth production and marketing operations, (c) both of the above, (d) neither of the above.

___ 3. Costs that are usually relevant to the inventory decision include: (a) carrying costs, (b) acquisition costs, (c) both of the above, (d) neither of these.

___ 4. EOQ is the optimum: (a) level of inventory, (b) time to order, (c) purchase quantity.

___ 5. EOQ is the quantity that would minimize the total relevant annual inventory carrying cost: (a) true, (b) false.

___ 6. The optimum size of a material-purchase order is the size that would minimize the total annual purchase-order cost: (a) true, (b) false.

___ 7. Small variations in cost predictions usually have: (a) significant effects on inventory decisions, (b) no effects on inventory decisions.

___ 8. A production manager would usually prefer: (a) short production runs, (b) long production runs.

___ 9. A decrease in quantity discounts offered by suppliers would tend to have the following effect on the economic order quantity: (a) increase, (b) no effect, (c) decrease.

___ 10. Examples of inventory costs that would usually not be relevant to inventory decisions include: (a) imputed interest on investment in inventories, (b) salaries of storekeepers and clerks, (c) both of the above, (d) neither of the above.

___ 11. The inventory reorder point would tend to be increased by: (a) a decrease in the expected usage of material during lead time, (b) an increase in the expected usage of material during lead time, (c) neither of the above.

___ 12. The quantity of the safety stock plus average usage during lead time is equal to: (a) optimum inventory balance, (b) economic order quantity, (c) both of the above, (d) neither of the above.

___ 13. The optimum safety-stock level would minimize: (a) stockout costs, (b) inventory carrying costs, (c) the sum of the above, (d) the difference between (a) and (b).

___ 14. The "two-bin" inventory system is designed to: (a) identify responsibility for inventory, (b) signal reorder of inventory items, (c) both of the above, (d) neither of the above.

___ 15. When the "ABC method" is used for inventory control, the inventory items with the highest safety stocks would be: (a) type A, (b) type B, (c) type C.

___ 16. The increasing computerization of inventory control systems promises to eradicate completely the need for the use of human judgment in inventory control: (a) true, (b) false.

___ 17. Making choices between the FIFO and LIFO inventory methods will affect the transfer of: (a) specific inventory *units* to production or to customers, (b) inventory *costs* to production or sales, (c) both of the above, (d) neither of the above.

___ 18. Compared to the FIFO method, LIFO tends to: (a) leave the inventory valuation closer to current replacement costs, (b) match current costs more closely with current sales.

___ 19. During a period of rising prices, the use of the LIFO method, in comparison to FIFO, will tend to produce: (a) lower reported net income, (b) higher reported cost of goods sold, (c) both of the above, (d) neither of the above.

___ 20. The effects of price changes are automatically isolated for managerial use by: (a) the FIFO method, (b) the LIFO method, (c) the weighted-average method, (d) a standard-cost system.

II Complete each of the following statements:

1. The optimum level of inventory would minimize ______________________________

____

2. The optimum size of a normal purchase order for replenishing materials is called ______________

____

3. The interval between placing an order and receiving delivery is called ______________

____

4. The estimated minimum inventory quantity needed as a buffer or cushion against reasonable expected maximum usage is called ______________

____

5. In general the inventory reorder point is the sum of ______________________________

______________ and ______________

____

6. The "ABC method" ranks inventory items in ______________________________

order of ______________________________

______________________________ and divides all the items into ______________________________ groups.

7. During a period of rising prices, the use of the average method of costing inventories would tend to produce inventory costs above ______________ cost and below ______________ cost.

III Given for Material AOK of Precision Puzzle Company:

Total annual requirements	3,000 units
Relevant carrying costs per unit per year	$5
Relevant costs per purchase order	$300
Inventory level when each order arrives	zero

1. Using the form below, compute the total relevant costs associated with ordering one, two, five, ten, and twenty times per year:

Number of orders per year	One	Two	Five	Ten	Twenty
Order size					
Average inventory in units					
Relevant annual carrying cost					
Relevant annual purchase-order cost					
Total relevant annual costs					
2. Check one blank for least-cost order size					

3. Using the formula, compute the economic order quantity (EOQ):

4. Using the formula, compute the total relevant annual costs at the EOQ level:

IV Given for Material PDQ of Enigma, Incorporated:

Maximum daily usage	80 units
Average daily usage	70 units
Minimum daily usage	60 units
Lead time	22 days

1. Compute the safety stock ______ units

2. Determine the reorder point ______ units

V Given for Material RPM of Acceleration Manufacturing Company:

April 1 inventory: 40 units at $20 cost each $800

Purchases:

April 13, 50 units at $21 each
April 20, 80 units at $22 each
April 27, 30 units at $24 each

April 30 inventory: 60 units

Compute the following total costs:	FIFO	LIFO	Weighted Average
Cost of April 30 inventory	$	$	$
Cost of materials used in April	$	$	$
Total	$	$	$

23 Cost Accounting and Linear Programming

COST ACCOUNTING TODAY is not a narrow field, separate and distinct from other areas; it is an important part of the information system needed for executive decision making. For example, as we have seen in the preceding chapter, management decisions are often facilitated by various kinds of mathematical models that typically depend on accounting data for their usefulness.

This chapter deals with the fundamentals of another widely known mathematical decision model, **linear programming (LP).** This is a formal approach to the short-run assignment of limited productive resources for use in an optimal manner. As a modern management accountant, you should be able to recognize the situations for which LP would be feasible, to construct the appropriate models, to deal effectively with computer programmers in solving LP problems, and to understand the principal implications for managers and accountants.

REVIEW SUMMARY

A. *Linear programming* is a mathematical search procedure for finding the optimum solution to certain types of short-run problems.

1. The objective of LP is to determine, for a fixed set of available resources, the combination of products or services that maximizes profits or minimizes costs.
   - **a.** For example, a typical problem is the determination of the optimal quantity of two or more products to process through a series of manufacturing operations.
   - **b.** The basic idea was described in Chapter 11: to determine these quantities on the basis of the maximum contribution per unit of the *scarce resource* or *constraining factor,* such as total available machine-hours.
   - **c.** However, in practice there is usually more than one constraint—often many—and it is these situations for which the LP model is appropriate.
2. The most crucial step in solving an LP problem is to build the LP model.
   - **a.** Essentially this means the formulation of the *simultaneous linear equations* to express the relationships of numerous variables.
   - **b.** Most LP problems have so many variables that these equations must be solved by digital computers (typically with the aid of computer programmers).

c. The formulation of the equations is, of course, the most crucial step, not the mechanics of the solution.

3. Your most helpful key to understanding how to set up the LP equations is the textbook example on which most of the chapter is based.
   a. The first step is to construct an equation to express the objective. This equation is an *objective function* to be maximized or minimized.
   b. The second step is to determine the basic relationships: to construct in mathematical form the *inequalities* to reflect the applicable *constraints* imposed by scarce resources.
   c. Your understanding of these constraints can be greatly aided if you trace them to the graph in textbook Exhibit 23–1.
4. The textbook refers to three different ways for solving an LP problem:
   a. The graphic approach (Exhibit 23–1) is practicable only in the simplest of situations, but it is used here mainly to help you grasp the principal idea that the optimal solution is typically at a corner of the "area of feasible production combinations," the polygon bounded by straight lines representing constraints.
   b. Manual trial-and-error computations can be used to arrive at the optimal solution in a simple case like the textbook example. You should carefully follow these computations and trace them to the graphic solution in Exhibit 23–1.
   c. However, the solution to most LP problems requires digital computers for performing an *iterative* (step-by-step) process called the *simplex method.*
   d. Accountants and managers should concentrate on a careful and accurate construction of the LP model, because solutions obtained through linear programming are, of course, no more reliable than the data used in formulating the LP equations.

B. All approaches to solving LP problems are based, in essence, on the *substitution of the scarce resource* (productive capacity) among two or more products that can be processed through a particular operation.
   1. Moving from one corner of the polygon of feasible solutions to another corner involves giving up the contribution margin of one product and adding the contribution margin of another product.
   2. You should be certain to understand this key concept. See the related corners in the graph (Exhibit 23–1).

C. LP problems have important implications for managers and accountants.
   1. It is, of course, impossible to predict (or measure) accurately all relevant revenues, costs, and technical coefficients in an LP model.
      a. Thus, managers and accountants need to know the possible effects on the optimal solutions that may be due to errors of prediction (or measurement).
      b. These effects can be determined by making a *sensitivity analysis* in order to find the *cost of the prediction error* for selected differences in predicting certain data.
      c. In some cases, although the total contribution margin will be affected by prediction errors, there may be no change in the selection of the optimal combination of products to make.
      d. Sensitivity analysis can also reveal how much prediction error can be tolerated before the optimal choice (decision) would change.
   2. Prediction errors can often be reduced by spending more money to obtain better information or to implement predictions; thus, a *cost-benefit approach* is often appropriate.
   3. The determination of possible changes in total contribution margins *by expanding capacity* can be facilitated by computations of *shadow prices.*
      a. These are opportunity costs that measure contributions foregone by failing to have an additional unit of a scarce resource in a particular situation.
      b. Shadow prices are customarily provided by LP computer programs.

4. The use of LP techniques requires at least two basic assumptions, and these are important limitations that managers must face in deciding whether to use an LP approach in a given case:
   a. All relationships between capacity and production are *linear.*
   b. All data used in the equations for the LP model are *stated in certain terms.* (Probability factors do not *appear* in the equations, although probabilities may have been *used* to forecast the data appearing in the equations.)

SELF-TEST AND PRACTICE EXERCISES

I For each of the following multiple-choice and true-false statements, select the most appropriate answer and enter its identification letter in the space provided:

____ 1. The most appropriate use for LP models is for long-term decisions involving linear relationships and probability factors: (a) true, (b) false.

____ 2. A typical objective of linear programming is: (a) to measure the quality of production, (b) to control the quality of production, (c) to forecast completion dates for special projects, (d) none of the above.

____ 3. The most critical phase of linear programming is using digital computers in solving simultaneous linear equations: (a) true, (b) false.

____ 4. LP models typically have: (a) no constraints, (b) one constraint, (c) two constraints, (d) more than two constraints.

____ 5. In an LP model there is usually only one: (a) objective function, (b) feasible alternative, (c) both of these, (d) neither of these.

____ 6. All of the equal total-contribution-margin lines on an LP graph show the slope of the objective function: (a) true, (b) false.

____ 7. Sensitivity analysis can be used in LP situations to: (a) find the cost of the prediction error, (b) determine how much prediction error can be tolerated before the optimal choice would change, (c) both of these, (d) neither of these.

____ 8. The assumptions or requirements that underlie the use of LP techniques include: (a) nonlinear relationships between capacity and production, (b) statement of equations in probabilistic terms, (c) both of the above, (d) neither of the above.

____ 9. In practice, the optimum solution to an LP problem is usually determined by: (a) a graphic approach, (b) the simplex method.

____ 10. In LP problems, there are typically several: (a) feasible alternatives, (b) constraints, (c) both of the above, (d) neither of the above.

____ 11. Solutions to most LP problems require: (a) digital computers, (b) an iterative process, (c) both of the above, (d) neither of the above.

II Complete each of the following statements:

1. Linear programming is a mathematical search procedure for finding the best solution to short-run problems for____________________

____

2. The equation that expresses the objective in an LP problem is called ____________________

____

3. The mathematical expressions of inequalities for an LP problem represent ____________________

____

4. The coefficients of the constraints are often called ____________________

____

5. Alternative LP solutions that are technically possible are called ______________________________

____

6. In the graphic solution to an LP problem, the optimal combination of resources generally lies at a polygon corner through which an ______________ ______________________ line can be drawn that is furthest from the origin.

7. Opportunity costs that measure contributions foregone by failing to have an additional unit of a scarce resource in a particular situation are called

____

III Effortless Perfume Company, which can produce either of two kinds of perfume called Explore and Encore, furnishes the following data:

Product	Daily Capacity in Product Units Process Q	Process T	Contribution Margin per Product Unit
Explore (*X*)	200	400	$ 7.00
or			
Encore (*Y*)	400	160	$ 8.00

Severe material shortages for Encore will limit its production to a maximum of 150 per day. Assuming that daily capacities in *total machine-hours* are 200 for Process Q and 400 for Process T, compute:

1. Process Q machine-hours required per *Y* product unit: . . . . ______ hours

2. Process T machine hours required per *Y* product unit: . . . . ______ hours

Develop the relevant equations for a linear programming solution:

3. Maximum total contribution margin = ______________________________

4. Process Q constraint: ______________________________

5. Process T constraint: ______________________________

6. Material shortage constraint: ______________________________

7. Negative production constraints: ______________________________

IV Thorough Soap Company has determined the exact coordinates of each corner of the area of feasible combinations for an LP problem to maximize total contribution margin for two products, P and Q, respectively:

(7, 2) (8, 11) (4, 3) (3, 9)

Contribution-margin rates per units of product are:

	Predicted	Actual
Product P	\$2	\$3
Product Q	\$7	\$5

1. Compute the cost of the prediction error.

2. Assume that the object is to minimize total direct-labor costs and that the actual predicted dollars shown above are direct-labor cost rates instead of contribution-margin rates. Compute the cost of the prediction error.

COST BEHAVIOR AND REGRESSION ANALYSIS 24

CHAPTER 9 INTRODUCED the important and complex problem of searching for cost-behavior patterns (**cost functions**) that can be useful for predicting costs under various circumstances. Explained were several methods for determining cost functions. However, each of these methods had some significant limitations.

This chapter goes further into the problem of making accurate predictions of costs. It explains **regression analysis** and the **least-squares method,** well-known mathematical techniques for measuring relationships among variables.

REVIEW SUMMARY

(Including Chapter Appendix)

A. The first step in determining cost functions is a survey and an examination of the ledger accounts.

   1. This is true whether the determination is to be made by the methods of Chapter 9 or by regression analysis.

B. An important technique for approximating cost functions is *regression analysis.*

   1. *Simple regression analysis* measures the average amount of change in one variable that is associated with unit increases in another variable.

   2. *Multiple regression analysis,* which uses more than one independent variable, can sometimes substantially improve predictions of cost made by simple regression analysis.

   3. This textbook chapter and its appendix deal almost exclusively with simple regression analysis.

C. For a helpful introduction to simple regression analysis, see the chapter appendix example of the historical sampling data regarding the relationship of direct-labor costs to batch size.

   1. The first step is to select two variables and plot them on a *scatter diagram* to detect any unusual features that need further investigation:

      x: batch size, the independent variable
      y: direct labor costs, the dependent variable

2. Second, use the mathematical *method of least squares* (if the function seems to be linear) as an objective way to determine the equation for the particular regression line.
3. The regression line is the line that will *most precisely fit* the data plotted for the two variables.
4. However, this line represents only an estimation of the *average* values of y for different x values.
5. A useful statistic that should be computed is the *coefficient of correlation,* a measure of the extent to which the independent variable accounts for the variability in the dependent variable.
6. In order to determine the accuracy of the regression line for prediction purposes, one may compute the *standard error of estimate,* a measure of the scatter of the actual observations about the regression line.
7. Digital computer programs are widely available for regression analysis and for the routine computations of such tests as the above, including *confidence intervals,* so that the accountant can more easily choose the most appropriate independent variable in a given instance.

D. As pointed out by the textbook chapter, managers and accountants should be aware of certain limitations and pitfalls in the use of regression analysis to predict costs.

1. Guidelines should be followed in choosing from various possible regressions that use different independent variables.
2. Three main criteria should be met in order for regression analysis to be useful:
   - **a.** Economic plausibility and correlation
   - **b.** Goodness of fit
   - **c.** Specification analysis
3. *Economic plausibility:* The regression should make economic sense to the manager and the accountant.
   - **a.** Physical relationships that can be implicitly determined through logic and a knowledge of operations are useful in meeting the plausibility test.
   - **b.** *A high correlation between two variables merely indicates that the two variables move together and does not prove a cause-and-effect relationship* (for example, church attendance and beer consumption!).
4. *Goodness of fit:* This criterion involves steps that help measure the degree of plausibility of the cost function.
   - **a.** Useful statistical tests include *r-square* (coefficient of determination) and the *t-value* for the slope of the regression line.
   - **b.** The "fixed-cost" part of the cost function must be interpreted cautiously, because the regression line is not necessarily valid in its extensions *beyond the relevant range.*
5. *Specification analysis:* This criterion deals with various statistical pitfalls to be guarded against or allowed for.
   - **a.** The use of canned computer programs without professional help from statisticians might result in the application of statistical tools inappropriate to the particular circumstances.
   - **b.** Regression analysis inherently assumes that the relationships will persist, and therefore it should not be used for *nonrepetitive operations.*
   - **c.** The validity of inferences from sample data about population relationships depends on four conditions, all of which must be satisfied:
     Linearity between x and y in the population. This can be easily checked by a scatter diagram.

Constant variance (homoscedasticity), the uniform and random scattering of deviations around the regression line. Again, the scatter diagram furnishes the easiest proof.

Independence from each other of the deviations from points about the regression line.

Normal distribution of points around the regression line.

SELF-TEST AND PRACTICE EXERCISES

I For each of the following multiple-choice and true-false statements, select the most appropriate answer and enter its identification letter in the space provided:

___ 1. Regression analysis is used in cost accounting for the primary purpose of: (a) increasing the precision of cost measurements, (b) determining cause-and-effect relationships, (c) aiding in cost prediction, (d) assisting in the assignment of cost responsibilities.

___ 2. The regression line determined by the least-squares method is: (a) straight, (b) curved.

___ 3. The first step that should be taken in a simple regression-analysis approach is: (a) to calculate the coefficient of correlation, (b) to make the least-squares computations, (c) to plot two variables on a scatter diagram, (d) to find the standard error of estimate.

___ 4. For making regression-analysis computations, digital computer programs are: (a) usually available, (b) seldom available.

___ 5. Canned computer programs for regression analysis can generally be used quite safely without professional help from statisticians: (a) true, (b) false.

___ 6. In cost accounting, regression analysis is appropriate for: (a) repetitive operations, (b) nonrepetitive operations, (c) both of the above, (d) neither of the above.

___ 7. A high degree of correlation between two variables is proof of a cause-and-effect relationship: (a) true, (b) false.

II Complete each of the following statements:

1. A mathematical technique that measures the average amount of change in one variable that is associated with unit increases in another variable is called ______________________

2. In the formula for a straight line, $y = a + bx$, b measures ______________________ and is called ______________________

____

3. The mathematical method for determining the equation for a particular regression line is called ______________________

____

4. The uniform and random scattering of deviations around the regression line is called ______________________

____

5. The regression line is not necessarily valid in its extensions beyond______________________

____

III An accountant for Perceptions, Unlimited made ten monthly observations of a certain cost as a basis for developing a cost-prediction formula. A scatter diagram indicates a mixed-cost behavior: **y = a + bx.** The observations and certain computations from them are condensed below:

Month	Hours	Cost	Hours Squared	Cost Squared	Hours Times Cost
1	30	$ 50	900	2,500	1,500
2	20	40	400	1,600	800
etc.	etc.	etc.	etc.	etc.	etc.
Totals	300	$400	7,000	15,000	9,600

1. Find the predicted variable cost per hour by the least-squares method.

2. Find the predicted amount of fixed cost by the least-squares method.

Some formulas: $\Sigma y = na + b(\Sigma x); \ \Sigma xy = a(\Sigma x) + b(\Sigma x^2)$

$$a = \frac{(\Sigma y)(\Sigma x^2) - (\Sigma x)(\Sigma xy)}{n(\Sigma x^2) - (\Sigma x)^2}$$

$$b = \frac{n(\Sigma xy) - (\Sigma x)(\Sigma y)}{n(\Sigma x^2) - (\Sigma x)^2}$$

3. What is the flexible-budget formula for this cost?

25 VARIANCES: MIX, YIELD, AND INVESTIGATION

VARIANCE ANALYSIS is usually more complicated than the relatively simple situations assumed previously, because most companies produce several types of products in different combinations or mixes and also utilize different mixes of materials in manufacturing a given type of product. For convenience in dealing with these and related problems, the chapter is divided into three major parts, each of which can be studied independently.

The first part demonstrates how computations of **sales-quantity** and **sales-mix variances** can be included in the analysis of the total difference between actual and budgeted contribution margins. The second part describes procedures for including **production-yield** and **production-mix variances** in the analysis of the difference between actual and budgeted manufacturing costs. The third part of the chapter distinguishes between variances or deviations due to chance (**random deviations**) and those due to other causes. This part also includes an approach to investigating variances that uses probabilities and predictions for comparing expected costs and benefits.

REVIEW SUMMARY

PART ONE: SALES-QUANTITY AND SALES-MIX VARIANCES

A. For management control purposes, it is useful to analyze the difference between the actual and budgeted amounts of a company's *contribution margin* (sales minus variable costs).

1. The simplest approach to explaining the total variance between budgeted and actual operations is to make a product-by-product analysis having three components: price, efficiency, and volume variances.

a. The central example for this part of the chapter (textbook Exhibit 25–1) shows variances that are due only to the *sales volume component.*

b. Note in this example that there are no changes from the static budget in product selling prices or variable costs per unit, and thus the unit contribution margin is unchanged for each of the two products, A and B.

2. As the example shows, the *total sales volume* in units did not change from the budget, but there were changes in the *physical proportions* of the two products, and hence a *sales mix variance.*
   a. Observe that the total contribution margin was $60,000 more than budgeted because a larger proportion of the higher-margin Product B was actually sold than was specified in the original mix.
   b. The *sales volume variance* in a situation like this could be subdivided into *quantity* and *mix* variances.
   c. However, a more straightforward analysis of the volume variance shows that the $60,000 improvement in total contribution margin was simply the excess of the $70,000 favorable variance in Product B's contribution margin over the $10,000 unfavorable variance in the contribution margin of Product A.
   d. The main point this example illustrates is that in using cost-volume-profit analysis, one must be aware of the effects of underlying assumptions, particularly as to the product mix.
   e. For example, if the specified proportions of Products A and B are maintained at various volume levels in this case, the *average* contribution margin per unit would not be affected by volume changes.

PART TWO: PRODUCTION-YIELD AND PRODUCTION-MIX VARIANCES

B. Manufacturing processes often involve different mixes of materials to make a specific product.
   1. *Mix* means the relative proportion or combination of the various ingredients of direct materials or of the components of a finished product line.
   2. *Yield* means the quantity of finished output produced from a predetermined or standard combination and amount of inputs such as direct material or direct labor.
   3. Changes in the specified mix of inputs will, of course, affect yield or output.
   4. The usual analysis can be made of the difference between actual inputs at actual prices and standard inputs allowed at standard prices, as shown by the textbook example of material costs:
      a. The *price variance* would be the difference between the actual inputs at actual prices and the actual inputs at standard prices.
      b. The *efficiency variance* would be the difference between actual inputs at standard prices and standard inputs allowed at standard prices.
   5. However, a manager may want a more exhaustive analysis of the efficiency variance (for example, the $763 favorable variance for materials):
      a. The *material yield variance* would be the difference between the units of input and the budgeted average price per unit of input ($1,863 F).
      b. The *material mix variance* would be the difference between the units of input multiplied by the difference between budgeted and average price per unit ($1,000 U).
      c. Note that these two variances account for the material efficiency variance:

$$\$1,863 - \$1,100 = \$763 \text{ F.}$$

      d. A similar analysis is illustrated in the textbook for direct-labor cost.
   6. You should especially try to understand the yield variance.
      a. This variance assumes that the standard combination of inputs is not changed.
      b. Thus, the yield variance is defined as the anticipated change in expected cost because output deviated from that expected for the total actual inputs.

C. Usually, of course, the actual costs of any process differ from the expected, budgeted, or standard costs.

1. The variances or deviations from standards may be classified into five types on the basis of their *causes,* or *sources,* each type involving different management decisions for corrective actions:

a. An *implementation deviation* is a human or mechanical failure to achieve a specific obtainable action. This is largely the *traditional concept* of cost variances.

b. A *prediction deviation* is an error in predicting a parameter value in the decision model.

c. A *measurement deviation* is an error measuring the actual cost of operating a process.

d. A *model deviation* is an error in the functional representation or formulation of the decision model.

e. A *random deviation* is a difference between actual cost and expected cost due to chance, which by definition is a deviation that calls for *no corrective action.*

2. When deviations from standards are reported in manufacturing processes, management must decide whether to investigate them.

a. Unfortunately, such deviations are often quite difficult to analyze, because *interdependencies* typically exist among the different kinds of processes, deviations, and investigations.

b. Conceptually, the decision to investigate performance deviations would be made if the expected benefits from the investigation exceeded the expected costs of the investigation.

c. The textbook example (see Exhibit 25–2) describes mathematical models that use probabilities and predicted costs in developing three critical figures that can aid the decision maker:

(1) The expected cost of the decision to investigate,

(2) The expected cost of the decision not to investigate,

(3) The level of the probability of being out of control that would equalize the expected costs of investigating and the expected costs of not investigating (*point of indifference,* or *breakeven point*).

d. The rules of thumb or intuition often used in practice are models that are simpler than these mathematical models, but they nevertheless implicitly recognize the same variables used in the mathematical models.

3. *Statistical quality control (SQC)* techniques are often used to distinguish between random deviations and other deviations as a first step in deciding whether to investigate deviations or variations from standards.

a. In practice, actual performance may vary from a *single* standard and yet fall within a *band,* or *range,* of acceptable results.

b. SQC offers means for distinguishing between deviations falling within the acceptable band (*random variances*) and those falling outside the band (*nonrandom variances*).

c. Random variances are due to chance, and they do not need investigation.

d. Nonrandom variances are due to other causes, and they do require investigation.

SELF-TEST AND PRACTICE EXERCISES

I For each of the following multiple-choice and true-false statements, select the most appropriate answer and enter its identification letter in the space provided:

PART ONE

___ 1. The sales volume variance is the difference between some initial or original budgeted or expected output and the actual output, multiplied by: (a) actual price, (b) standard price.

___ 2. A sales-mix variance is due to changes in: (a) total volume of product units sold, (b) prices of product units sold, (c) a combination of total volume and prices, (d) none of the above.

___ 3. The sales volume variance minus the sales mix variance would be equal to the sales quantity variance: (a) true, (b) false.

PART TWO

___ 4. In the context of this chapter, yield means: (a) budgeted net income or contribution margin, (b) changes in outputs caused by changes in the physical proportions of inputs, (c) quantity of outputs from a standard combination of inputs, (d) none of the above.

___ 5. Efficiency variance is the standard price multiplied by the difference between actual inputs and standard inputs allowed: (a) true, (b) false.

___ 6. The yield variance: (a) assumes that the standard combination of inputs is not changed, (b) is defined as the anticipated changes in expected cost because output deviated from that expected for the total actual inputs, (c) both of the above, (d) neither of the above.

PART THREE

___ 7. The traditional concept of cost variances from standard is represented by: (a) prediction deviations, (b) random deviations, (c) implementation deviations, (d) model deviations, (e) measurement deviations.

___ 8. A deviation in predicting a parameter value in the decision model is conceptually: (a) a model deviation, (b) a prediction deviation, (c) both of the above, (d) neither of the above.

___ 9. A random deviation of actual costs from standard costs: (a) is due to chance, (b) requires no corrective action, (c) both of the above, (d) neither of the above.

___ 10. The textbook mathematical models for determining whether to investigate performance deviations use: (a) probabilities, (b) predicted costs, (c) both of the above, (d) neither of the above.

___ 11. If the probability of being out of control exceeds the point of indifference, investigation of the deviation is generally: (a) desirable, (b) not desirable.

___ 12. In practice, the actual performance of manufacturing processes is usually acceptable: (a) only if it meets the single standard of performance, (b) if it falls within a predetermined band or range.

___ 13. The main objective of statistical quality control (SQC) is: (a) to classify products according to their quality, (b) to measure the total difference between standard costs and actual costs, (c) to distinguish between random and nonrandom variances from standard performance, (d) to measure individual variances from standard performance.

___ 14. It would not be necessary to seek causes for observations that fall within the normal band determined by SQC techniques: (a) true, (b) false.

II Complete each of the following statements:

PART ONE

1. The sales volume is composed of two elements:

(a) ________________________________

(b) ________________________________

2. The sales mix is defined as ____________________

____

____

3. The total variance in contribution margin is the difference between ____________________

____

PART TWO

4. The material price variance is the difference between the actual and standard unit price multiplied by ____________________

____

5. The yield variance is the difference between the standard combination of inputs for actual output at standard prices and ____________________

____

PART THREE

6. When the difference between actual cost and expected cost is due to chance, it is called ____________

____

7. Conceptually, the management decision to investigate performance deviations would be made if the ____________________ exceeded the ____________________

____

8. A useful first step in deciding whether to investigate variances from standard performances is to distinguish between ____________________ ____________ and ____________

____

9. ____________________ is a general approach that relies on classical statistics techniques for identifying random deviations and for deciding when to investigate deviations.

PART ONE

III This problem is based on the textbook case presented in Exhibit 25–1. However you need to use only the following data in working the problem:

Product	Unit Contribution Margin	Budgeted Unit Sales	Actual Unit Sales
A	$1.00	120,000	130,000
B	7.00	40,000	38,000
Weighted Average	2.50		

Assume that actual contribution margins for Products A and B are the same per unit as budgeted: $1.00 and $7.00.

1. Compute the following amounts:
   (a) Total budgeted contribution margin .... $ ________
   (b) Total actual contribution margin .... $ ________
   (c) Total variance to be accounted for .... $ ________
2. Prepare a detailed analysis of the sales volume variance:
   Product A: .... $ ________

Product B: .... $ ______

Total sales volume variance .... $ ______

3. Break the sales volume variance into these two subparts:
   (a) Quantity variance:
   Product A: .... $ ______

   Product B: .... $ ______

   Total quantity variance .... $ ______

   (b) Sales-mix variance:
   Product A: .... $ ______

   Product B: .... $ ______

   Total sales-mix variance .... $ ______

4. (a) Which of the analyses above seems more helpful in understanding what happened: 2 or 3? ______
   (b) Give reasons to support your answer:

PART TWO

IV Intricate Electronics Inc. presents the following data concerning its direct-materials cost:

Actual output:	
Actual inputs at actual prices	$59,100
Actual inputs at standard prices	$60,200
Standard inputs allowed at standard prices	$58,800
Standard cost of standard combination of inputs	$57,500

Compute the following material variances:

1. Flexible-budget variance .... $ ______

2. Price variance .... $ ______

3. Efficiency variance .... $ ______

4. Yield variance .... $ ______

5. Mix variance .... $ ______

PART THREE

V Given for the Balancing Process of the Candid Scales Company:

Cost of investigation (C)	$ 2,400
Cost of correcting the deviation (M)	$10,000
Present value of costs that could be saved by correcting the deviation (L)	$40,000
Probability of being out of control	.05

1. Summarize these data in a decision table.

2. Compute the expected cost of the decision to investigate .... $ ______

3. Compute the expected cost of the decision not to investigate.............. $ ______

4. Compute the out-of-control probability at the point of indifference (breakeven point) .... $ ______

26 Accounting for Payroll

ACCOUNTING FOR PAYROLL involves employees' earnings and related fringe-benefit costs, payroll taxes, and government requirements for keeping records and filing tax returns. This chapter presents the main accounting concepts and procedures for dealing with these matters and the accompanying payroll deductions and liabilities. The nature and cost effects of each type of payroll tax are explained, and the accounting treatment of each principal payroll transaction is described.

Textbook Exhibits 26–1 and 26–2 serve as useful summaries and checklists of the main payroll-tax matters: tax assessments, requirements for filing tax returns, and deadlines for making tax payments. The extended textbook illustration of typical payroll accounting entries can be quite helpful to you in tying together and understanding the main payroll transactions. Exhibit 26–3 is especially helpful in relating different kinds of incentive pay plans to types of organizations and their management styles.

REVIEW SUMMARY

A. Today, many subtractions must be made by employers from employees' *gross earnings* to arrive at their *net earnings* or *take-home pay.*

1. These subtractions, usually called *payroll deductions* or *withholdings,* are merely parts of an employee's gross earnings that are being transferred to third parties.
2. The main withholdings are two kinds of taxes levied on employees and deducted from their earnings by employers, who serve in effect as tax-collection agents.
    - **a.** Government schedules show the amounts of estimated *income taxes* on employees that should be withheld for the many different combinations of gross earnings and dependents.
    - **b.** The Social Security tax, or Federal Insurance Contributions Act tax (*F.I.C.A. tax* or *F.O.A.B. tax*), on employees, designed primarily to provide retirement pensions, is computed by applying a specified percent to gross earnings, the 1981 rate being 6.7% of the first $29,700 of gross earnings per employee in the calendar year. (These figures increase almost yearly.)

3. In addition to the two tax deductions described above, there are many other payroll withholdings not required by law, such as employee contributions to group life insurance plans, group hospitalization insurance plans, pension funds, and employee savings plans; payment of union dues; and donations to charities.
4. The accounting for payroll deductions may be accomplished in three steps:
   a. When the employer records labor costs incurred, debit the appropriate cost accounts (for example, the accounts for work in process, factory overhead, selling and administrative expense) with gross earnings, which, of course, include all payroll deductions. Credit Accrued Payroll for the total gross earnings owed to employees.
   b. Debit Accrued Payroll and credit the separate liability accounts for the various items deducted from gross earnings.
   c. When the employer pays each payroll-related liability, debit the appropriate liability account and credit the cash account.

B. Labor costs incurred *by employers* include, in addition to the gross earnings of employees, two other kinds of costs (*fringe labor costs*) that typically amount to a large fraction of total employment costs:

1. Payroll taxes are assessed against employers.
   a. *Federal and state unemployment taxes* apply only to the first $6,000 earned by each employee each calendar year (1981).
   b. *F.I.C.A. taxes* apply only to the first $29,700 earned by each employee each calendar year (1981). This is *in addition* to the equal amount of F.I.C.A. taxes assessed against employees and deducted from their gross earnings.
2. Other labor costs are borne by employers.
   a. These include workmen's compensation insurance, vacations and paid holidays, and employers' contributions to pension funds and to health and life insurance plans.
   b. These costs are in addition to those borne by employees through payroll deductions.
3. When these fringe labor costs accrue, debits are made to appropriate cost accounts and credits are made to the related liability accounts.
   a. *In theory,* these fringe costs should be charged to the *same accounts* to which the gross earnings are charged; for example, the Work-in-Process account for direct-labor costs.
   b. *In practice,* however, the fringe labor costs for *all* factory labor, both direct and indirect, are usually charged to the *Factory Overhead Control account.*
4. Each liability account is, of course, debited when paid in cash.

C. A separate payroll bank account facilitates the control, preparation, and reconciliation of huge numbers of payroll checks.

D. In use today are a wide variety of *incentive wage plans* that provide additional compensation to employees for part of the cost savings that employees make possible by increasing their rates of production.

1. Although these plans generally add to clerical costs and may tend to increase spoilage costs, they often produce favorable net results.
2. In no event, however, would an incentive wage plan automatically substitute for adequate management as the most effective way of controlling labor costs.
   a. The choice of an incentive plan depends heavily on the type of organization and its style of management.
   b. See the excellent textbook Exhibit 26–3 for four important organization factors and their relationship to different kinds of incentive pay plans.

SELF-TEST AND PRACTICE EXERCISES

I For each of the following multiple-choice and true-false statements, select the most appropriate answer and enter its identification letter in the space provided.

___ 1. Accounting for payroll is significantly involved with: (a) payroll taxes, (b) employment fringe benefits, (c) both of the above, (d) neither of the above.

___ 2. Typically, there is little difference between an employee's gross earnings and his net earnings after payroll deductions: (a) true, (b) false.

___ 3. Payroll withholdings for taxes should be charged to tax-expense accounts: (a) true, (b) false.

___ 4. The Social Security tax is also called: (a) the F.I.C.A. tax, (b) the F.O.A.B. tax, (c) both of the above, (d) neither of the above.

___ 5. Payroll taxes that are ordinarily borne by both employees and their employers include: (a) the F.I.C.A. tax, (b) the Federal Unemployment Insurance tax, (c) both of the above, (d) neither of the above.

___ 6. Deductions for payroll taxes are the only deductions that are allowed to be made from the gross earnings of employees: (a) true, (b) false.

___ 7. In general, there is no upper limit to the annual amount of employees' earnings subject to: (a) F.I.C.A. taxes, (b) Federal Unemployment taxes, (c) both of the above, (d) neither of the above.

___ 8. Fringe labor costs of employers would generally include part of the: (a) F.I.C.A. taxes, (b) individual federal income taxes, (c) both of the above, (d) neither of the above.

___ 9. The fringe labor costs incurred by employers could include: (a) part of the cost of life insurance on lives of employees, (b) all of the federal unemployment taxes, (c) both of the above, (d) neither of the above.

___ 10. The amounts of fringe labor costs in relation to gross earnings of employees are typically: (a) quite large, (b) very small.

___ 11. Most companies treat fringe costs on direct labor as overhead costs: (a) true, (b) false.

___ 12. Federal and state unemployment taxes apply to no more than the statutory maximum of earnings paid to the employee in a calendar year: (a) true, (b) false.

___ 13. In effect, equal amounts of taxes are assessed against employees and employers for: (a) federal unemployment taxes, (b) state unemployment taxes, (c) both of the above, (d) neither of the above.

___ 14. In practice, employer payroll taxes are usually allocated by employers over the year, using a leveled rate: (a) true, (b) false.

___ 15. Theoretically, employers' payroll taxes should be accrued as wages are earned by employees: (a) true, (b) false.

___ 16. Incentive wage plans automatically substitute for adequate management as the most effective way of controlling labor costs: (a) always, (b) often, (c) occasionally, (d) never.

___ 17. The make-up pay for piecework in a common incentive wage plan would ordinarily be charged as factory-overhead cost: (a) true, (b) false.

II Complete each of the following statements:

1. The subtractions made from the gross earnings of employees are usually called ________________

____

2. The two kinds of taxes ordinarily deducted from the gross earnings of employees are the

____________________ tax and the

____________________ tax.

3. Under the textbook accounting method, when an employer records labor costs incurred, he should

credit the ____________________

account for the ________________ earnings owed to employees.

4. The labor costs incurred by employers in addition to the gross earnings of employees are called

____

____

5. The two kinds of *federal* payroll taxes typically assessed against employers are ____________

____________ taxes and ____________ taxes.

6. Theoretically, the fringe costs pertaining to direct labor should be charged to the ____________

____________________ account.

7. Usually, equal amounts of taxes are assessed against employees and employers for ____________ taxes.

8. The usual practice in accounting for payroll taxes tends to result in a ratio of payroll taxes to employee earnings that is ____________ in the earlier months than in the later months of the

____________________ year.

III Scrooge and Cratchit Clerical Supplies uses for its payday the last day of each month. The firm's labor summary for a month included the following data:

Gross earnings of employees:	
Direct labor	$20,000
Indirect labor	5,000
Selling expense	3,000
Administrative expense	2,000
Total	$30,000
Vacation pay	5.0%
F.I.C.A. tax	6.0
Federal unemployment tax	0.5
State unemployment tax	2.5
Total	14.0%
All earnings are subject to the above rates.	
Employee's income taxes withheld	$ 4,000

1. Prepare the journal entry to record the *incurrence of all payroll costs* for the month:

Calculations:

2. Prepare the journal entry to record the *payment of the payroll* for the month:

Calculations:

27 Accounting Systems and Internal Control

A FIRM OF INDEPENDENT ACCOUNTANTS may conduct an audit and express a formal opinion concerning the fairness and consistency of a company's financial statements and their conformity with generally accepted reporting standards. However, the **primary responsibility** for the financial statements still rests with the **company's management.** This idea has recently been reinforced and expanded by the U.S. Foreign Corrupt Practices Act.

The systems and techniques for carrying out this important management responsibility are called **internal accounting controls.** They are aimed at improving the accountability for actions, the accuracy and reliability of records, the safeguarding of assets, and the overall efficiency of operations. Internal accounting controls are designed also to minimize errors, waste, and fraud. A key role in achieving these goals is played today by a company's **audit committee.** This chapter presents some methods and procedures for accomplishing internal control.

REVIEW SUMMARY

A. Today *internal control* is considered so important that most annual reports of corporations include definite statements of management's basic responsibilities for the financial reports.

  1. For example, see the excerpt from the report of General Motors Corporation in textbook Exhibit 27–1.

  2. Additional heavy emphasis on these responsibilities has been required by recent legislation in the United Sates: the *Foreign Corrupt Practices Act.*

  3. The immensity of the problem of internal control is apparent when one realizes how voluminous transactions have become and how rapidly the technology has developed for conducting and recording huge quantities of transactions (for example, the growing use of electronic data-processing equipment).

  4. Therefore we necessarily cover here *only the general features* of internal control systems, features that are applicable to many different kinds of operations.

B. We survey *internal accounting controls.*

  1. These controls are concerned primarily with the *execution and recording of transactions* and such directly related matters as

    a. Accuracy and reliability of records and reports

b. Safeguarding all kinds of assets (cash, receivables, inventory, equipment)
c. Authorization and accountability for actions
d. Maximizing overall efficiency
e. Minimizing errors, waste, and fraud

2. A distinction should be observed between such accounting controls and the *administrative controls* not covered here: the administrative organization within an entity, planning, performance evaluation, and so forth.

C. The Foreign Corrupt Practices Act of 1977 is much broader than its title indicates.

1. The act directly impacts the internal control systems of all American companies, whether or not they conduct business outside the United States.
2. Specific prohibitions against bribery and other corrupt practices are included.
3. Perhaps even more important, however, are the requirements for maintaining appropriate accounting records and an effective system of internal accounting controls.
   a. These requirements place the primary responsibility for internal control on a company's *management,* not on the independent external auditors.
   b. This is implemented largely by a mandatory documentation of all internal control activities, including plans, procedures, and evaluation of the system.

D. A recent important development that is a key element of internal control has been the formation of *audit committees* in the 1970s.

1. These committees usually consist of "outside" members of the board of directors, who are *not part of the corporate management.*
2. Because of their higher degree of *independence,* they are entrusted with the responsibilities of:
   a. Selecting *external auditors* and dealing directly with them
   b. Overseeing the entire *internal auditing* function of the company
3. Note also in the textbook Exhibit 27–2 how the lines of authority extend from the board of directors down through the audit committee to the chief financial officer and to the internal auditing department.

E. Although no internal control system can prevent fraud completely or result in operating perfection, some general principles and procedures can help an organization move toward these ideals. A *checklist* is provided:

1. Hiring and training *reliable personnel* with *clearly defined responsibilities.*
2. Maintaining an appropriate *separation of duties* of all individuals involved in the various processes of authorization, custody, recording, and so forth.
   a. For example, recordkeeping and physical handling of assets should be assigned to separate persons instead of combining the two functions in a job for one person.
3. Requiring *proper authorization* for all policies and procedures.
4. Preparing *adequate documents.* This means to systematize the handling of transactions, especially sales, to help ensure that they are recorded on documents immediately, adequately, and in a tamper-proof manner (document control).
5. Establishing *proper procedures,* that is, using uniform routines for repetitive activities in order to permit specialization of effort, division of duties, and automatic checks.
6. Using *physical safeguards:* safes, locks, watchmen, and limited access.
7. Observing certain precautions for key personnel: *bonding, vacations,* and *rotation of duties.*
8. Providing for *independent checks* through periodic reviews of the system by both internal and external auditors.
9. Using the *cost-benefit approach,* avoiding procedures with monetary or psychological costs in excess of benefits.

F. *Electronic computers* have important implications for internal control.

1. Although electronic data systems can have high degrees of reliability, efficiency, and effectiveness, they are *less flexible* than manual systems.
2. The checklist for internal control also applies to electronic computer systems, especially to such items as:
   a. Careful selection of employees
   b. Rotation of employees' duties
   c. Separation of recordkeeping and cash-handling responsibilities

G. Reliable reports from many sources point to an alarming increase in retail *inventory shrinkage* or *shortage.*
1. These merchandise losses, which are due primarily to shoplifting by customers and embezzling by employees, can make disastrous inroads on slim profit margins.
2. Although the best deterrent is an alert employee at the point of sale, other methods are increasingly being used to cope with such thefts; for example, surveillance by television cameras and placing sensitized tags on merchandise.

H. The *retail inventory method* is widely used as a control device, especially in situations of wide merchandise variety, high sales volume, and low unit values of products (food stores, for example).
1. The retail inventory method is helpful in measuring the inventory shortages for which store managers bear prime responsibility.
2. Best results from this method are obtained when it is used in conjunction with close supervision and spot checks by branch managers.
3. The method is also used to obtain an inventory valuation for financial statement purposes.

I. The examples in the textbook Appendix 27A show in detail some of the typical procedures for the routine processing of certain common types of business documents.
1. Exhibit 27–3 shows the routing of various papers involved in the *purchase of merchandise.* Note that this diagram reflects *all* of the nine items in the controls checklist previously described.

J. The textbook Appendix 27B describes additional specialized techniques for accumulating accounting data.
1. The use of *branch ledgers* tied to home-office ledgers by *reciprocal control accounts* helps to integrate all company accounts in a manner that minimizes duplications, omissions, and other errors (Exhibit 27–5).

SELF-TEST AND PRACTICE EXERCISES

I For each of the following multiple-choice and true-false statements, select the most appropriate answer and enter its identification letter in the space provided.

___ 1. The primary responsibility for a company's financial statements rests upon: (a) the independent outside auditors, (b) the company's management, (c) neither of the above.

___ 2. The U.S. Foreign Corrupt Practices Act pertains to the internal control systems of: (a) only foreign companies, (b) only publicly held domestic companies that do business outside the United States, (c) all publicly held domestic companies, (d) none of the above.

___ 3. The growing use of electronic data-processing hardware has virtually eliminated the need for internal accounting controls: (a) true, (b) false.

___ 4. Administrative control includes: (a) budgetary procedures, (b) performance evaluation, (c) both of the above, (d) neither of the above.

___ 5. Accounting control includes: (a) authorization of transactions, (b) accountability for actions, (c) both of the above, (d) neither of the above.

___ 6. In a large corporation, it is feasible for an internal control system to: (a) prevent fraud completely, (b) provide verification of all transactions, (c) both of the above, (d) neither of the above.

___ 7. In general, internal control systems involve, in addition to accounting procedures and the processing of business documents: (a) employee selection, (b) physical safeguards, (c) both of the above, (d) neither of the above.

___ 8. If an internal control system is properly designed, there should be no need for: (a) internal auditors, (b) external auditors, (c) both of the above, (d) neither of the above.

___ 9. In general, it is desirable that only one employee should have sole control over the recordkeeping and physical handling for the individual transactions that are assigned to him or her: (a) true, (b) false.

___ 10. In a certain company, one employee maintains both the cash receipts journal and the accounts receivable ledger. For a good system of internal control, this would be: (a) an undesirable combination, (b) an acceptable combination.

___ 11. In general, the textbook checklist for internal control would be applicable to: (a) electronic computer systems, (b) manual systems, (c) both of the above, (d) neither of the above.

___ 12. The audit committee of a corporation is typically selected from the corporation's: (a) stockholders, (b) full-time employees, (c) outside auditing firm, (d) outside directors.

___ 13. The functions of a corporation's audit committee include making plans, judgments, and decisions concerning the activities of: (a) the external auditing firm, (b) the internal auditing department, (c) both of the above, (d) neither of the above.

___ 14. EDP systems are less flexible than manual systems: (a) true, (b) false.

___ 15. Electronic computer systems: (a) can have high degrees of reliability, efficiency, and effectiveness, (b) are more flexible than manual systems, (c) both of the above, (d) neither of the above.

___ 16. In general, the nine-item checklist for internal control would be applicable to: (a) electronic computer systems, (b) manual systems, (c) both of the above, (d) neither of the above.

___ 17. Retail inventory shortages seem to be: (a) increasing, (b) decreasing, (c) remaining about the same.

___ 18. In general, shoplifting has a significant effect on profits: (a) true, (b) false.

___ 19. The retail inventory method is useful: (a) as a control device, (b) for obtaining an inventory valuation for financial-statement purposes, (c) both of the above, (d) neither of the above.

___ 20. Use of the retail inventory method automatically eliminates merchandise thefts by employees: (a) true, (b) false.

___ 21. The classification and coding of accounts in a large organization is intended primarily to: (a) protect confidential information, (b) increase the speed and accuracy of recordkeeping.

___ 22. When reciprocal control accounts are used for a factory ledger and the home-office ledger as described in the chapter appendix, the purchase of direct materials would require: (a) a credit to Factory Ledger Control, (b) a debit to Home Office Ledger Control, (c) a credit to Home Office Ledger Control, (d) all of the above, (e) none of the above.

II Complete each of the following statements:

1. Internal accounting control systems are designed to minimize:

(a) ____________________

(b) ______________________________

(c) ______________________________

2. A desirable feature of an internal control system is the assignment to separate persons of the functions or duties of:

(a) ______________________________

(b) ______________________________

3. Systematizing the handling of transactions to help ensure that they are recorded on documents immediately, adequately, and in a tamper-proof manner is called ______________________________

4. Ordinarily, the original copies of purchase orders are sent to ______________________________

5. In a system for controlling purchase-related transactions, the purchase invoice is usually compared with two other documents or copies of them:

(a) ______________________________

(b) ______________________________

6. In a good internal control system, the duties of cash paying and cash receiving should be ______________________________

7. Typically, large retail inventory shrinkages and shortages are caused primarily by ______________________________ and ______________________________

8. The retail inventory method is particularly useful as a control device in situations of wide merchandise variety, high ______________________________ and low ______________________________

9. When reciprocal control accounts are used to tie a branch factory ledger to the home-office ledger, the Home Office Ledger Control account is included in the ______________________________ ledger and normally has a ______________________________ balance.

III Internal Control System

For each of the following pairs of employee functions, indicate whether it is an acceptable combination (A) or an unacceptable combination (U) for only one employee to perform in a good system of internal control.

____ 1. Maintaining general ledger; handling and depositing cash receipts.

____ 2. Maintaining general ledger; reconciling bank account.

____ 3. Handling and depositing cash receipts; issuing credits on returns and allowances.

____ 4. Handling and depositing cash receipts; preparing checks for signature.

____ 5. Maintaining accounts payable ledger; maintaining accounts receivable ledger.

____ 6. Maintaining cash disbursements journal; maintaining accounts payable ledger.

____ 7. Reconciling bank account; handling and depositing cash receipts.

____ 8. Issuing credits on returns and allowances; maintaining accounts receivable ledger.

IV Given for High-Margin Stores:

	Retail Prices
Beginning merchandise inventory (physical count)	$ 9,000
Merchandise purchases	60,000
Merchandise sales	50,000
Markups	4,000
Markdowns	10,000
Allowable inventory shrinkage	2,000
Ending merchandise inventory (physical count)	10,700

Using the retail method of inventory control, determine the amount of inventory shortage (in excess of allowable inventory shrinkage) . . . . $ ________

28 Cost Accounting in Professional Examinations

MANY READERS of the textbook plan to become Certified Public Accountants or Certified Management Accountants and to take the CPA and CMA examinations. Because cost accounting is one of the most important topics in these and other professional examinations, many of the previous chapters in this book can be quite useful for study and review.

However, the accounting terminology in the examinations is not uniform, and some problem situations appear somewhat strange to candidates. Moreover, alternative solutions are acceptable for some problems. Candidates who understand and anticipate these differences are better prepared for the examinations. Therefore, we take up in this chapter and its appendix several of the alternative terms, accounting procedures, and solution approaches for examination problems dealing with cost accounting.

REVIEW SUMMARY

A. Because the professional examinations include problems from many sources and are given on a nationwide basis, they have two characteristics that should be recognized by candidates:

1. A meaning may be expressed by different terms; for example:

a. *Factory overhead* may be called *factory burden, manufacturing expenses, indirect manufacturing costs,* or *manufacturing overhead.*

b. *Cost of goods sold* and *cost of sales* are used interchangeably.

c. *Direct materials* are often referred to as *raw materials.*

d. *Denominator volume* is our textbook term for the level of activity used for computing predetermined overhead rates, but this is often called *normal* or *standard volume.*

e. *Efficiency variance* may be called *usage* or *quantity variance.*

f. *Price variance* may be called *rate variance.*

2. Alternative solutions may be acceptable for full grading credit in some cases.

a. When solving problems, candidates should always use terminology that is *consistent* with the problem terminology.

b. In general, candidates should interpret problem requirements *literally.*

c. If a candidate thinks it is desirable to make an assumption—and this is *rarely necessary*—he or she should state the assumption clearly and support it with adequate reasons.

B. As shown by textbook Exhibit 28-3, several alternative methods are used for accumulating manufacturing costs in general-ledger accounts.

1. When direct materials are issued for production or direct-labor costs are incurred, they may be charged immediately to the Work in Process account, or they may be carried first through intermediate accounts called Direct Materials Used or Direct Labor, respectively.
2. The materials-efficiency variance and the direct-labor price variance may be recognized either when costs are charged to the Work in Process account or when costs are transferred to the Finished Goods account.
3. When factory-overhead costs are incurred, they may be charged directly to a single control account, or they may be carried first through several intermediate accounts for functional types of costs, such as Depreciation, Repairs, and Power.

C. Alternative procedures for standard costs are in use:

1. The Work in Process account can be charged on any of three different bases:
   a. Actual quantities at actual prices
   b. Actual quantities at standard prices
   c. Standard quantities at standard prices
2. Overhead variances are computed in different ways:
   a. The recommended approach described in Chapter 7 breaks the total variance into a production volume variance and a budget variance, the latter being subdivided into a spending variance and an efficiency variance (Alternative 1 in Chapter 28).
   b. A second method for analyzing variances is sometimes used, but it has the serious shortcomings described in this textbook chapter.

SELF-TEST AND PRACTICE EXERCISES

I For each of the following multiple-choice and true-false statements, select the most appropriate answer and enter its identification letter in the space provided:

___ 1. CPA and CMA examinations seem to virtually exclude: (a) the management-decision aspects of cost accounting, (b) quantitative methods and techniques, (c) measurements of inventory and income, (d) all of the above, (e) none of the above.

___ 2. In the professional accounting examinations: (a) alternative solutions may be acceptable, (b) terminology may not be uniform, (c) both of the above, (d) neither of the above.

___ 3. An acceptable alternative term for factory overhead is manufacturing expenses: (a) true, (b) false.

___ 4. In general, it would not be unwise to use acceptable alternative terminology in solving CPA and CMA problems, even though such terminology is inconsistent with that used in the problem: (a) true, (b) false.

___ 5. When solving CPA and CMA problems, candidates should make assumptions: (a) always, (b) frequently, (c) rarely, (d) never.

___ 6. When direct-labor costs are incurred, they may be charged first to: (a) the Work in Process account, (b) Direct Labor, (c) either of the above, (d) neither of the above.

___ 7. The materials-efficiency or usage variance may be recognized when costs are charged to: (a) the Work in Process account, (b) the Finished Goods account, (c) either of the above, (d) neither of the above.

___ 8. The charges to the Work-in-Process account under a standard cost accounting system may be made on the basis of: (a) standard quantities at standard prices, (b) standard quantities at actual prices, (c) either of the above, (d) neither of the above.

___ 9. Published solutions to CPA exams have included some unsound methods for analyzing overhead variances: (a) true, (b) false.

II Complete each of the following statements:

1. An acceptable alternative term for cost of goods sold is ______________________________

____

2. An acceptable alternative term for denominator volume is ______________________________

3. When direct materials are issued for production, debits may be made either to the ______________ ______________ account or to ______________ ______________ account.

4. The direct-labor price or rate variance may be recognized either when costs are charged to the ______________________________ account or when costs are transferred to the ______________________________ account.

5. In the recommended approach for analyzing overhead variances, the budget variance is subdivided into ______________________________ variance and ______________________________ variance.

Solutions

CHAPTER 1

I	1 d	5 d	9 d	13 b	17 d
	2 b	6 c	10 a	14 a	18 c
	3 b	7 b	11 b	15 b	19 a
	4 a	8 d	12 e	16 d	20 c .

II 1 Management accounting or managerial accounting; 2 Certificate in Management Accounting; 3 management by exception; 4 (a) budgets, (b) performance reports; 5 feedback; 6 feedback; 7 cost-benefit approach; 8 the controller; 9 "watchdog" role and "helper" role

III	1 AD	2 SK	3 PS	4 SK	5 SK	6 AD

IV	1 SK	2 AD	3 PS	4 SK	5 AD

V	1 L	3 L	5 N	7 L	9 N
	2 S	4 L	6 S	8 S	10 N

VI	1 S	3 P	5 S	7 S	9 P
	2 S	4 S	6 P	8 S	10 P

CHAPTER 2

I	1 d	4 c	7 c	10 c	13 b	16 b	19 c	22 c
	2 d	5 a	8 c	11 b	14 b	17 a	20 a	
	3 c	6 b	9 a	12 e	15 a	18 a	21 d	

Computations:

2 $80,000 ÷ 8,000 = $10 per unit (d)
3 $120,000 ÷ 15,000 = $8 per unit (c)
21 (45 − 40) ($18 − $12) = 5 × $6 = $30 (d)
22 (48 − 40) ($18 ÷ 2) = 8 × $9 = $72 (c)

II 1 A resource sacrificed or foregone to obtain a specific objective; 2 (a) management planning and control decisions, (b) inventory valuation and income determination; 3 a cost objective; 4 cost accumulation; 5 cost functions; 6 (a) direct material, (b) direct labor; 7 conversion cost; 8 indirect materials (or supplies); 9 gross margin (or gross profit); 10 inventoriable costs; 11 (a) direct materials inventory, (b) work-in-process inventory, (c) finished goods inventory; 12 payroll fringe costs; 13 cost of goods sold (or cost of sales); 14 cost of goods available for sale

III Queensview Corporation

(a) $84,000 + $68,000 = $152,000
(b) $84,000 + $44,000 + $20,000 = $148,000
(c) $84,000 + $68,000 + $44,000 + $20,000 = $216,000
(d) $64,000 + $36,000 + $8,000 + $24,000 = $132,000

IV Glen Lakes Company

1 VN	3 FI	5 VI	7 FI	9 VI
2 VI	4 FN	6 FN	8 FN	10 FN

V Sphinx Company

Let DM = direct material
DL = direct labor
FO = factory overhead

Then: Conversion cost − Prime cost = $180,000 − $132,000
(DL + FO) − (DL + DM) = $48,000
FO − DM = $48,000
But: FO = 1.5 (DM)
Therefore: 1.5 (DM) − DM = $48,000
.5 (DM) = $48,000
DM = $96,000 (a)
FO = 1.5 ($96,000) = $144,000 (c)
DL = Prime cost − DM = $132,000 − $96,000 = $36,000 (b)
or
DL = Conversion cost − FO = $180,000 − $144,000 = $36,000 (b)
Proof: Prime cost = $96,000 + $36,000 = $132,000
Conversion cost = $36,000 + $144,000 = $180,000

VI Rather Corporation

Manufacturing costs incurred	$250,000
Less increase in work in process	28,000
Cost of goods manufactured	$222,000 (a)
Add decrease in finished goods	23,000
Cost of goods sold	245,000 (b)

VII Board Game Manufacturing Company

1

BOARD GAME MANUFACTURING COMPANY

Schedule of Cost of Goods Manufactured
For Year Ended December 31, 19__2

Direct materials:		
Inventory, December 31, 19__1	$ 22,000	
Purchases of direct materials	88,000	
Cost of direct materials available for use	$110,000	
Inventory, December 31, 19__2	20,000	
Direct materials used		$ 90,000
Direct labor		70,000
Factory overhead:		
Indirect labor	$ 28,000	
Supplies	2,000	
Heat, light, and power	3,000	
Depreciation, machinery	4,000	
Rent, factory building	12,000	
Miscellaneous	1,000	50,000
Manufacturing costs incurred during 19__2		$210,000
Add work-in-process inventory, December 31, 19__1		18,000
Manufacturing costs to account for		$228,000
Less work-in-process inventory, December 31, 19__2		12,000
Cost of goods manufactured (to Income Statement)		$216,000

2

BOARD GAME MANUFACTURING COMPANY
Income Statement
For Year Ended December 31, 19__2

Sales		$350,000
Less cost of goods sold:		
Finished goods, December 31, 19__1	$ 39,000	
Cost of goods manufactured (see schedule)	216,000	
Cost of goods available for sale	$255,000	
Finished goods, December 31, 19__2	45,000	
Cost of goods sold		210,000
Gross margin		$140,000
Less selling and administrative expenses (detailed)		120,000
Net income		$ 20,000

CHAPTER 3

I

1 b	5 d	9 a	13 a	17 b	21 a	25 b	29 c
2 c	6 c	10 d	14 c	18 e	22 a	26 d	30 d
3 d	7 b	11 c	15 b	19 a	23 b	27 a	
4 c	8 d	12 d	16 a	20 b	24 c	28 c	

Computations:

3 (500,000 − 350,000) ÷ 500,000 = 30% (d)

4 135,000 ÷ 30% = $450,000 (c)

7 Selling price: 650 ÷ 130 = $5; variable cost per unit: 390 ÷ 130 = $3; contribution margin: 5 − 3 = $2 per unit; breakeven sales: 330 ÷ 2 = 165 units; 165 × 5 = $825 (b)

8 (330 + 70) ÷ 2 = 200 units (d)
13 Contribution margin: (600,000 − 180,000) ÷ 600,000 = 70%; breakeven sales: 399,000 ÷ 70% = $570,000 (a)
14 (399,000 + 42,000) ÷ 70% = $630,000 (c)
25 530 − 220 = $310 (b)
26 530 − (220) (1/2) − (270) (2/3) = 530 − 110 − 180 = $240 (d)
27 (5 × $4) + $10 = $30; $30 ÷ (5 + 1) = $5 average contribution margin per unit; $21,000 ÷ $5 = 4,200 total units (a)
28 $14,000 ÷ (1 − 40%) = $14,400 ÷ 60% = $24,000 profit before 40% income taxes; $24 − $16 = $8; ($48,000 + $24,000) ÷ $8 = $72,000 ÷ $8 = 9,000 units (c)

II 1 Contribution margin; 2 activity volume (or level of activity); 3 relevant range; 4 activity volume (or level of activity); 5 sensitivity analysis; 6 increase; 7 sales mix; 8 sales minus manufacturing cost of goods sold; 9 sales minus variable expenses; 10 fixed expenses

III Country Corporation

(a) $96,000	(c) $90,000	(e) $4	(g) $144,000	(i) $90,000
(b) $4	(d) $3.75	(f) $3	(h) $4	(j) $2.50

Computations:

(a) 24,000 ($120,000 ÷ 30,000) = 24,000 × $4 = $96,000
(b) $120,000 ÷ 30,000 = $4
(c) $90,000 given
(d) $90,000 ÷ 24,000 = $3.75
(e) $120,000 ÷ 30,000 = $4
(f) $90,000 ÷ 30,000 = $3
(g) 36,000 ($120,000 ÷ 30,000) = 36,000 × $4 = $144,000
(h) $120,000 ÷ 30,000 = $4
(i) $90,000 given
(j) $90,000 ÷ 36,000 = $2.50

IV Flexible Products, Inc.:

1 Unit contribution margin is unit selling price less unit variable expenses: $70 − $50 = $20.
2 Breakeven sales in units is total fixed expenses divided by unit contribution margin: $4,800 ÷ $20 = 240 units.
3 Unit sales to produce a target net income would be the sum of the total fixed expenses and the target net income divided by the unit contribution margin: ($4,800 + $1,200) ÷ $20 = $6,000 ÷ $20 = 300 units.
4 If the target net income is 20% of sales, the target net income per product unit would be: (20%) ($70) = $14 per unit. Therefore, the dollars per product unit available for coverage of the total fixed expenses would be the unit sales price less the unit net income less the unit variable costs: $70 − $14 − $50 = $6 per unit. Dividing this into the total fixed expenses gives us the required sales in units: $4,800 ÷ $6 = 800 units.
5 Each unit would contribute $20 toward total fixed expenses. Therefore, net income would be: ($20) (600) − $4,800 = $12,000 − $4,800 = $7,200.
6 The new unit contribution margin would be $70 − ($50 + $5) = $15 per unit. The new total fixed expenses would be: $4,800 − $1,200 = $3,600. Therefore, the new breakeven sales in units would be: $3,600 ÷ $15 = 240 units.

7 The necessary unit contribution margin to cover *both* the target net income and the total fixed expenses would be: ($1,800 + $4,800) ÷ 300 = $6,600 ÷ 300 = $22 per product unit. Therefore, the selling price per unit would be the variable cost per unit plus this unit contribution margin: $50 + $22 = $72.

V Monument Sales Company:

1 Sales less fixed and variable expenses: $60,000 – $12,000 – $42,000 = $6,000.
2 Contribution-margin ratio: ($60,000 – $42,000) ÷ $60,000 = $18,000 ÷ $60,000 = 30%.
3 Breakeven sales are total fixed expenses divided by the contribution-margin ratio: $12,000 ÷ 30% = $40,000.
4 Divide the sum of the fixed expenses and the desired net income (target net income) by the contribution-margin ratio: ($12,000 + $9,000) ÷ 30% = $21,000 ÷ 30% = $70,000.
5 These sales would be total fixed expenses divided by the excess of the contribution-margin ratio (or percent) over the net-income ratio (or percent): $12,000 ÷ (30% – 20%) = $12,000 ÷ 10% = $120,000. Another approach would be to set up an equation with *S* for the required sales and using the 70% variable-expenses percentage and the 20% net income percentage:

$$S = \$12{,}000 + 70\%\ S + 20\%\ S = \$12{,}000 + 90\%\ S$$
$$10\%\ S = \$12{,}000$$
$$S = \$12{,}000 \div 10\% = \$120{,}000$$

6 The new total fixed expenses would be: $12,000 – $2,000 = $10,000. The new variable-cost percentage (*to total dollar sales*) would be: $42,000 ÷ ($60,000 – 10% of $60,000) = $42,000 ÷ $54,000 = 7/9. Therefore, the new contribution-margin ratio would be 2/9. The new breakeven sales would then be the new total fixed expenses divided by the new contribution-margin ratio: $10,000 ÷ 2/9 = $10,000 × 9/2 = $45,000.

VI Paper Toys, Inc.

1 $400 × 40% = $160
2 $400 – $160 = $240
3 $300 × 30% = $90
4 $300 – $90 = $210
5 $160 + $90 = $250
6 $240 + $210 = $450
7 $750 – $400 = $350
8 $750 – $450 = $300
9 $350 – $300 = $50; or $300 – $250 = $50; or $750 – $400 – $300 = $50

VII Canasta Products, Inc.

Contribution margins are $18 – $13 = $5 for J and $10 – $7 = $3 for K.

1 (3 × $5) + $3 = $18; $18 ÷ (3 + 1) = $4.50 average contribution margin per unit; $31,500 ÷ $4.50 = 7,000 total units
2 (3 × $3) + $5 = $14; $14 ÷ (3 + 1) = $3.50; $31,500 ÷ $3.50 = 9,000 total units
3 (5 × $5) + (3 × $3) = $34; $34 ÷ (5 + 3) = $4.25; $31,500 ÷ $4.25 = 7,412 total units

VIII Iconoclast Potteries

Let X = number of units to be sold

$$50X = 30X + 16{,}000 + \frac{9{,}000}{1 - .4}$$

$$20X = 16{,}000 + \frac{9{,}000}{.6}$$

$$20X = 16{,}000 + 15{,}000 = 31{,}000$$

$$X = 31{,}000 \div 20 = 1{,}550 \text{ units}$$

Proof:

Sales: 1,550 × $50		$77,500
Less expenses:		
Variable: 1,550 × $30	$46,500	
Fixed	16,000	62,500
Income before income tax		$15,000
Less 40% income tax		6,000
Net income		$ 9,000

IX 1

DUAL-VIEW LENS CORPORATION

Income Statement
For the Year Ended December 31, 19__8

Sales		$365,000
Less manufacturing cost of goods sold		200,000
Gross profit (or gross margin)		$165,000
Less selling and administrative expenses:		
Selling expenses	$100,000	
Administrative expenses	40,000	140,000
Operating income		$ 25,000

2

DUAL-VIEW LENS CORPORATION

Income Statement
For the Year Ended December 31, 19__8

Sales		$365,000
Less variable expenses:		
Manufacturing	$120,000	
Selling	80,000	
Administrative	10,000	210,000
Contribution margin		$155,000
Less fixed expenses:		
Manufacturing	$ 80,000	
Selling	20,000	
Administrative	30,000	130,000
Operating income		$ 25,000

3

Operating income, as above	$ 25,000
Add 10% of contribution margin: 10% × 155,000	15,500
Operating income after a 10% increase in sales volume	$ 40,500

CHAPTER 4

I

1 d	6 b	11 a	16 b	21 a	26 e	31 a
2 a	7 c	12 d	17 d	22 c	27 a	32 c
3 c	8 d	13 c	18 a	23 d	28 b	33 b
4 b	9 a	14 a	19 c	24 d	29 a	
5 d	10 b	15 b	20 a	25 a	30 b	

Computations:

25 \$621,000 overhead incurred minus \$614,000 applied is equal to \$7,000 underapplied (a)

31 \$3,200 ÷ (550 + 150 × 60%) = \$3,200 ÷ 640 = \$5.00 per unit (a)

32 \$2,450 ÷ (550 + 150) = \$2,450 ÷ 700 = \$3.50 per unit (c)

33 (150 × \$3.50) + (150) (60%) (\$5.00) = \$525 + \$450 = \$975 (b)

II 1 Job-order, process; 2 cost centers or departments; 3 cost sheets for uncompleted jobs; 4 the stores requisition; 5 Work-in-Process, job-cost sheets; 6 budgeted factory-overhead, budgeted direct-labor cost (or budgeted machine hours); 7 the predetermined overhead rate, the actual (or historical) amount of the overhead rate base; 8 credit, Cost of Goods Sold, Finished Goods, Work-in-Process

III Prognosis Instruments, Inc.

1 The predetermined overhead rate is budgeted factory-overhead cost divided by budgeted direct-labor hours: \$550,000 ÷ 440,000 = \$1.25 per hour.

2 Applied factory-overhead cost is actual direct-labor hours times the predetermined overhead rate: (460,000) (\$1.25) = \$575,000.

3 Overapplied factory-overhead cost is applied overhead cost minus actual overhead cost: \$575,000 − \$562,000 = \$13,000.

IV Prolific Production Company:

1	(e)	April 1 balance of stores	\$ 32,000
		Add materials purchased (b)	42,000
		Materials available for use	\$ 74,000
		Less April 30 balance of stores	30,000
		Materials used in April	\$ 44,000
		Less direct materials used (c)	39,000
		Indirect materials used in April	\$ 5,000
	(f)	Factory payroll paid (l)	\$ 22,000
		Add accrued payroll, April 30	3,000
		Total payroll incurred in April	\$ 25,000
		Less direct factory labor incurred (d)	16,000
		Indirect factory labor incurred in April	\$ 9,000
	(j)	Direct factory labor incurred (d)	\$ 16,000
		Multiply by predetermined overhead rate (j)	125%
		Applied factory overhead cost for April	\$ 20,000

(m)	April 1 balance of work in process	$ 41,000
	Add:	
	Direct materials used (c)	39,000
	Direct labor incurred (d)	16,000
	Factory overhead applied (j)	20,000
	Total	$116,000
	Less April 30 balance of work in process	47,000
	Cost of goods manufactured in April	$ 69,000
(n)	April 1 balance of finished goods	$148,000
	Add cost of goods manufactured (m)	69,000
	Cost of goods available for sale in April	$217,000
	Less April 30 balance of finished goods	152,000
	Cost of goods sold in April	$ 65,000

2

Cash

Debit	Credit
10,000	k) 49,000
a) 105,000	l) 22,000

Factory Department Overhead Control

Debit	Credit
62,000	
e) 5,000	
f) 9,000	
g) 300	
h) 1,700	
i) 3,000	

Unexpired Insurance

Debit	Credit
1,000	g) 300

Factory Overhead Applied

Debit	Credit
	63,000
	j) 20,000

Allowance for Depreciation

Debit	Credit
	70,000
	h) 1,700

Work-in-Process Control

Debit	Credit
41,000	m) 69,000
c) 39,000	
d) 16,000	
j) 20,000	

Accounts Payable

Debit	Credit
k) 49,000	27,000
	b) 42,000
	i) 3,000

Finished Goods Control

Debit	Credit
148,000	n) 65,000
m) 69,000	

Accrued Payroll

Debit	Credit
l) 22,000	-0-
	d) 16,000
	f) 9,000

Cost of Goods Sold

Debit	Credit
200,000	
n) 65,000	

Stores Control

Debit	Credit
32,000	c) 39,000
b) 42,000	e) 5,000

Sales

Debit	Credit
	310,000
	a) 105,000

V Adherence Glue Works

1 4,800 + 40% (1,200) = 5,280
2 4,800 + 100% (1,200) = 6,000
3 $17,952 ÷ 5,280 = $3.40
4 $13,200 ÷ 6,000 = $2.20
5 4,800 ($3.40 + $2.20) = $26,880
6 1,200 ($2.20) + 1,200 ($3.40) (40%) = $2,640 + $1,632 = $4,272
7 Proof: $26,880 + $4,272 = $31,152

CHAPTER 5

I

1 d	5 c	9 a	13 c	17 c
2 b	6 a	10 b	14 e	18 c
3 c	7 e	11 a	15 a	19 b
4 c	8 d	12 b	16 d	20 d

Computations

5 64,500 + 14,500 − 20,000 = 59,000 units (c).
10 126,000 + 219,000 − 143,500 = $201,500 (b).
11 179,000 + 10,000 − 143,500 = $45,500 (a).
16 (84,000 × 2.5) − (40% × 120,000) = 210,000 − 48,000 = 162,000 units (d).

II 1 Pro Forma; 2 plans, plans; 3 continuous; 4 sales; 5 the desired ending inventory of finished goods, the beginning inventory of finished goods; 6 deficiencies, idle; 7 financial planning models (or total models); 8 cost-benefit; 9 responsibility; 10 variances, exception; 11 controllable costs

III Eight Seas Company:

Cost + 70% Cost = $510,000; 170% Cost = $510,000; Cost = $510,000 ÷ 1.7 = $300,000

Expected cost of goods sold	$300,000
Add desired ending inventory at cost	145,000
Total needs	$445,000
Less beginning inventory at cost	120,000
Budgeted purchases	$325,000

IV Mort Sanger Stores:

1 Collections in March:

January sales: 20% × $300,000	$ 60,000
February sales: 30% × $250,000	75,000
March sales: 50% × 98% × $400,000	196,000
Total	$331,000

2 March 31 accounts receivable:

(20% × $250,000) + (50% × $400,000)	$250,000

V Gabbert Tapestries:

	Case 1	Case 2
Beginning cash balance	$ 4,200	$ 2,700
Add expected cash receipts	98,000	73,600
(a) Total available before current financing	$102,200	$ 76,300
Expected cash disbursements	$ 87,000	$ 80,800
Add minimum ending cash balance desired	8,000	8,500
(b) Total cash needed	$ 95,000	$ 89,300
1. Necessary to borrow (b − a)		$ 13,000
2. Available for repayment of loans and interest (a − b)	$ 7,200	

VI Summ-Totall Material Company:

		Material A	Material B
1	Number of Product X units to be produced	2,000	2,000
	Multiply by number of material units needed per Product X unit	× 10	× 20
	(a) Total	20,000	40,000
	Number of Product Y units to be produced	3,000	3,000
	Multiply by number of material units needed per Product Y unit	× 15	× 6
	(b) Total	45,000	18,000
	Total number of material units needed for production of both products (a + b)	65,000	58,000
2	Multiply above by unit purchase prices of materials	× $4	× $6
	Cost of materials needed for production	$260,000	$348,000
3	Number of material units desired in ending inventories	10,000	8,000
	Add number of material units needed for production	65,000	58,000
	Total material units needed	75,000	66,000
	Less number of material units in beginning inventories	6,000	15,000
	Number of material units to be purchased	69,000	51,000
4	Multiply above by unit purchase prices of materials	× $4	× $6
	Cost of materials to be purchased	$276,000	$306,000

VII Adam Taylor Company:

	Variable Cost	Controllable Cost By Controller	By Punch Press Foreman	By Production Superintendent	By Mfg. Vice-Pres.
1 Direct material used in drill press department	Yes	No	No	Yes	Yes
2 Salary of personnel vice-president	No	No	No	No	No
3 Supplies used by purchasing agent	Yes	No	No	No	Yes
4 Straight-line depreciation in punch-press department	No	No	No*	No*	No*
5 Secretary's salary in controller's department	No	Yes	No	No	No
6 Direct labor used in punch press department	Yes	No	Yes	Yes	Yes

*Perhaps controllable over a longer span of time.

Note: Although each of several executives can often regard a given cost item as being within his or her control, usually there is only one manager in the whole company who bears primary responsibility for control. This is usually the manager who is closest to overseeing the day-to-day action that influences costs. Nevertheless, all costs that are controllable by that manager are also regarded as being controllable by the manager's superior line executives.

CHAPTER 6

I

1 a	6 b	11 a	16 b	21 d
2 a	7 d	12 d	17 c	22 a
3 b	8 c	13 a	18 a	23 b
4 c	9 c	14 b	19 b	24 a
5 a	10 b	15 b	20 b	25 b

Computations:

1 Unit cost is $140,000 ÷ 8,000 = $17.50; $17.50 × 9,000 = $157,500 (a)
2 $48,000 − $40,000 = $8,000 U (a)
3 Unit cost is $40,000 ÷ 8,000 = $5; $5 × 10,000 = $50,000
$50,000 − $48,000 = $2,000 F (b)
4 Unit cost is $180,000 ÷ 20,000 = $9; $9 × 18,000 = $162,000; $170,000 − $162,000 = $8,000 U (c)
7 Unit cost is $210,000 ÷ 6,000 = $35; $35 × 5,000 = $175,000; $185,000 − $175,000 = $10,000 U (d)
8 Unit cost is $240,000 ÷ 6,000 = $40; $40 × 5,000 = $200,000; $240,000 − $200,000 = $40,000 F (c)
10 1,800 × $4 × 10 = $72,000 (b)
11 Actual quantity of material: 1,800 × 11 = 19,800 pounds; ($5 − $4) × 19,800 = $19,800 U (a)
12 Standard quantity of material used: 1,800 × 10 = 18,000 pounds; (19,800 − 18,000) × $4 = $7,200 U (d)

II Flexible budget amounts and the static (master) budget amounts; 2 (a) good outputs, (b) inputs allowed per unit of output, (c) standard unit price of inputs; 3 attainment of a predetermined goal; 4 (a) usage variance, (b) quantity variance; 5 rate variance; 6 (a) efficiency variances, (b) price-variances; 7 unit, total; 8 purchased, issued (or used); 9 purchasing; 10 standard, first-in, first-out, or last-in, first-out; 11 hours, wage-rates

III Neato Corporation

	Actual	Flexible Budget Variances	Flexible Budget	Sales Volume Variances	Static Budget
Physical units of output	12,000	–	12,000	2,000 F	10,000
Revenue (sales)	$735,000	$15,000 F	$720,000	$120,000 F	$600,000
Variable costs	496,000	8,000 F	504,000	84,000 U	420,000
Contribution margin	239,000	23,000 F	216,000	36,000 F	180,000
Fixed costs	153,000	3,000 U	150,000	–	150,000
Operating income	$ 86,000	$20,000 F	$ 66,000	$ 36,000 F	$ 30,000

IV Mustang Leather Corporation:

1 Analysis Framework

Actual Inputs at Actual Prices	Actual Inputs at Standard Prices	Standard Inputs Allowed for Actual Outputs at Standard Prices
Actual Inputs	Actual Inputs	Standard Hours
× Actual Rate:	× Standard Rate:	Allowed
(550) ($11)	(550) ($12)	× Standard Rate:
=	=	(200) (2.5) ($12) =
$6,050	$6,600	(500) ($12) = $6,000

Price Variance
$6,600 − $6,050 = $550 F
or (550) ($12 − $11)
= $550 F

Efficiency Variance
$6,600 − $6,000 = $600 U
or ($12) (550 − 500) =
($12) (50) = $600 U

Flexible-Budget Variance
$6,050 − $6,000 = $50 U
or $600 − $550 = $50 U

2 Journal

Work in process	6,000	
Direct-labor efficiency variance	600	
Direct-labor price variance		550
Accrued payroll		6,050

V Peruna Medicinal Products, Inc.:

1 Analysis Framework

Actual Inputs at Actual Prices	Actual Inputs at Standard Prices (Purchases)	Actual Inputs at Standard Prices (Usage)	Standard Inputs Allowed for Actual Outputs at Standard Prices
Actual Quantity	Actual Quantity	Actual Quantity	Units Produced
× Actual Price:	× Standard Price:	× Standard Price:	× Standard Price:
(4,000) ($1.80)	(4,000) ($2.00)	(3,500) ($2.00)	(300) (10) ($2.00)
=	=	=	= (3,000) ($2.00)
$7,200	$8,000	$7,000	= $6,000

Price Variance
$8,000 − $7,200 = $800 F
or (4,000) ($2.00 − $1.80)
= (4,000) ($0.20) = $800 F

Efficiency Variance
$7,000 − $6,000 = $1,000 U
or ($2.00) (3,500 − 3,000)
= ($2.00) (500) = $1,000 U

2 Journal

a) Stores	8,000	
Direct-material price variance		800
Accounts payable		7,200
b) Work in process	6,000	
Direct-material efficiency variance	1,000	
Stores		7,000

CHAPTER 7

I	1 b	5 b	9 c	13 a	17 b	21 d	25 a
	2 d	6 a	10 b	14 b	18 c	22 c	26 b
	3 b	7 d	11 c	15 a	19 a	23 b	27 a
	4 b	8 b	12 b	16 e	20 c	24 a	28 a

Computations:

5 (8,500 − 8,000) × \$5 = \$2,500 unfavorable (b)
6 Flexible budget: 8,000 × \$5 = \$40,000; flexible-budget variance: \$44,500 − \$40,000 = \$4,500 unfavorable; price variance: \$4,500 − \$2,500 = \$2,000 unfavorable (a)
12 \$2,500 − (− \$2,500) = \$2,500 + \$2,500 = \$5,000 favorable (b)
17 \$24,000 − \$20,000 = \$4,000 unfavorable (b)
18 \$24,000 − \$22,500 = \$1,500 favorable (c)
19 Predetermined rate: \$44,000 ÷ 2,000 = \$22 per hour; \$22 × 2,200 = \$48,400 (a)
20 \$48,400 − \$44,000 = \$4,400 favorable (c)
21 \$46,000 − \$44,000 = \$2,000 unfavorable (d)
22 \$48,400 − \$42,000 = \$6,400 overapplied (c)

II 1 Price variance, 2 production-volume variance, 3 debit, Variable Factory Overhead Control; 4 Work-in-Process Control, Variable Factory Overhead Applied; 5 Fixed Factory Overhead Control; Accrued Payroll, Allowance for Depreciation, etc.; 6 spending (or price), efficiency; 7 flexible-budget, favorable; 8 denominator level; 9 budget, production-volume; 10 Fixed Factory Overhead Control, Fixed Factory Overhead Applied.

III N.I.K. Shaving Utensils, Inc.:

1 (a) Actual direct-labor hours used	700 hours
Multiply by standard overhead rate per hour	× \$2
Actual labor hours used at standard overhead rate	\$1,400
(b) Actual product units made	400 units
Multiply by standard variable-overhead cost per unit: 1.5 hours @ \$2 per hour	× \$3
Actual units made at standard cost (variable-overhead cost applied)	\$1,200
(c) Inputs at actual prices: Actual variable-overhead cost incurred (given)	\$1,350
Outputs at standard prices: Variable-overhead cost applied (b)	1,200
Flexible-budget variance	\$ 150 U
(d) Inputs at standard prices: Actual labor hours used at standard overhead rate (a)	\$1,400
Inputs at actual prices: Actual variable-overhead cost incurred (given)	1,350
Variable-overhead spending variance (or price variance)	\$ 50 F
(e) Inputs at standard prices: Actual labor hours used at standard overhead rate (a)	\$1,400
Outputs at standard prices: Variable-overhead cost applied (b)	1,200
Variable-overhead efficiency variance	\$ 200 U
or	
Actual direct-labor hours used	700 hours
Standard hours allowed: (1.5) (400)	600 hours
Excess hours used	100 hours

Multiply by standard variable-overhead rate per hour (given) ...		× $2.00
Variable-overhead efficiency variance ...		$ 200 U

2 Variable factory-overhead control ...	1,350	
Accounts payable, accrued payroll, etc. ...		1,350
To record actual variable-overhead incurred.		
Work in process ...	1,200	
Variable factory-overhead applied ...		1,200
To record variable-overhead applied.		

IV Stamp Pest Eradicators:

1 (a) Budgeted fixed-overhead cost ...	$1,800
Divide by denominator level of activity ...	300 hours
Standard rate for fixed overhead ...	$ 6.00 per hour
(b) Standard hours allowed for work done on product units manufactured ...	280 hours
Multiply by standard rate (a) ...	$ 6.00
Applied fixed-overhead cost ...	$1,680
(c) Actual fixed-overhead cost (given) ...	$1,750
Applied fixed-overhead cost (b) ...	1,680
Underapplied fixed-overhead cost ...	$ 70 U
(d) Budgeted fixed-overhead cost (given) ...	$1,800
Actual fixed-overhead cost (given) ...	1,750
Fixed-overhead budget variance ...	$ 50 F
(e) Budgeted fixed-overhead cost (given) ...	$1,800
Applied fixed-overhead cost (b) ...	1,680
Fixed-overhead production-volume variance ...	$ 120 U
or:	
Denominator hours used (given) ...	300 hours
Standard hours allowed (given) ...	280 hours
Excess hours used ...	20 hours
Multiply by standard fixed-overhead rate per hour (a) ...	$ 6.00
Fixed-overhead production-volume variance ...	$ 120 U

2 Fixed factory-overhead control ...	1,750	
Accrued payroll, allowance for depreciation, etc. ...		1,750
To record actual fixed overhead incurred.		
Work in process ...	1,680	
Fixed factory overhead applied ...		1,680
To record fixed overhead applied.		

CHAPTER 8

I	1 d	5 a	9 a	13 b	17 b	21 b	25 b
	2 c	6 e	10 b	14 b	18 a	22 c	26 a
	3 c	7 b	11 c	15 d	19 c	23 b	
	4 a	8 a	12 b	16 a	20 b	24 a	

II 1 Manufacturing costs and nonmanufacturing costs; 2 variable costs and fixed costs; 3 contribution margin, gross margin; 4 direct-materials cost, direct-labor cost, variable-overhead costs; 5 fixed factory overhead, fixed and variable selling expenses, fixed and variable administrative expenses; 6 external reporting, income-tax purposes; 7 sales volume is greater than production volume; 8 practical capacity or practical attainable capacity; 9 capacity utilization that is also called master-budget volume; 10 master-budget volume; 11 normal volume; 12 cost of goods sold, gross margin; 13 Work in Process, Finished Goods, Cost of Goods Sold; 14 decreased

III 1 (a)

HUDSON COMPANY

Income Statement
For the Year Ending December 31, 198__

Sales: (80,000) (15)		$1,200,000
Less cost of goods sold:		
Beginning inventory: (10,000) (10)	$ 100,000	
Cost of goods manufactured (90,000) (10)	900,000	
Cost of goods available for sale	$1,000,000	
Less ending inventory: (20,000) (10)	200,000	
Cost of goods sold		800,000
Gross margin on sales		$ 400,000
Less total selling and administrative expenses: 200,000 + 100,000		300,000
Net income		$ 100,000

(b)

HUDSON COMPANY

Income Statement
For the Year Ending December 31, 198__

Sales: (80,000) (15)		$1,200,000
Less variable costs:		
Beginning inventory: (10,000) (8)	$ 80,000	
Variable cost of goods manufactured: (90,000) (8)	720,000	
Available for sale	$ 800,000	
Less ending inventory: (20,000) (8)	160,000	
Variable manufacturing cost of goods sold	$ 640,000	
Add variable selling and administrative expenses	200,000	
Total variable costs charged against sales		840,000
Contribution margin		$ 360,000
Less fixed costs:		
Fixed manufacturing costs: (90,000) (2)	$ 180,000	
Fixed selling and administrative costs	100,000	
Total fixed costs		280,000
Net income		$ 80,000

2 Net income:

Absorption-costing method (a)	$ 100,000
Direct-costing method (b)	80,000
Difference to be accounted for	$ 20,000
Ending inventory	20,000 units
Less beginning inventory	10,000 units
Increase in inventory	10,000 units
Multiply by fixed-overhead cost per unit	$ 2.00
Increase in inventory, as above	$ 20,000

(Current year's addition to the fixed-overhead costs that are carried forward as an asset)

IV Bouchard Company:

1 (a)	Budgeted fixed factory overhead	$ 72,000
	Divide by expected annual activity	12,000 hr
	Fixed overhead rate per hour	$ 6.00
(b)	Standard hours allowed for work done	13,000 hr
	Multiply by predetermined rate (a)	$ 6.00
	Fixed overhead applied	$ 78,000
(c)	Fixed overhead applied (b)	$ 78,000
	Less actual fixed overhead	74,000
	Overapplied fixed overhead	$ 4,000
2 (a)	Budgeted fixed overhead	$ 72,000
	Divide by normal activity	16,000 hr
	Fixed-overhead rate per hour	$ 4.50
(b)	Standard hours allowed for work done	13,000 hr
	Multiply by predetermined rate (a)	$ 4.50
	Fixed overhead applied	$ 58,500
(c)	Actual fixed overhead	$ 74,000
	Less fixed overhead applied	58,500
	Underapplied fixed overhead	$ 15,500

3 (a) Master-budget volume basis
(b) Normal-volume basis

V Stage Corporation

VARIANCE-PRORATION SCHEDULE

Type of Variance	Total Variance	To Stores	To Material Efficiency	To Finished Goods	To Cost of Goods Sold
Material-price	$ 1,600 (a)	$320	$ 80	$ 360	$ 840
Material-efficiency:					
Unadjusted balance	320		320		
Adjusted balance			$400 (b)	120	280
Labor-price	2,000 (b)			600	1,400
Labor-efficiency	3,000 (b)			900	2,100
Factory-overhead	5,000 (b)			1,500	3,500
Totals	$11,920	$320		$3,480	$8,120
Proration Percentages:					
(a) Given:	100%	20%	5%	22.5%	52.5%
(b) See below:	100%			30%*	70%†

* (18,000) ÷ (18,000 + 42,000) = 18,000 ÷ 60,000 = 30%
† (42,000) ÷ (18,000 + 42,000) = 42,000 ÷ 60,000 = 70%

VI Rice Company:

1 Sales		$ 25,000
Less standard cost of goods sold:		
Standard cost of goods manufactured	$ 20,000	
(Cost per unit: $20,000 ÷ 2,000 = $10)		
Less standard cost of ending inventory: (400) (10)	4,000	
Cost of goods sold: (1,600) (10)		16,000

Gross margin			$ 9,000
Less selling and administrative expenses			6,000
Net income before variances			$ 3,000
2	Unfavorable variances: $700 + $900 =	$ 1,600	
	Less favorable variances: $500 + $300 =	800	
	Net unfavorable variance		$ 800
3 (a)	Net income before variances (1)		$ 3,000
	Less net unfavorable variance (2)		800
	Net income		$ 2,200
(b)	Standard cost of goods manufactured		$ 20,000
	Divide by product units manufactured		2,000 units
	Standard cost per product unit		$ 10
	Multiply by ending inventory		400 units
	Standard cost of ending inventory		$ 4,000
4 (a)	Net income before variances (1)		$ 3,000
	Less proration of variance to cost of goods sold: (800) (1,600 ÷ 2,000)		640
	Net income		$ 2,360
(b)	Standard cost of ending inventory (3, b)		$ 4,000
	Add proration of variance to inventory: (800) (400 ÷ 2,000)		160
	Actual cost of ending inventory		$ 4,160

5 3 a
6 4 b

CHAPTER 9

I	1 a	5 b	9 d	13 b	17 c	21 a
	2 d	6 a	10 a	14 b	18 c	22 b
	3 c	7 c	11 a	15 b	19 a	23 a
	4 c	8 b	12 a	16 b	20 b	24 b

II 1 Cost functions; 2 dependent, independent; 3 variable, fixed, mixed (or semivariable); 4 scatter diagram, visual-fit; 5 simple regression analysis; 6 the slope coefficient of the line; 7 the method of least squares; 8 the relevant range

III Provost Corporation

1 (a) y; (b) x; (c) $50; (d) $y = 200 + (50)(30) = \$1{,}700$; (e) $y = 200 + (50)(0) = \$200$

2 (a) no; (b) no.
Although a cost function estimated for a mixed cost (as in this case) may yield a good approximation to the actual cost function over the relevant range, such a relevant range rarely includes zero activity. Therefore, the *intercept* (200 in this case) would probably be neither the expected cost at zero activity nor a valid estimate of fixed cost, because the actual observations probably did not include the point where activity was zero and the cost function was probably not linear beyond the relevant range.

IV Vee-Lee Company

1 Difference in total cost per month: $12,000 − $9,500 = $2,500
Difference in direct-labor hours: 40,000 − 30,000 = 10,000 hours

Variable cost rate per direct-labor hour: $2,500 ÷ 10,000 = $0.25

2	Total cost at 30,000 hours per month	$ 9,500
	Less variable cost: (30,000) ($0.25)	7,500
	Fixed cost per month	$ 2,000
	or:	
	Total cost at 40,000 hours per month	$12,000
	Less variable cost: (40,000) ($0.25)	10,000
	Fixed cost per month	$ 2,000

V Airpoint Corporation

	Lots Produced		
	A	**B**	**C**
Quantity (in units):			
Per lot	200	200	400
Cumulative	200	400	800
Cumulative average labor costs per unit:*			
A: 20 hours × $15	$300		
B: 16 hours × $15		$240	
C: 12.8 hours × $15			$192
Cumulative total labor costs:†			
A: 200 × $300	$60,000		
B: 400 × $240		$96,000	
C: 800 × $192			$153,600
Additional total labor cost of each lot:			
A:	$60,000		
B: $96,000 − $60,000		$36,000	
C: $153,600 − $96,000			$57,600

Answer: B + C = $36,000 + $57,600 = $93,600 (or $153,600 − $60,000 = $93,600)

* 4,000 ÷ 200 = 20 labor hours per unit
20 × 80% = 16 hours
16 × 80% = 12.8 hours

† Cumulative quantity times cumulative average labor cost per unit

CHAPTER 10

I

1 b	4 c	7 d	10 c	13 d	16 b	19 d	22 a
2 b	5 c	8 b	11 a	14 d	17 a	20 c	23 b
3 b	6 d	9 c	12 a	15 c	18 b	21 b	

II 1 Cost-benefit; 2 congruence and effort; 3 organization, informal group, individual; 4 group norms; 5 self-satisfaction; 6 responsibility centers, performance evaluation, rewards; 7 managed costs and programmed costs; 8 negotiated static budgets; 9 committed costs; 10 engineered costs; 11 zero-base budgets; 12 priority incremental budgets; 13 control-factor units; 14 Planning, Programming, and Budgeting

III Umbrella Insurance Company

1 Actual cost: 30 × ($600 + 5 × $20) = 30 × $700 = $21,000
Budgeted cost: $21,000
Variance: none

2 Standard rate per claim: $700 ÷ (4 × 5) = $700 ÷ 20 = $35 per claim
Flexible-budget: 580 × $35 = $20,300
Variance: $21,000 − $20,300 = $700 U

3 One claim adjuster's quota would be 4 × 5 = 20 claims per week at $35 per claim. This would be $35 × 20 = $700, which is equal to the unfavorable cost variance for the week. However, a claim adjuster should not necessarily be fired, because this particular week may have a below-average volume. Moreover, the claims may vary considerably in their size and complexity.

CHAPTER 11

I

1 c	5 b	9 a	13 c	17 c	21 a	25 a
2 b	6 a	10 b	14 b	18 a	22 b	26 c
3 b	7 b	11 c	15 c	19 a	23 c	27 b
4 c	8 b	12 b	16 c	20 b	24 c	

Computations:

10	Total cost of 10,000 units: $19 × 10,000	=	$190,000
	Less total cost of 9,000 units: $20 × 9,000	=	180,000
	Incremental cost of 1,000 units		$ 10,000
	Unit incremental cost: $10,000 ÷ 1,000	=	$ 10

This is lower than the $18 selling price (b)

11 See above: $10 (c)

16 Variable cost per unit: $200,000 ÷ 5,000 = $40;
Total cost of 5,500 units: $275,000 + (5,500 × $40) = $495,000;
Average cost per unit: $495,000 ÷ 5,500 = $90 (c)

17 Incremental cost per unit: $200,000 ÷ 5,000 = $40; or
($495,000 − $275,000 − $200,000) ÷ 500 = $20,000 ÷ 500 = $40 (c)

18 The $75 selling price exceeds $40 (a)

21 Two units of Product A can be made for each unit of Product B
A: $80 × 40% × 2 = $64. B: $80 × 70% = $56. Product A would produce a larger total contribution margin per hour (a)

22 A: $50 × 40% × 2 = $40. B: $60 × 70% = $42. Product B would produce a larger contribution margin per hour (b)

II 1 Relevant; 2 expected future (or predicted), will differ (or will be different); 3 Historical (or Past), the decision itself; 4 contribution approach; 5 lessen or eliminate competition; 6 full manufacturing costs (or a full-costing approach, or the absorption-costing approach), fixed; 7 to profit per unit of constraining factor; 8 opportunity cost

III Wild-Flower Products

1	Total cost of current production plus special order: (20,000 + 4,000) × $22.50	$540,000
	Less total cost of current production only: 20,000 × $24	480,000
	Total incremental cost of special order	$ 60,000
	Incremental cost per unit: $60,000 ÷ 4,000	$ 15.00
2	Incremental profit: ($18.00 − $15.00) × 4,000	$ 12,000

IV Belknap Products

1 Variable cost per unit: $660,000 ÷ 15,000 = $44

Total costs:	
Fixed costs:	$ 720,000
Variable: (15,000 + 3,000) × $44	792,000
Total amount	$1,512,000
Average cost per unit: $1,512,000 ÷ 18,000	$ 84.00
2 Incremental cost per unit: $660,000 ÷ 15,000	$ 44.00
3 Incremental profit: ($70 − $44) × 3,000	$ 78,000

V Cody Corporation:

Yes:

Special-order sales: (600) (30)		$ 18,000
Less variable expenses:		
Manufacturing: (600) (23)	$13,800	
Sales commissions: (600) (2)	1,200	15,000
Addition to company profit		$ 3,000

VI The Grimes Company:

Cash outflow to buy the new machine	$193,000
Less cash inflow from sale of the old machine	15,000
Net cash outflow to change machines	$178,000
Net cash inflow from annual power-expense savings: (10) (19,000)	190,000
Difference in favor of buying the new machine	$ 12,000

VII Redbird Corporation:

	C	D
Selling price per unit	$ 40	$ 85
Less variable expenses per unit	18	35
Contribution margin per unit	$ 22	$ 50
Multiply by number of units that can be manufactured per hour	9	5
Contribution to profit per hour of plant capacity	$198	$250

All 1,300 hours should be devoted to the manufacture of product D, because it would make the larger profit contribution per unit of the constraining factor (hours of plant capacity).

VIII

1

HOUMA NOVELTY COMPANY

Pro Forma Operating Statement
Giving Effect to Discontinuance of Product T Operations
($000 omitted)

	L	C	Total
Sales	150	180	330
Variable costs and expenses	90	100	190

Fixed costs and expenses:	L	C	Total
Annual salaries of product-line supervisors	20	23	43
Total company-wide fixed costs allocated equally to product lines	45	45	90
Total costs and expenses	155	168	323
Operating income (loss)	(5)	12	7

2 No, because the company's operating income would be reduced from $30,000 to $7,000 without any reduction in the total assets used by the company.

CHAPTER 12

I

1 c	5 b	9 b	13 a	17 c	21 a	25 c
2 a	6 a	10 b	14 b	18 b	22 a	26 c
3 b	7 a	11 b	15 a	19 c	23 c	27 a
4 c	8 a	12 a	16 a	20 b	24 d	28 c

Computations:

26 Depreciation is $120,000 ÷ 8 = $15,000 per year.
Accrual accounting rate of return is
($45,000 − $15,000) ÷ $120,000 = 25% (c)

II 1 Hurdle rate; 2 more; 3 time-adjusted rate of return; 4 negative; 5 sensitivity analysis; 6 will differ between alternatives; 7 dividing the annual cash inflow by the initial cash investment (or dividing 100 percent by the payback period); 8 future annual net income, required investment; 9 cash-flow differences between the two projects

III

DCF: discounted cash flow
NPV: net present value
IRR: internal rate of return
RRR: required rate of return

IV Implement Manufacturing Company:

	Annual savings in cash operating expenses	$15,000	
	Multiply by present value of $1 annuity	5.197	
1	Present value of annual cash savings		$77,955
	Predicted residual value of machine	$ 6,000	
	Multiply by present value $1	0.168	
2	Present value of machine residual value		1,008
3	Total present value of expected net cash inflows		$78,963
	Less initial investment		80,000
4	Net present value (negative)		$(1,037)

V Good Accessories, Inc.:

Payback period is: $\frac{\$120{,}000 \text{ initial cost}}{\$\ 20{,}000 \text{ annual cash savings}} = 6.000$

Rates of Return	Present Value Factors	
14%	6.142	6.142
Internal rate		6.000
16%	5.575	
2%	.567	.142

Internal rate: 14% + (2%) (.142 ÷ .567) = 14% + (2%) (.25) = 14% + .5% = 14.5%

VI Wrangler Industries:

1	Initial cost of proposed new equipment	$180,000
	Divide by predicted annual cash savings	40,000
	Payback period	4.5 years
2	The payback reciprocal is 100% divided by the 4.5 years payback period	22.2%
3	Initial cost of equipment less residual value	$160,000
	Divide by predicted useful life	8 years
	Straight-line depreciation expense per year	$ 20,000
4	Predicted annual cash savings in operating expenses	$ 40,000
	Less annual depreciation expense	20,000
	Predicted increase in future average annual net income	$ 20,000
5	Predicted increase in annual net income	$ 20,000
	Divide by initial investment	180,000
	Accounting rate of return based on initial investment	11.1%
6	Predicted increase in annual net income	$ 20,000
	Divide by average investment: ($180,000 + $20,000) ÷ 2	100,000
	Accounting rate of return based on average investment	20%

CHAPTER 13

I

1 a	4 a	7 a	10 c	13 c	16 c	19 b	22 b
2 c	5 b	8 a	11 b	14 c	17 a	20 d	
3 b	6 a	9 d	12 d	15 d	18 b	21 c	

Computations:

1 60% × $5,000 = $3,000 (a)

2 Income before income tax: $60,000 − $40,000 − $5,000 = $15,000; Net Income: $15,000 − 60% ($15,000) = $15,000 − $9,000 = $6,000 (c)

3 $6,000 + $5,000 = $11,000 (b); or $60,000 − $40,000 − $9,000 = $11,000 (b); or 40% ($60,000 − $40,000) + 60% ($5,000) = $8,000 + $3,000 = $11,000 (b)

9 Advertising: $10,000 − 40% ($10,000) = $6,000 outflow; Depreciation: $10,000 (40%) = $4,000 inflow (d)

12 Denominator of depreciation fraction: 1 + 2 + 3 + 4 + 5 + 6 + 7+ 8 = 36; $72,000 ÷ 36 = $2,000; depreciation: $2,000 × 8 = $16,000 (d); or $72,000 (8/36) = $16,000

13 100% ÷ 8 = 12.5%; 12.5% × 2 = 25%; depreciation: 25% × $72,000 = $18,000 (c)

16 Annual depreciation: ($130,000 − $10,000) ÷ 10 = $12,000; net book value when sold: $130,000 − 8 ($12,000) = $34,000; gain on sale: $44,000 − $34,000 = $10,000 (c)

17 Tax on gain: 40% × $10,000 = $4,000; after-tax cash: $44,000 − $4,000 = $40,000 (a)

II 1 (a) Risk-free element, (b) business-risk element, (c) inflation element; 2 required rate of return; 3 (a) sum-of-year's digits, (b) double-declining balance; 4 the reinvestment of the cash proceeds at the end of the shorter project life; 5 capital rationing; 6 cost of capital

III Mrs. Brady's Bread Company:

1

Sales		$800,000
Less:		
Depreciation	$ 40,000	
Other expenses	700,000	740,000
Income before income taxes		$ 60,000
Less 45% income tax		27,000
Net income		$ 33,000

2 $33,000 + $40,000 = $73,000, or $800,000 − $700,000 − $27,000 = $73,000, or 55% ($800,000 − $700,000) + 45% ($40,000) = $55,000 + $18,000 = $73,000

IV Cases A and B:

	Case A	**Case B**
Depreciation per year:		
($300,000 − $20,000) ÷ 8	$ 35,000	
($270,000 − $30,000) ÷ 10		$ 24,000
Accumulated depreciation when sold:		
6 × $35,000	$210,000	
7 × $24,000		$168,000
Book value when sold:		
$300,000 − $210,000	$ 90,000	
$270,000 − $168,000		$102,000
Selling price	$120,000	$ 82,000
Gain on sale: $120,000 − $90,000	$ 30,000	
Loss on sale: $102,000 − $82,000		$ 20,000
Tax on sale: 60% × $30,000	$ 18,000	
Tax saving on sale: 40% × $20,000		$ 8,000
After-tax cash effect of sale:		
$120,000 − $18,000	$102,000	
$ 82,000 + $ 8,000		$ 90,000

V Shield Corporation:

	Salaries	**Depreciation**
Cash paid for expense	$100,000	none
Income tax saving:		
55% × $100,000	$ 55,000	$ 55,000
After-tax cash outflow:		
$100,000 − $55,000	$ 45,000	
After-tax cash inflow		$ 55,000

VI Fractionating Company:

1 (a) $72,000 ÷ 8 = $9,000.

(b) 1 + 2 + 3 + 4 + 5 + 6 + 7 + 8 = 36;
$72,000 ÷ 36 = $2,000; $2,000 × 7 = $14,000; or $72,000 (7/36) = $14,000

(c) 100% ÷ 8 = 12.5%; 2 × 12.5% = 25%; 25% × 72,000 = $18,000; 25% × ($72,000 − $18,000) = 25% × $54,000 = $13,500.

2 (a) 60% ($14,000 − $9,000) = 60% × $5,000 = $3,000 saving

(b) 60% ($13,500 − $9,000) = 60% × $4,500 = $2,700 saving

VII Flex-Tex Company:

1 $50,000 − 60% ($50,000) = $50,000 − $30,000 = $20,000;
$20,000 × 1.10 × .833 = $22,000 × .833 = $18,326.

2 $50,000 × 60% = $30,000;
$30,000 × .833 = $24,990.

VIII Centre Company:

1

Annual savings in cash operating costs	$30,000	
Less income tax at 60%	18,000	
After-tax effect of annual cash savings		$ 12,000
Annual depreciation ($100,000 ÷ 10 years)	$10,000	
Multiply by income tax rate	60%	
Annual tax savings from depreciation		6,000
Total annual after-tax net cash inflow		$ 18,000
Cost of special equipment		$100,000
Payback period (100,000 ÷ 18,000)		5.56 years

2

	Rate of Return	Discount Factor	Rate of Return	Discount Factor
	12%	5.65	12%	5.65
		–	True rate	5.56
	14%	5.22	–	–
Differences	2%	0.43	?	0.09

By interpolation the true rate, or internal rate of return, is:
12% + (2%) (0.09 ÷ 0.43) = 12% + (2%) (0.2) = 12% + 0.4% = 12.4%

3

See 1 for predicted annual after-tax net cash inflow	$ 18,000
Multiply by present value of an annuity of $1 at 10%	6.15
Total present value of expected after-tax net cash inflows	$110,700
Less cost of the investment	100,000
Net present value of the investment	$ 10,700

IX Optional Corporation:

1

Project	Net Present Value	Excess-Present-Value Index
A	$6,000	140%
B	4,000	150
C	2,500	150
D	2,400	160
E	1,500	175
F	900	190

2

Project	Total Cost	Present Value	Net Present Value	Excess-Present-Value Index
A	$15,000	$21,000	$ 6,000	140%
C	5,000	7,500	2,500	150
D	4,000	6,400	2,400	160
F	1,000	1,900	900	190
Totals	$25,000	$36,800	$11,800	147%

No other combination within the $25,000 total budget constraint would show as much net present value as the above combination. Note that Project E is not included even though its 175% excess-present-value index is higher than three of the included projects.

3 (a)

Project	Total Cost	Present Value	Net Present Value	Excess-Present-Value Index
B	$ 8,000	$12,000	$ 4,000	150%
C	5,000	7,500	2,500	150
D	4,000	6,400	2,400	160
E	2,000	3,500	1,500	175
F	1,000	1,900	900	190
Totals	$20,000	$31,300	$11,300	156.5%

It is not necessary to utilize the full $24,000 available budget in order to maximize net present value. For example, two combinations that do use the entire $24,000 but which have *lower* net present values are shown below:

(b)

Project	Total Cost	Present Value	Net Present Value	Excess-Present-Value Index
A	$15,000	$21,000	$ 6,000	140%
B	8,000	12,000	4,000	150
F	1,000	1,900	900	190
Totals	$24,000	$34,900	$10,900	145%

(c)

Project	Total Cost	Present Value	Net Present Value	Excess-Present-Value Index
A	$15,000	$21,000	$ 6,000	140%
C	5,000	7,500	2,500	150
D	4,000	6,400	2,400	160
Totals	$24,000	$34,900	$10,900	145%

CHAPTER 14

I	1 b	3 c	5 a	7 a	9 c	11 c	13 c
	2 b	4 b	6 c	8 c	10 c	12 a	

II 1 Predicts changes in total costs; 2 an intermediate, a final; 3 the cost allocation base; 4 variable, fixed; 5 predetermined or budgeted; 6 greatest, least

III Innovation Emanators, Inc.

INNOVATION EMANATORS, INC.

Budgeted Allocation of Factory-Overhead Costs ($000 omitted)

	Service Departments			Production Departments		
	A	B	C	X	Y	Z
Overhead costs before allocation	300	210	240	160	110	105
Costs allocated from Dept. A to others	300	30	60	90	45	75
Costs allocated from Dept. B to others		240	30	90	30	90
Costs allocated from Dept. C to others			330	110	110	110
Total overhead of production departments				450	295	380
Divide by total direct-labor hours				300	100	190
Predetermined overhead rates for product costing				1.50	2.95	2.00

IV All-Energy Company

1 *Budgeted* fixed costs should be allocated on the basis of *long-run demand* (total KWH: 300,000 + 200,000 = 500,000):

Dept. A (300,000/500,000) × $80,000 = $48,000
Dept. B (200,000/500,000) × $80,000 = $32,000

2 Variable costs should be allocated by using the $.05 *predetermined rate* and *actual KWH used:*

Dept. A 230,000 × $.05 = $11,500
Dept. B 190,000 × $.05 = $ 9,500

(Unallocated actual costs for 19__6 may be written off to cost of sales at end of year.)

V OK Products

	Service Depts.		Production Depts.	
	J	K	1	2
Overhead costs before allocation	$50,000	$90,000	$ 34,000	$ 43,000
Dept. J (see below)	(74,359)	7,436	29,744	37,179
Dept. K (see below)	24,359	(97,436)	48,718	24,359
Total overhead costs			$112,462	$104,538
Machine hours			2,500	4,000
Rate per hour			$44.9848	$26.1345

J = $50,000 + .25 K
K = $90,000 + .10 J
K = $90,000 + .10 ($50,000 + .25 K)
K = $90,000 + $5,000 + .025 K
.975 K = $95,000
K = $95,000/.975 = $97,436
J = $50,000 + .25 ($97,436)
J = $50,000 + 24,359 = $74,359

CHAPTER 15

I

1 a	4 e	7 b	10 c	13 d	16 c	19 e
2 c	5 b	8 b	11 b	14 a	17 c	
3 a	6 c	9 b	12 b	15 b	18 a	

II 1 Contribution, costs controllable by division managers; 2 controllable by division (or segment) managers, controllable by others; 3 sales revenue; 4 potential or budgeted sales rather than actual sales; 5 incremental or variable costs plus allocation of fixed costs; 6 Cost Accounting Standards Board; 7 cause-and-effect, misleading; 8 homogeneous; 9 direct-labor costs and direct-labor hours

III

GENERAL OMNIBUS COMPANY

Contribution-Approach Income Statement by Segments
($000 omitted)

	Company Total	Alpha Division	Omega Division
Net revenues	$900	$500	$400
Less variable manufacturing cost of goods sold	450	300	150
Manufacturing contribution margin	$450	$200	$250
Less variable selling and administrative costs	130	60	70
Contribution margin	$320	$140	$180
Less fixed costs controllable by segment managers	140	60	80
Contribution controllable by segment managers	$180	$ 80	$100
Less fixed costs controllable by others	70	30	40
Contribution by segments	$110	$ 50	$ 60
Less unallocated costs	75		
Income before income taxes	$ 35		

CHAPTER 16

I

1 a	4 a	7 b	10 c	13 a	16 a	19 a
2 d	5 a	8 b	11 d	14 b	17 c	
3 d	6 c	9 a	12 c	15 a	18 a	

II 1 Joint products; 2 the stage of production at which the different individual products can be identified; 3 the revenue-producing properties or abilities of the separate products; 4 relative-sales-value; 5 costs beyond the split-off point, predicted sales values of the fully processed products; 6 product costing; 7 the costs beyond the split-off point; 8 by-products

III Steer Wheeling Corporation:

		Product REV	Product ROL	Total
	Quantities produced and processed	150 yd	300 yd	
	Multiply by unit selling prices	$40	$10	
1	Total sales values when completed	$6,000	$3,000	$9,000
	Less further processing costs	1,500	1,500	3,000
	Approximate values at split-off	$4,500	$1,500	$6,000
	Allocation of $4,000 joint costs:			
	To REV: (4,500/6,000) (4,000)	$3,000		
	To ROL: (1,500/6,000) (4,000)		$1,000	

2

	Product REV	Product ROL	Total
Sales (computed above)	$6,000	$3,000	$9,000

Less production costs:	Product REV	Product ROL	Total
Joint costs (computed above)	$3,000	$1,000	$4,000
Further processing costs	1,500	1,500	3,000
Total costs	$4,500	$2,500	$7,000
Gross profit on sales	$1,500	$ 500	$2,000

3

	Product REV	Product ROL
Unit selling prices of completely processed products	$ 40	$ 10
Unit selling prices at split-off	32	4
Increase in unit selling prices from further processing	$ 8	$ 6
Multiply by number of units	150	300
Differential revenue from further processing	$1,200	$1,800
Less differential costs (costs of further processing)	1,500	1,500
Differences	($300)	$ 300
Decisions	Sell at Split-off	Process beyond split-off

4 Sales:

Product REV at split-off point: 150 yds. at $32 each		$4,800
Product ROL at end of further processing: 300 yds. at $10 each		3,000
Total sales		$7,800
Less costs:		
Joint costs	$4,000	
Product ROL costs of further processing	1,500	5,500
Gross profit on sales		$2,300

(Note that this gross profit is greater than the $2,000 gross profit based upon the further processing of both products as computed in 2 above.)

5 No, because the total joint costs of $4,000 would not be affected by further-processing decisions. Note that because the joint costs would be the same for each of the following four possible combinations of further-processing decisions, the differences in gross profit would be caused only by the incremental costs and revenues:

	Process Both Products	Process REV Only	Process ROL Only	Process Neither Product
Sales: REV	$6,000	$6,000	$4,800	$4,800
ROL	3,000	1,200	3,000	1,200
Total sales	$9,000	$7,200	$7,800	$6,000
Less Costs:				
Joint costs	$4,000	$4,000	$4,000	$4,000
REV processing costs	1,500	1,500	–	–
ROL processing costs	1,500	–	1,500	–
Total costs	$7,000	$5,500	$5,500	$4,000
Gross profit	$2,000	$1,700	$2,300	$2,000

IV N. C. Dental Products Company:

Sales		$75,000
Less cost of goods sold:		
Gross production costs	$50,000	
Less net realizable value of by-product produced	2,000	
Net production costs of main product	$48,000	
Less ending inventory of main product (10%)	4,800	
Net cost of main product sold		43,200
Gross margin on sales		$31,800

CHAPTER 17

I

1 c	4 e	7 a	10 a	13 a	16 b	19 b
2 a	5 a	8 b	11 b	14 b	17 c	
3 d	6 a	9 c	12 b	15 d	18 b	

Computations:

1 (100% − 40%) (5,000) + (24,000 − 5,000) + (1,000) (50%) = 3,000 + 19,000 + 500 = 22,500 units (c)
2 22,500 + (40%) (5,000) = 24,500 units (a)
3 (24,000 − 5,000) + 1,000 = 20,000 units (d)
4 20,000 + 5,000 = 25,000 (e)

II 1 Operation costing; 2 equivalent units produced; 3 Finished Goods; Work in Process; 4 FIFO and weighted average; 5 FIFO; 6 standard costing

III EQ Manufacturing Process

	Material Costs	Conversion Costs
FIFO:		
Completed from beginning inventory	–	60*
Started and completed currently: 600 − 200	400	400
Ending inventory in process	300	180†
Equivalent units produced	700	640
*(100% − 70%) (200) = 60 †(60%) (300) = 180		
Weighted-average:		
Totals from FIFO above	700	640
Work on beginning inventory in previous period	200	140‡
Equivalent units produced	900	780
‡(70%) (200) = 140		

IV WA manufacturing process:

Step 1—Units of Physical Flow

Work in process, beginning	300 (40%)	Units completed	700
Units transferred in	600	Work in Process, end	200 (50%)
Units to account for	900	Units accounted for	900

Step 2—Equivalent Units	Transferred-in Costs	Conversion Costs
Completed from beginning inventory	–	180*
Started and completed currently: 700 – 300	400	400
Ending inventory in process	200	100†
Work done in current period only	600	680
Work on beginning inventory in previous period	300	120‡
Equivalent units produced	900	800

* (100% – 40%) (300) = 180
† (50%) (200) = 100
‡ (40%) (300) = 120

Step 3—Summary of Total Costs to Account for	Transferred-in Costs	Conversion Costs	Total Costs
Work-in-process, beginning	$3,000	$ 2,000	$ 5,000
Current costs	5,100	3,600	8,700
Total costs to account for	$8,100	$ 5,600	$13,700

Step 4—Unit Costs	Transferred-in Costs	Conversion Costs	Total Costs
Total costs to account for (Step 3)	$8,100	$ 5,600	
Divide by equivalent units (Step 2)	900	800	
Unit costs	$ 9.00	$ 7.00	$ 16.00

Step 5—Total Costs of Work Completed and in Process		
Units completed: (700) ($16)		$11,200
Work-in-process, end:		
Transferred-in-costs: (200) ($9)	$1,800	
Conversion costs: (200) (50%)($7)	700	2,500
Total costs accounted for		$13,700

V FI manufacturing process:

Step 1—Units of Physical Flow	
Work-in-process, beginning	200 (75%)
Units transferred in	600
Units to account for	800
Units completed and transferred out during February	500
Work in process, end	300 (50%)
Units accounted for	800

Step 2—Equivalent Units	Transferred-in Costs	Conversion Costs
Completed from beginning inventory	–	50*
Started and completed currently: 500 – 200	300	300
Ending inventory in process	300	150†
Equivalent units produced	600	500

*(100% – 75%) (200) = 50 †(50%) (300) = 150

Step 3—Summary of Total Costs to Account for	Transferred-in Costs	Conversion Costs	Total Costs
Work-in-process, beginning	$ 2,200	$ 1,300	$ 3,500
Current costs	6,000	4,000	10,000
Total costs to account for	$ 8,200	$ 5,300	$13,500

Step 4—Unit Costs	Transferred-in Costs	Conversion Costs	Total Costs
Current costs only	$6,000	$ 4,000	
Divide by equivalent units (Step 2)	600	500	
Unit Costs	$10.00	$ 8.00	$ 18.00

Step 5—Total Costs of Work Completed and in Process		
Units completed:		
From beginning inventory (Step 3)		$ 3,500
Current costs added:		
Conversion costs: (200) ($8) (100% − 75%)		400
Total from beginning inventory		$ 3,900
Started and completed: (500 − 200) ($18)		5,400
Total costs transferred out (Average unit cost: $9,300 ÷ 500 = $18.60)		$ 9,300
Work in process, end:		
Transferred-in costs: (300) ($10)	$3,000	
Conversion costs: (300) (50%) ($8)	1,200	4,200
Total costs accounted for		$13,500

CHAPTER 18

I	1 b	4 a	7 a	10 d	13 c	16 d
	2 d	5 a	8 b	11 a	14 c	17 a
	3 d	6 b	9 b	12 d	15 a	

II 1 Spoilage, quality, disposal value (or salvage value); 2 costs accumulated to the point of rejection, disposal value of the spoiled goods; 3 measurable but relatively minor; 4 net cost of normal; 5 factory-overhead cost; 6 the disposal value of the spoiled goods; 7 Factory Overhead; 8 Work in Process; 9 Factory Overhead, Work in Process; 10 spoilage random fluctuations, exceeds the top of

III Coronado & Cunningham, Inc.

	Debit	Credit
1 Normal spoilage common to all jobs:		
Stores	200	
Factory Overhead	700	
Work in Process		900
2 Normal spoilage due to the nature of particular jobs:		
Stores	200	
Work in Process		200

	Debit	Credit
3 Abnormal spoilage:		
Stores	200	
Special Loss from Abnormal Spoilage	700	
Work in Process		900
4 Normal defective work common to all jobs:		
Factory Overhead	600	
Stores, Accrued Payroll, Factory Overhead Applied		600
5 Normal defective work due to the nature of particular jobs:		
Work in Process	600	
Stores, Accrued Payroll, Factory Overhead Applied		600
6 Abnormal defective work:		
Special Loss from Abnormal Defective Work	600	
Stores, Accrued Payroll, Factory Overhead Applied		600
7 Normal scrap common to all jobs:		
Stores	150	
Factory Overhead		150
8 Abnormal scrap due to the nature of particular jobs:		
Stores	150	
Work in Process		150

IV Melding Process of Amorphous Products, Inc.

1 Lost from normal spoilage	40 units
Lost from abnormal spoilage	60
Good units transferred out	540
Ending work in process: (3/4) (80)	60
Equivalent units for conversion costs	700 units
2 Conversion costs in beginning inventory	$ 2,000
Add current conversion costs	9,200
Total conversion costs	$11,200
Divide by equivalent units	700
Unit conversion cost	$ 16
3 Lost from normal spoilage	40 units
Multiply by unit conversion cost	$ 16
Total conversion costs of normal spoilage	$ 640
4 Lost from abnormal spoilage	60 units
Multiply by unit conversion cost	$ 16
Total conversion costs of abnormal spoilage	$ 960
5 Good units transferred out	540 units
Multiply by unit conversion cost	$ 16
Conversion costs before adding normal spoilage	$ 8,640
Add conversion costs of normal spoilage	640
Total conversion costs transferred out to next process	$ 9,280
6 Ending work in process	80 units
Multiply by completion fraction	3/4
Equivalent units in ending work in process	60 units
Multiply by unit conversion cost	$ 16
Total conversion costs in ending work-in-process inventory	$ 960

Recapitulation or proof (not required by problem):

Conversion costs in beginning inventory	$ 2,000
Current conversion costs	9,200
Total conversion costs to account for	$11,200
Conversion costs of abnormal spoilage	$ 960
Conversion costs transferred out to next process	9,280
Conversion costs in ending inventory of work in process	960
Total conversion costs accounted for	$11,200

CHAPTER 19

I	1 d	5 a	9 b	13 b	17 c
	2 a	6 c	10 d	14 a	18 a
	3 b	7 c	11 d	15 c	19 a
	4 c	8 b	12 b	16 a	20 b

II 1 Interdependence among subunits; 2 goal congruence, managerial effort, subunit autonomy; 3 competitive, minimal; 4 dysfunctional; 5 buying (or purchasing); 6 independent, dysfunctional decision making; 7 cost, external, payables, cost of goods sold, gross profit in inventories

III Abacus Calculator Equipment, Inc.:

1

	(a)	(b)
Variable costs per unit	$ 40	$ 40
Outside market price per unit	43	36
Benefit (detriment) per unit	($3)	$4
Multiply by number of units	5,000	5,000
Total benefit (detriment) to the company	($15,000)	$20,000

(The fixed costs are irrelevant.)

2

	(a)	(b)
Benefit (detriment) as above, before considering alternative use of facilities	($15,000)	$20,000
Benefit from alternative use	26,000	26,000
Total benefit to the company	$11,000	$46,000

(The fixed costs are irrelevant.)

IV Manifold Company:

1 Alternative computations all indicate an advantage of outside purchase of $9 per unit (which is $9,000 total):

(a) $15 − $6 = $9

(b) Buy outside: $98 (net outflow)
Buy inside: $70 + ($98 − $70) + ($15 − $6) = $107 (net outflow)
$107 − $98 = $9

(c) Buy outside: $98 − ($98 − $70) − ($15 − $6) = $61*
Buy inside: $70
$70 − $61 = $9

(d) Buy outside: $98 − ($15 − $6) = $89
Buy inside: $70 + ($98 − $70) = $98
$98 − $89 = $9

See next page.

*A diagram is helpful:

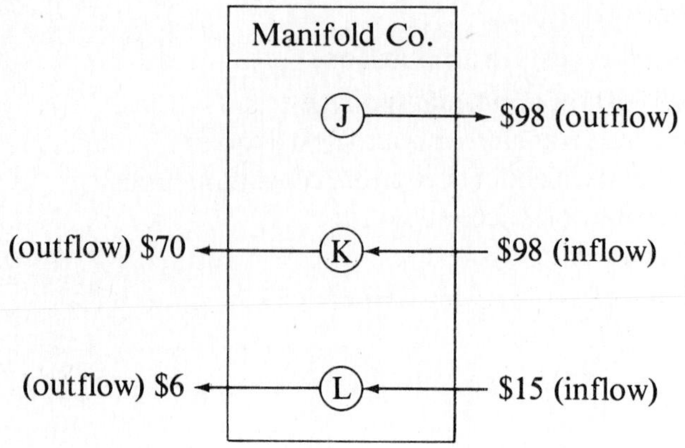

$$\$98 + \$70 + \$6 - \$98 - \$15 = \$61$$

2 $\$70 + (\$15 - \$6) + (\$98 - \$70) = \$70 + \$9 + \$28 = \$107$

CHAPTER 20

I					
	1 b	5 d	9 b	13 b	17 c
	2 a	6 d	10 a	14 b	18 b
	3 b	7 e	11 b	15 c	19 c
	4 c	8 d	12 a	16 c	20 b

Computations:

3 Net income: 12% × $3,000,000 = $360,000.
Sales: $360,000 ÷ 4% = $9,000,000 (b).

4 Capital turnover: $9,000,000 ÷ $3,000,000 = 3 times (c).

6 Imputed interest: $500,000 − $180,000 = $320,000.
Invested capital: $320,000 ÷ 16% = $2,000,000 (d).

7 ROI: $500,000 ÷ $2,000,000 = 25% (e).

II 1 Capital turnover, net-income percentage of sales; 2 the imputed interest on its invested capital; 3 the investment controllable by him; 4 current disposal, total present; 5 replacement cost

III Three Companies:

1 (a)	Sales of Capover Company	$900,000
	Divide by invested capital	200,000
	Capital turnover	4.5 times
(b)	Net income	$ 27,000
	Divide by sales	900,000
	Net income percentage of sales	3%
(c)	Net income	$ 27,000
	Divide by invested capital	200,000
	Return on investment	13.5%

(Or: Capital Turnover times Net Income Percentage of Sales:
(4.5) (3%) = 13.5%)

2 (a)	Invested capital of Investurn Company	$300,000
	Multiply by return on investment	10%
	Net income	$ 30,000
(b)	Net income	$ 30,000
	Divide by net income percentage of sales	4%
	Sales	$750,000
(c)	Sales	$750,000
	Divide by invested capital	300,000
	Capital turnover	2.5 times
3 (a)	Sales of Marsales Company	$600,000
	Divide by capital turnover	5
	Invested capital	$120,000
(b)	Net income	$ 24,000
	Divide by sales	600,000
	Net income percentage of sales	4%
(c)	Net income	$ 24,000
	Divide by invested capital	120,000
	Return on investment	20%

(Or: Capital Turnover times Net Income Percentage of Sales: (5) (4%) = 20%)

IV Key Division of Hard Lock Company:

1	Net income	$ 99,000
	Divide by invested capital	450,000
	ROI	22%
2	Net income	$ 99,000
	Less 18% of $450,000	81,000
	Residual Income	$ 18,000

3 (a) No, because the additional project would reduce overall ROI.
(b) Yes, because the additional project would increase Residual Income.

V Astute Computer Company:

1	Annual net cash inflows from operations	$ 38,344
	Less annual depreciation: 200,000 ÷ 10	20,000
	Operating income	$ 18,344

(a) ROI on gross cost for each year: 18,344 ÷ 200,000 = 9.2%
(b) ROI on net book value:
For first year: 18,344 ÷ 200,000 = 9.2%
For sixth year: 18,344 ÷ 100,000 = 18.3%

2 Note the difference between the 14% internal rate of return and the 9.2% ROI. Although 14% might exceed the minimum desired ROI, a division manager might tend to reject this project, knowing that his subsequent earnings performance would be evaluated by the traditional accrual accounting method and would show only a 9.2% ROI, using the original investment. This example shows that it would be inconsistent—and might therefore induce dysfunctional decisions—to use DCF models to guide the original investment decision but the traditional accrual accounting models to evaluate the performance resulting from those decisions.

3 Gross cost would be preferred as a basis for comparing divisional performances. The

increasing ROI rates on net book value (from 9.2% to 18.3%) show that a possibly deceptive higher ROI might be reflected in later years, despite a level operating income ($18,344 per year), or even a declining operating income.

CHAPTER 21

I	1 c	3 b	5 c	7 d	9 c	11 d
	2 d	4 a	6 c	8 a	10 a	

II 1 Objective function; 2 profit, cost (or loss); 3 states, states of nature; 4 exhaustive, exclusive; 5 specific courses of action, specific events; 6 expected future; 7 uncertainty; 8 events or states of nature, probability; 9 the standard deviation; 10 payoffs, its probability of occurrence; 11 the standard deviation, the expected value

III Precision Automatix:

1 Expected value:

$(\$10 \times .2) + (\$30 \times .3) + (\$40 \times .3) + (\$50 \times .2) =$

$\$2 + \$9 + \$12 + \$10 = \underline{\underline{\$33}}$

2 Standard deviation:

$(33 - 10)^2 \times .2 = (23)^2 \times .2 = 529 \times .2 =$	105.8
$(33 - 30)^2 \times .3 = (3)^2 \times .3 = 9 \times .3 =$	2.7
$(33 - 40)^2 \times .3 = (7)^2 \times .3 = 49 \times .3 =$	14.7
$(33 - 50)^2 \times .2 = (17)^2 \times .2 = 289 \times .2 =$	57.8
Total	181.0

$\sqrt{181.0} = \underline{\underline{\$13.45}}$

3 Coefficient of variation: $\$13.45 \div \$33 = \underline{\underline{.41}}$

IV Kismet Fortune Cookies, Inc.:

1 $(.1)(10) + (.4)(5) + (.3)(0) + (.2)(-10) = 1 + 2 + 0 - 2 = \$1.00$
2 $(.1)(15) + (.4)(10) + (.3)(5) + (.2)(-5) = 1.5 + 4 + 1.5 - 1 = \$6.00$
3 $(.1)(20) + (.4)(15) + (.3)(0) + (.2)(0) = 2 + 6 + 0 + 0 = \$8.00$
4 $(.1)(30) + (.4)(10) + (.3)(0) + (.2)(-15) = 3 + 4 + 0 - 3 = \$4.00$
5 $(.1)(30) + (.4)(15) + (.3)(5) + (.2)(0) = 3 + 6 + 1.5 + 0 = \$10.50$
6 Action 3.
7 Item 5 minus item 3 = $10.50 − $8.00 = $2.50

CHAPTER 22

I	1 e	5 b	9 c	13 c	17 b
	2 c	6 b	10 b	14 b	18 b
	3 a	7 b	11 b	15 c	19 c
	4 c	8 b	12 d	16 b	20 d

II 1 Total long-run costs; 2 the economic order quantity; 3 lead time; 4 the safety stock; 5 the average usage during lead time, the safety stock; 6 descending (or decreasing), total consumption costs, three; 7 LIFO, FIFO

III Material AOK of Precision Puzzle Company:

	One	Two	Five	Ten	Twenty
1 Number of orders per year	One	Two	Five	Ten	Twenty
Order size (3,000 divided by number of orders per year)	3,000	1,500	600	300	150
Average inventory in units (order size divided by 2)	1,500	750	300	150	75
Relevant annual carrying cost (average inventory multiplied by $5)	$7,500	$3,750	$1,500	$ 750	$ 375
Relevant annual purchase-order cost (number of orders multiplied by $300)	$ 300	$ 600	$1,500	$3,000	$6,000
Total relevant annual costs	$7,800	$4,350	$3,000	$3,750	$6,375
2 Least-cost order size			×		

3 E = least-cost order size = $\sqrt{\frac{2AP}{S}}$

A = annual quantity used	3,000 units
P = cost per purchase order	$ 300
S = annual cost of carrying one unit one year	$ 5

Substitute in formula:

$$E = \sqrt{\frac{(2)\,(3{,}000)\,(300)}{5}} = \sqrt{\frac{1{,}800{,}000}{5}}$$

$E = \sqrt{360{,}000} = \underline{\underline{600}}$ units, the EOQ

Optimum number of orders per year would therefore be 3,000 ÷ 600 = 5 (as above in 1)

4 $C = \sqrt{2APS} = \sqrt{(2)(3{,}000)(300)(5)} = \sqrt{9{,}000{,}000} = \$3{,}000$
(as above in 1)

IV Material PDQ of Enigma, Incorporated:

1 Maximum daily usage	80 units
Less average daily usage	70 units
Excess usage per day	10 units
Multiply by lead time	22 days
Safety stock	220 units
2 Safety stock	220 units
Add average usage during lead time: 70 units for 22 days	1,540 units
Reorder point (inventory level at which additional units should be ordered)	1,760 units
Or, the reorder point may be computed as the maximum usage during lead time: 80 units for 22 days	1,760 units

V Material RPM of Acceleration Manufacturing Company:

Summary of April Activity:

	Units	Unit Cost	Total Cost
April inventory	40	$20	$ 800
Purchases:			
April 13	50	21	1,050
April 20	80	22	1,760
April 27	30	24	720
Total available for April	200		$4,330

Weighted-Average Method:

Weighted-average cost per unit: \$4,330 ÷ 200 units =	\$21.65	
Multiply by April 30 inventory	60	units
April 30 inventory cost, 60 units	\$1,299	
Material used in April: 200 − 60 =	140	units
Multiply by weighted-average cost per unit	\$21.65	
Cost of materials used in April, 140 units	\$3,031	

FIFO Method

April 27, 30 units at \$24	\$ 720
April 20, 30 units at \$22	660
April 30 inventory cost, 60 units	\$1,380
April 1 inventory, 40 units at \$20	\$ 800
April 13, 50 units at \$21	1,050
April 20, 50 units at \$22	1,100
Cost of materials used in April, 140 units	\$2,950

LIFO Method:

April 1 inventory, 40 units at \$20	\$ 800
April 13, 20 units at \$21	420
April 30 inventory cost, 60 units	\$1,220
April 27, 30 units at \$24	\$ 720
April 20, 80 units at \$22	1,760
April 13, 30 units at \$21	630
Cost of materials used in April, 140 units	\$3,110

Recapitulation:

	FIFO	LIFO	Weighted Average
Cost of April 30 inventory	\$1,380	\$1,220	\$1,299
Cost of materials used in April	2,950	3,110	3,031
Total	\$4,330	\$4,330	\$4,330

CHAPTER 23

I

1 b	3 b	5 a	7 c	9 b	11 c
2 d	4 d	6 a	8 d	10 c	

II The optimum allocation of scarce resources; 2 the objective function; 3 the constraints of scarce resources; 4 technical coefficients; 5 feasible alternatives; 6 equal total-contribution-margin; 7 shadow prices

III Effortless Perfume Company:

1 $200 \div 400 = .5$ hour
2 $400 \div 160 = 2.5$ hours
3 $7X + 8Y = TCM$
4 $X + .5Y \leqslant 200$; or $2X + Y \leqslant 400$
5 $X + 2.5Y \leqslant 400$; or $.4X + Y \leqslant 160$
6 $Y \leqslant 150$
7 $X \geqslant 0$ and $Y \geqslant 0$

IV Thoroughing Soap Company:

1 Contribution margin totals with predicted rates:
(a) (7,2): $(7 \times \$2) + (2 \times \$7) = \$28$ (minimum)
(b) (8,11): $(8 \times \$2) + (11 \times \$7) = \$93$ (maximum)
(c) (4,3): $(4 \times \$2) + (3 \times \$7) = \$29$
(d) (3,9): $(3 \times \$2) + (9 \times \$7) = \$69$

Contribution margin totals with actual rates:
(a) (7,2): $(7 \times \$3) + (2 \times \$5) = \$31$
(b) (8,11): $(8 \times \$3) + (11 \times \$5) = \$79$ (maximum)
(c) (4,3): $(4 \times \$3) + (3 \times \$5) = \$27$ (minimum)
(d) (3,9): $(3 \times \$3) + (9 \times \$5) = \$54$

In each case the optimum is (b), the maximum; therefore a zero cost of the prediction error.

2 See above: optimum is the minimum labor cost total: (a), using predicted rates, but (c) using actual rates; therefore, cost of prediction error is $\$31 - \$27 = \$4$ (not $\$29 - \$27$).

CHAPTER 24

I 1 c 2 a 3 c 4 a 5 b 6 a 7 b

II 1 Simple regression analysis; 2 the slope coefficient of the line, the regression coefficient; 3 the method of least squares; 4 constant variance or homoscedasticity; 5 the relevant range

III Perceptions, Unlimited:

Be sure you interpret correctly the column headings given in this problem:
Hours: x
Cost: y
Hours squared: x^2
Cost squared: y^2 (not relevant here)
Hours times cost: xy

1 $$b = \frac{10\,(9{,}600) - 300\,(400)}{10\,(7{,}000) - (300)^2} = \frac{96{,}000 - 120{,}000}{70{,}000 - 90{,}000} = \$1.20 \text{ per hour}$$

2 $$a = \frac{(400)\,(7{,}000) - (300)\,(9{,}600)}{(10)\,(7{,}000) - (300)^2} = \frac{2{,}800{,}000 - 2{,}880{,}000}{70{,}000 - 90{,}000} = \$4$$

3 The flexible-budget formula would be:
$y = a + bx$
$y = \$4.00 + \$1.20$ per hour
(Other formulas may be used for requirements 1 and 2)

CHAPTER 25

I	1 b	4 c	7 c	10 c	13 c
	2 d	5 a	8 b	11 a	14 a
	3 a	6 c	9 c	12 b	

II 1 Quantity variance and mix variance; 2 physical proportions of the products sold; 3 actual and budgeted contribution margins; 4 the actual quantity of material used; 5 the adjusted expectations; 6 a random deviation; 7 expected benefits from the investigation, expected costs of the investigation; 8 random deviations, nonrandom deviations; 9 Statistical quality control (or SQC).

III Textbook-Based Problem:

1 (a) (120,000 × \$1) + (40,000 × \$7) = \$120,000 + \$280,000	=	\$400,000
(b) (130,000 × \$1) + (38,000 × \$7) = \$130,000 + \$266,000	=	\$396,000
(c) \$400,000 − \$396,000 = \$4,000 U		
2 Product A: (130,000 − 120,000) × \$1	=	\$10,000 F
Product B: (38,000 − 40,000) × \$7	=	\$14,000 U
Total sales volume variance		\$ 4,000 U
3 (a) Product A: (130,000 − 120,000) × \$2.50	=	\$25,000 F
Product B: (38,000 − 40,000) × \$2.50	=	\$ 5,000 U
Total quantity variance		\$20,000 F
(b) Product A: (130,000 − 120,000) (\$1.00 − \$2.50)	=	\$15,000 U
Product B: (38,000 − 40,000) (\$7.00 − \$2.50)	=	\$ 9,000 U
Total sales-mix variance		\$24,000 U

4 (a) The detailed volume variance in 2 is more helpful.
(b) It is easier to understand; it seems more direct and simpler. It does not need to use the \$2.50 weighted-average unit contribution margin, which would, of course, be altered by any change in sales mix.

IV Intricate Electronics Inc.:

1 Flexible-budget variance: \$59,100 − \$58,800	=	\$ 300 U
2 Price variance: \$59,100 − \$60,200	=	\$1,100 F
3 Efficiency variance: \$60,200 − \$58,800	=	\$1,400 U
4 Yield variance: \$58,800 − \$57,500	=	\$1,300 F
5 Mix variance: \$1,400 U − \$1,300 F		\$2,700 U
(or \$60,200 − \$57,500 = \$2,700 U)		

V Balancing Process of Candid Scales Company:

1 Decision Table:

State of nature	In Control	Out of Control
Probability of state of nature	.95	.05
Payoffs for actions:		
Investigate	C = 2,400	C + M = 12,400
Do not investigate	0	L = 40,000

2 Expected cost of decision to investigate:
(2,400) (.95) + (12,400) (.05) = 2,280 + 620 = \$2,900;
or (2,400) (1.00) + (10,000) (.05) = 2,400 + 500 = \$2,900

3 Expected cost of decision not to investigate:
0 + (40,000) (.05) = \$2,000

4 Out-of-control probability at the point of indifference:

$$\frac{C}{L - M} = \frac{2{,}400}{40{,}000 - 10{,}000} = \frac{2{,}400}{30{,}000} = .08$$

CHAPTER 26

I	1 c	4 c	7 d	10 a	13 d	16 d
	2 b	5 a	8 a	11 a	14 b	17 a
	3 b	6 b	9 c	12 a	15 a	

II 1 Payroll deductions or withholdings; 2 individual federal income, Social Security (or F.I.C.A., or F.O.A.B.); 3 Accrued Payroll, gross; 4 fringe labor costs; 5 unemployment, F.I.C.A. (or F.O.A.B.); 6 Work in Process Control; 7 F.I.C.A.; 8 higher, calendar

III Scrooge and Cratchit Clerical Supplies:

1 Work-in-process	20,000	
Factory overhead control: 5,000 + (14%) (5,000 + 20,000)	8,500	
Selling expense control: 3,000 + (14%) (3,000)	3,420	
Administrative expense control: 2,000 + (14%) (2,000)	2,280	
Accrued payroll		30,000
Estimated liability for vacation pay: (5%) (30,000)		1,500
Employer's F.I.C.A. taxes payable: (6%) (30,000)		1,800
Federal unemployment taxes payable: (0.5%) (30,000)		150
State unemployment taxes payable: (2.5%) (30,000)		750
2 Accrued payroll	30,000	
Employee's income taxes payable		4,000
Employee's F.I.C.A. taxes payable (6%) (30,000)		1,800
Cash: 30,000 – 4,000 – 1,800		24,200

CHAPTER 27

I	1 b	5 c	9 b	13 c	17 a	21 b
	2 c	6 d	10 a	14 a	18 a	22 c
	3 b	7 c	11 c	15 a	19 c	
	4 c	8 d	12 d	16 c	20 b	

II 1 Waste, errors, and fraud; 2 recordkeeping and physical handling of assets; 3 document control; 4 vendors or sellers; 5 receiving reports and purchase orders; 6 separated or assigned to different employees; 7 shoplifting by customers, embezzling by employees; 8 sales volume, unit values of products; 9 factory, credit

III Internal Control System

1 U 2 A 3 U 4 A 5 A 6 U 7 U 8 U

IV High-Margin Stores

		Retail Prices
Beginning merchandise inventory (physical count)		$ 9,000
Merchandise purchases		60,000
Additional retail price changes:		
Markups		4,000
Markdowns		(10,000)
Total merchandise to account for		$63,000
Less:		
Sales	$50,000	
Allowable inventory shrinkage	2,000	52,000
Ending inventory should be		$11,000
Less ending inventory (physical count)		10,700
Inventory shortage		$ 300

CHAPTER 28

I 1 e 3 a 5 c 7 c 9 a
2 c 4 b 6 c 8 a

II 1 Cost of sales; 2 normal volume (or standard volume); 3 Work-in-Process, Direct Materials Used; 4 Work-in-Process, Finished Goods; 5 a spending, an efficiency